Praise for *Lean-Agile Acceptanc* *Development*

"*Lean-Agile Acceptance Test-Driven Development* tells a tale about three fictive project stakeholders as they use agile techniques to plan and execute their project. The format works well for the book; this book is easy to read, easy to understand, and easy to apply."

—*Johannes Brodwall, Chief Scientist, Steria Norway*

"Agile development, some say, is all about pairing, and, yes, I'm a believer in the power of pairing. After reading this book, however, I became a fan of the 'triad'—the customer or business analyst + the developer + the tester, who work collaboratively on acceptance tests to drive software development. I've written some patterns for customer interaction and some patterns for testing and I like what Ken Pugh has chosen to share with his readers in this down-to-earth, easy-to-read book. It's a book full of stories, real case studies, and his own good experience. Wisdom worth reading!"

—*Linda Rising, Coauthor of* Fearless Change: Patterns for Introducing New Ideas

"The Agile Manifesto, Extreme Programming, User Stories, and Test-Driven Development have enabled tremendous gains in software development; however, they're not enough. The question now becomes 'How can I ensure clear requirements, correct implementation, complete test coverage, and more importantly, customer satisfaction and acceptance?' The missing link is acceptance as defined by the customer in their own domain language. *Lean-Agile Acceptance Test-Driven Development* is the answer."

—*Bob Bogetti, Lead Systems Designer, Baxter Healthcare*

"Ken Pugh's *Lean-Agile Acceptance Test-Driven Development* shows you how to integrate essential requirements thinking, user acceptance tests and sounds, and lean-agile practices, so you can deliver product requirements correctly and efficiently. Ken's book shows you how table-driven specification, intertwined with requirements modeling, drives out acceptance criteria. *Lean-Agile Acceptance Test-Driven Development* is an essential guide for lean-agile team members to define clear, unambiguous requirements while also validating needs with acceptance tests."

—*Ellen Gottesdiener, EBG Consulting, www.ebgconsulting.com, Author of* Requirements by Collaboration *and* The Software Requirements Memory Jogger

"If you are serious about giving Agile Testing a chance and only have time to read one book, read this one."

—David Vydra, http://testdriven.com

"This book provides clear, straightforward guidance on how to use business-facing tests to drive software development. I'm excited about the excellent information in this book. It's a great combination of the author's experiences, references to other experts and research, and an example project that covers many angles of ATDD. A wide range of readers will learn a lot that they can put to use, whether they work on projects that call themselves lean or agile or simply want to deliver the best possible software product."

—Lisa Crispin, Agile Tester, ePlan Services, Inc., Author of Agile Testing

Lean-Agile Acceptance Test-Driven Development

Lean-Agile Acceptance Test-Driven Development

Better Software Through Collaboration

Ken Pugh

Addison-Wesley

Upper Saddle River, NJ • Boston • Indianapolis • San Francisco
New York • Toronto • Montreal • London • Munich • Paris • Madrid
Capetown • Sydney • Tokyo • Singapore • Mexico City

The publisher offers excellent discounts on this book when ordered in quantity for bulk purchases or special sales, which may include electronic versions and/or custom covers and content particular to your business, training goals, marketing focus, and branding interests. For more information, please contact:

U.S. Corporate and Government Sales
(800) 382-3419
corpsales@pearsontechgroup.com

For sales outside the United States, please contact:

International Sales
international@pearson.com

Visit us on the Web: informit.com/aw

Library of Congress Cataloging-in-Publication Data

Pugh, Kenneth.
Lean-agile acceptance test driven development : better software through collaboration / Ken Pugh.
p. cm.
Includes bibliographical references and index.
ISBN-13: 978-0-321-71408-4 (pbk. : alk. paper)
ISBN-10: 0-321-71408-3 (pbk. : alk. paper) 1. Agile software development.
2. Computer software--Testing. 3. Computer software—Quality control.
4. Cooperation. I. Title.
QA76.76.D47P837 2011
005.1’4--dc22

2010042906

ISBN-13: 978-0-321-71408-4
ISBN-10: 0-321-71408-3

Text printed in the United States on recycled paper at R.R. Donnelley in Crawfordsville, Indiana.
First printing December 2010

Editor-in-Chief
Karen Gettman

Executive Editor
Chris Guzikowski

Senior Development Editor
Chris Zahn

Managing Editor
Kristy Hart

Project Editor
Jovana San Nicolas-Shirley

Copy Editor
Karen Gill

Indexer
Cheryl Lenser

Proofreader
Sheri Cain

Editorial Assistant
Raina Chrobak

Cover Designer
Alan Clements

Compositor
Nonie Ratcliff

*I'd like to dedicate this book to three people.
My brother Bob inspired me to become an engineer.
I recall one time when he was home from college and presented me with the N-body problem [Wiki01] and the four color map problem [Wiki02]. My high school science teacher, Mr. Sanderson, spurred me on to explore topics such as why there is air. My mechanical engineering professor at Duke, Dr. George Pearsall, encouraged exploration. In his strength of materials class, I discovered why my guitar strings broke. To each of them, I give thanks.*

Contents

Acknowledgments

Over my two-fifths of a century in software, I've have the opportunity to interact with a wide range of people. Many of the ideas expressed in this book have come from them—from their books, their talks, and personal conversations. Albert Einstein said, "Creativity is knowing how to hide your sources." I would like not to hide these people. The only problem is I can't always remember what I got from whom. The list includes in no particular order: Cem Kaner, Jerry Weinberg, James Bach, Michael Bolton, Brian Marick, Ellen Gottesdiener, Karl Wiegers, Ward Cunningham, Jim Shore, Rick Mugridge, Lisa Crispin, Janet Gregory, Kent Beck, Gerard Meszaros, Alistair Cockburn, Andy Hunt, Bob Martin, Dale Emery, III, Michael Feathers, Mike Cohn, Jim Highsmith, Linda Rising, Ron Jeffries, Mary Poppendieck, Jim Coplien, Norm Kerth, Scott Ambler, Jared Richardson, Dave Thomas, Martin Fowler, Bill Wake, Tim Lister, Eric Evans, Bret Pettichord, Brian Lawrence, Jeff Patton, David Hussman, Rebecca Wirfs-Brock, Joshua Kerievsky, Laurie Williams, Don Gause, James Grenning, Tom DeMarco, Danny Faught, Jeff Sutherland, David Astels, Lee Copeland, Elisabeth Hendrickson, Bob Galen, Gary Evans, George Dinwiddie, Jutta Eckstein, Bob Hartman, David Chelimsky, Dan North, Lasse Koskela, Cedric Beust, and Larry Constantine.

I'd like to thank Rob Walsh of EnvisionWare for the case study of a library print server, Robert Martin for the Cucumber style example in Slim, Markus Gaertner for the Slim example, Dale Emery for the Robot example, and John Goodsen for the Cucumber example. I appreciate Gerard Meszaros for permission to use his testing matrix graphic. Thanks to Dawn Cannan, Gabriel Le Van, Stephen Cresswell, Jared Richardson, Ian Cooper, Greg McNelly, and Gary Marcos for their ATDD stories in the Epilogue. I'd like to acknowledge the Net Objectives gang: Alan Shalloway, Jim Trott, Scott Bain, Amir Kolsky, Cory Foy, and Alan Chedalawada. Also thanks to Omie and Tammi for keeping me sane.

In helping make this book a reality, I thank the people at Addison-Wesley, Pearson Technology Group: Chris Guzikowski, Chris Zahn, Raina Chrobak, Kristy Hart, Jovana San Nicolas-Shirley, Karen Gill, Nonie Ratcliff, Cheryl Lenser, and Sheri Cain. And to reviewers Andrew Binstock, Graham Oakes, Lisa Crispin, Linda Rising, Bill Wake, Robert Bogetti, Johannes Brodwall, Peter Kurpis, SGuy Ge, Tom Wessel, Kody Shepler, Jinny Batterson, Julian Harty, and III.

Last but not least, I thank Leslie Killeen, my wife. She is a weaver. Software is not her field. She reviewed my drafts, gave helpful hints, and supported me through the creation process.

About the Author

Kenneth Pugh has over two-fifths of a century of software experience. Previously a principal at Pugh-Killeen Associates, he is now a fellow consultant for Net Objectives. He has developed software applications ranging from radar tracking to financial analysis. Responsibilities have included everything from gathering requirements to testing. After the start of the new millennium, he has worked with teams to create software more effectively with lean and agile processes. He has spoken at numerous national conferences; consulted and taught all over the world; and testified on technology topics. This is his seventh book. In 2006, his book *Prefactoring* won the Jolt Award [DrDobbs01]. In his spare time, he snowboards, windsurfs, and backpacks. Between 1997 and 2003, he completed the Appalachian Trail. The cover photograph of Mount Katahdin, the northern end of the trail, was taken by the author from Abol Bridge in Maine.

Introduction

"Context is all."

Margaret Atwood, *The Handmaid's Tale*

The context for the tale is introduced. A brief background of acceptance test-driven development (ATDD) is presented.

Testable Requirements

Developing software with testable requirements is the theme of this book. A testable requirement is one with an acceptance test. Acceptance tests drive the development of the software. As many development groups have experienced, creating acceptance tests prior to implementing requirements decreases defects and improves productivity. (See the Epilogue for examples.) A triad—the customer/business analyst, developer, and tester—collaborates on producing these tests to clarify what is to be done. In creating a high-quality product, ATDD is as much about this clarification as it is about the actual testing.

As an example, do you have criteria in mind as to whether this book will meet your needs? If you finish this book, how will you know whether it has met those criteria? This book represents an implementation of something that should meet your needs. Because you are reading this book after its completion, you don't have an opportunity to influence the acceptance criteria. But let me list the criteria here and see if this is what you are after.

In English classes, the teacher emphasized that a story should contain a who, what, when, where, why, and how. So I've made that the goal of this book. It explains

- Who creates acceptance tests
- What acceptance tests are
- When the acceptance tests should be created
- Where the acceptance tests are used
- Why acceptance test-driven development is beneficial
- How the acceptance tests are created

By the end of this book, the expectation is that you should understand how testable requirements can make the software development process more enjoyable (or at least less painful) and help in producing higher-quality products., Let's begin with a brief discussion on the why, what, where, and who issues.

Why ATDD Is Beneficial

Let's start with the answer to the why question. Jeff Sutherland, the cocreator of Scrum, has metrics on software productivity [Sutherland01]. He has found that adding a quality assurance person to the team and creating acceptance tests prior to implementation doubles the team's productivity. Your actual results may vary, but teams adopting ATDD have experienced productivity and quality increases. Mary Poppendieck says that creating tests before writing code is one of the two most effective and efficient process changes for producing quality code. (The other is frequent feedback.) [Poppendieck01] Customer-developer-tester collaboration reduces unnecessary loops in the development process. As Jerry Weinberg and Don Gause wrote, "Surprising, to some people, one of the most effective ways of testing requirements is with test cases very much like those for testing the completed system" [Weinberg01].

If you are going to test something and document those tests, it costs no more to document the tests up front than it does to document them at the end. But these are more than just tests. As stated in Chapter 3, "Testing Strategy," "The tests clarify and amplify the requirements." An acceptance test is "an authoritative and reliable source of what the software should do functionally" [Adzic01].

What Are Acceptance Tests?

Acceptance tests, as used in this book, are defined by the customer in collaboration with the developer and tested and created prior to implementation. They are not the traditional user acceptance tests [Cimperman01], which are performed after implementation "by the end user to determine if the system is working according to the specification in the contract." [Answers01] They are also not system tests which are usually independently written by testers by reading the requirements to ensure that the system meets those requirements. [Answers02] All three are related in that they are all black box tests—that is, they are independent of the implementation. It is the time and manner of creation in which they differ.

Where Are Acceptance Tests Used?

The concept of an acceptance test is defined by the intent of the test, not its implementation. You can apply an acceptance test at the unit, integration, or user interface level. You can use it as a validation test, which allows input to or produces outputs from an application installed in the customer's environment. Further, you can use it as a design verification test that ensures a unit or component meets it intended responsibility. In either case, the test makes certain the application is acceptable to the customer.

Who Creates the Acceptance Tests?

This book refers to a triad: the customer, developer, and tester. The power of three people working together [Crispin01] can create the bests acceptance tests.

If the triad writes the tests together, the distinction between user acceptance tests and system tests is practically eliminated. As will be shown, the three roles of customer, developer, and tester may be played by different individuals or by the same individual with different focuses.

What Types of Software Are Covered?

The acceptance tests covered in this book revolve mainly around requirements that have determinable results. These results are typical in business situations. You place an order, and the order total is determinable. On the other hand, you have a requirement to find the shortest possible path that goes through a number of points. For example, you want to determine the shortest driving trip that travels over every road in the United States. For a small number of roads (such as the interstate highways), the result is determinable by brute force. However, for a large number of roads, the answer is not determinable. You can have a test that checks the output of one way of solving the problem against the output of another way. But that does not guarantee that the shortest solution has been found.

How Will We Get to ATDD?

The answers to how and when the acceptance tests should be created are shown by a continuous example throughout this book. Each step in their creation and use is covered. Some books are devoted entirely to a single step and go into much greater detail than does this book. In particular, the references offer links for tools to automate the acceptance tests, to the agile process itself, to requirement elicitation, and to testing the other qualities of a software system (usability, performance, and so on).

The continuous example for Sam's CD Rental Store follows Sam's story in *Prefactoring—Extreme Abstraction, Extreme Separation, Extreme Readability*. That book used the tale as the context for examples of good design. *Prefactoring* covered some of the aspects of developer-customer interaction, because a good design requires understanding the customer's needs. *Prefactoring*'s focus was on the internal software quality. This book's focus is on externally visible quality. The two books complement each other.

Organization

The material is presented in six parts. The first part documents the tale of the triad members—customer, developer, tester—as they create a software system. It shows how acceptance testing permeates the entire process, from the project charter to individual stories. The second part covers details in acceptance testing, as simplification by separation. The third part explores general subjects, such as test presentation and valuation. The fourth part includes case studies from real-life situations. In some instances, the studies have been simplified to show only the relevant parts. The fifth part involves more technical issues, as how to handle test setup. The sixth part offers the appendices, which give additional information on topics as business value and test automation. For those who want to get the quick summary of ATDD and its benefits, read Chapter 25, "Retrospective and Perspective." Those who want to read the experiences of others, see the Epilogue.

Example Tables

The book presents tests with examples in tables rather than in narrative form. These tables follow the concepts of David Parnas, who states, "The tables constitute a precise requirements document" [Parnas01]. Some people prefer free text over tables. Those who prefer the narrative can easily convert tables to this form. The reverse is usually more difficult. Tables are familiar to spreadsheet users. Many business rules have conditions that are more easily tested with a table. From an analysis point of view, you can often find missing conditions by examining the values in a table's columns.

Automation After Communication

I emphasize acceptance tests as customer-developer-tester communication. If you don't have an acceptance test, you have nothing to automate. I do not advocate a particular test automation framework. When you automate an acceptance test that includes its accompanying requirement, you get what many term an executable specification [Melnik02], [Melnik03].

Acceptance tests can be manual. But if they are automated, you can use them as regression tests to ensure that future changes to the system do not affect previously implemented requirements. So the most effective use of the tests is as an executable specification. Appendix C, "Test Framework Examples," shows examples of test automation using several frameworks. The code for the examples is available online at http://atdd.biz.

ATDD Lineage

A Chinese proverb says, "There are many paths to the top of the mountain, but the view is always the same." And many of the paths share the same trail for portions of the journey. Although acceptance testing has been around for a long time, it was reinvigorated by extreme programming [Jefferies01]. Its manifestations include ATDD as described in this book, example-driven development (EDD) by Brian Marick [Marick01], behavior-driven development (BDD) by Dan North [Chelimsky01], story test-driven development (SDD) by Joshua Kerievsky of Industrial Logic [Kerievsky01], domain-driven design (DDD) by Eric Evans [Evans01], and executable acceptance test-driven development (EATDD) [EATDD01]. All these share the common goal of producing high-quality software. They aid developers and testers in understanding the customer's needs prior to implementation and customers being able to converse in their own domain language.

Many aspects are shared among the different approaches. ATDD in this book encompasses aspects of these other approaches. I've documented the parts that come specifically from the other driven developments (DDs), including Brian Marick's examples, Eric Evan's ubiquitous language, and Dan North's given-when-then template. The most visible differences are that the tests here are presented in table format rather than in a more textual format, such as BDD's Cucumber language, and they concentrate on functionality instead of the user interface. This book's version of ATDD matches closely that described by

Lasse Koskela [Koskela01] and Gojko Adzic [Adzic01] and follows the testing recommendations of Jim Coplien [Coplien01].

One of the most well-known DDs is test-driven development (TDD) by Kent Beck [Beck01]. TDD encompasses the developer's domain and tests the units or modules that comprise a system. TDD has the same quality goal as ATDD. The two interrelate because the acceptance tests can form a context in which to derive the tests for the units. TDD helps creates the best design for an application. A TDD design issue would be assigning responsibilities to particular modules or classes to pass all or part of an acceptance test.

> Acceptance test driven development:
> The answer is 42. Now implement it.

Summary

- Testable requirements have acceptance tests associated with them.
- ATDD involves developing requirement tests prior to implementation.
- ATDD can improve productivity.
- Acceptance tests are developed collaboratively between the customer, developer, and tester.

PART I

The Tale

This part tells the tale of a team developing a project. It starts with an exploration of testing. The team develops a charter followed by a set of high-level requirements. Requirements are broken down into stories. Stories are detailed with use cases and business rules. Acceptance tests are developed for every business rule and every scenario.

Chapter 1

Prologue

"Begin at the beginning," the King said, very gravely, "and go on till you come to the end; then stop."

Lewis Carroll, *Alice's Adventures in Wonderland*

Say hello to testable requirements. You are introduced to acceptance tests and discover the benefits of using them. You are also introduced to the team that will create them.

Ways to Develop Software

Different teams have different ways to develop software. Here are examples of two ways.

One Way

It's the last day of the iteration. Tom, the tester, is checking the implementation that Debbie, the developer, handed over to him earlier that day. He goes through the screens, entering the test case data he created. He discovers that the results aren't what he had assumed they should be. He's unable to contact Cathy, the customer, for clarification as to whether he made the correct assumptions. There's nothing left to do but write up a defect to be addressed during the next iteration, leaving less time to develop new features.

Another Way

It's the last day of the iteration. Debbie, the developer, has run through the acceptance tests that Cathy, Debbie, and Tom created prior to Debbie starting implementation. Tom quickly runs through the same acceptance tests and then starts doing more testing to get a feeling for how the implementation fits into the entire workflow. At the review the next morning, Cathy agrees that the story is complete.

The Difference

What's the difference between the first way and the second way? In the first case, no tests were created upfront. The developer had nothing to test against, so she relied on the tester to perform verification. The tester needed more details from the customer. Feedback as to success or failure of a requirement implementation was delayed. Every requirement story in the second situation has one or more tests associated with it, making each a testable requirement. The tests were developed by the customer, tester, and developer prior to implementation. As we will see in later chapters with detailed examples, these tests clarify the requirements. They provide a measure of doneness to all the parties.

If a requirement does not have a test, it is not yet demonstrated to be a testable requirement. If you cannot test that a requirement has been fulfilled, how do you know when it has been met? This does not mean that the test is easy to perform. Nor can tests be fully specified; there are always assumptions. But there must be at least an objective test so that the customer, developer, and tester have a common understanding of what meeting the requirement means.

The Importance of Acceptance Tests

In my classes, I often start with a dialogue to emphasize the importance of acceptance tests. It usually goes something like this:

I ask, "Does anyone want a fast car?"

Someone always says, "Yes, I want one."

"I'll build you one," I reply. I turn around and work furiously for 5 seconds. I turn back around and show the student the results. "Here's your car," I state.

"Great," the student answers.

"It's really fast. It goes from 0 to 60 in less than 20 seconds," I proudly explain.

"That's not fast," the student retorts.

"I thought it was fast. So give me a test for how fast you want the car to be," I reply.

"0 to 60 in less than 4.5 seconds," the student states.

I turn back around, again work quickly, and then face the student again. "Here it is: 0 to 60 in 4.5 seconds. Fast enough?" I ask.

"Yes," the student answers.

"Oh, by the way: 60 is the top speed," I state.

"That's not fast," the student retorts.

"So give me another test," I ask.

"The top speed should be 150," the student demands.

Again, I quickly create a new car. "Okay, here it is: 0 to 60 in 4.5 seconds. Top speed of 150. Fast enough?" I again ask.

"That should be good," the student retorts.

"Oh, by the way: It takes two minutes to get to 150," I let slide.

By this time, my point has been made. Getting just a requirement for a "fast car" is not sufficient for knowing what to build. The customer needs to create some tests for that requirement that clarify what exactly is meant by "fast." Without those tests, the engineers may go off and create something that they think meets the requirement. When they deliver it to the customer, the customer has a negative reaction to the creation. The item does not meet his needs, as he thought he had clearly stated in saying, "the car must be fast."

Having acceptance tests for a requirement gives developers a definitive standard against which to measure their implementation. If the implementation does not meet the tests, they do not have to bother the customer with something that is noncompliant. If each acceptance test represents a similar effort in creating the implementation, the number of passing tests can be used as a rough indication of how much progress has been made on a project.

Absolute Tests Are Not Absolutely Fixed

Although the tests are absolute, such as "0 to 60 in less than 4.5 seconds," they also form a point of discussion between the customer and the engineers. If the engineers work for a while and the car accelerates in 4.6 seconds, they can discuss with the customer whether this is sufficient. In particular, this would occur when the engineers discover that getting the time down to 4.5 seconds might take considerably more development time. In the end, the customer is the decision maker. If 4.5 seconds is an absolute requirement to sell the car, the extra development cost is worth it. If it is not, money will be saved.[1]

I'd like to clarify a couple of terms that are used throughout the book: acceptance criteria and acceptance tests. *Acceptance criteria* are general conditions of acceptance without giving specifics. For the car example, these might be "acceleration from one speed to another," "top speed," and "must feel fast." *Acceptance tests* are specific conditions of acceptance, such as "0 to 60 in less than

1. If you can agree up front how much that extra 0.1 second is worth, developers can make quick decisions. See Don Reinertsen [Reinertsen01] for lean economic models.

4.5 seconds." Each acceptance test has unstated conditions. For example, an unstated condition could be that the acceleration is measured on a flat area, with little wind. You could be very specific about these conditions: an area that has less than .1 degree of slope and wind less than 1 mile per hour. If necessary for regulatory or other purposes, you could add these to the test. But you should avoid making the test a complex document.

A few facets that differentiate acceptance tests from other types of tests, such as unit tests, are

- The customer understands and specifies acceptance tests.
- Acceptance tests do not change even if the implementation changes.

System and Team Introduction

The principles and practices of acceptance test-driven development (ATDD) are introduced through the tale of the development of a software system. The story originated in my book *Prefactoring—Extreme Abstraction, Extreme Separation, Extreme Readability* [Pugh02]. That book emphasizes how developers can create a high-quality solution for the system. This book highlights the customer-developer-tester interaction in creating and using acceptance tests in developing the system.

The System

Sam, the owner of Sam's Lawn Mower Repair and CD Rental Store, had a lawn mower repair shop for a number of years. He noticed that people coming into the shop had circular devices hanging on their bodies. It turned out they were Sony Discmans. Being the inquisitive type, he discovered that his customers liked to listen to music while they mowed the lawn. So he added CD rental to the services his store offered.

Business has been booming, even though the Sony Discman is no longer being used. People are now coming in with little rectangular boxes hanging around their necks or sitting in their pockets. They are renting more CDs than ever and returning them quickly—in as little as an hour. Sam's paper system is having a hard time keeping up, and it is becoming difficult to produce the reports needed to track the inventory. Sam is planning to open a second store. Before he does that, he figures that he needs to obtain a software system, or his issues will just double.

Sam got a recommendation and called Debbie. She works with Tom in an agile development shop. Sam selected that shop to develop the system.

The People

Sam represents the project sponsor for the new system. His wife Cathy takes care of the logistic side of the business. She does the bookkeeping, handles the inventory, and places orders for new CDs. Cathy plays the role of customer—the one requesting the application. Along the way, as you'll see, Cathy is introduced to software development and in particular to ATDD. Other interested parties include Sam's sister Mary and his brother-in-law Harry, who frequently help out at the store. Their son Cary is a clerk at the store. He will be using the new system.

Debbie is the developer and Tom is the tester. They work as a pair to understand and implement what Cathy needs. The terms *developer* and *tester* are often related to titles. In this book, these terms refer to what Debbie and Tom focus on. The development focus is to create an implementation that does what it is supposed to do. The testing focus is to check that the implementation does precisely that and does not do what it should not.

Focus may not be correlated with the titles developer and tester. In many agile processes, such as Scrum, there are no titles on teams [Larman01]. Any two people may pair together, with one focusing on testing and one on implementing. It's possible that a single person may focus both ways on a particular requirement. The entire team is shown in Figure 1.1.

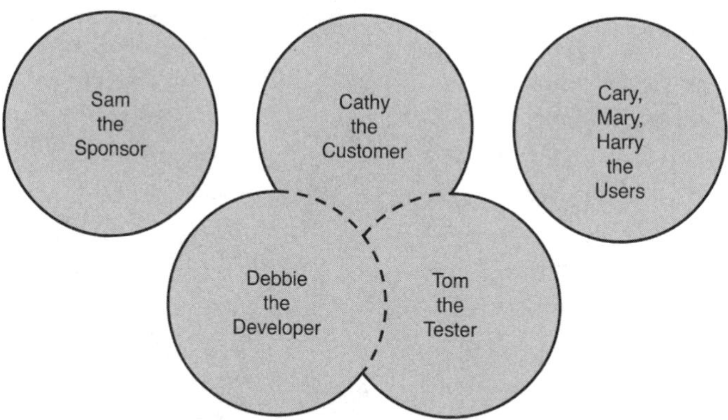

Figure 1.1 *The Team*

Summary

- A testable requirement has one or more acceptance tests.
- An acceptance test is a standard to measure the correctness of the implementation.
- Acceptance tests are created in collaboration with the customer.

Chapter 2

Lean and Agile

"You're a lean, mean, fighting machine!"

Bill Murray as John Winger in *Stripes*

The triad of Cathy the customer, Debbie the developer, and Tom the tester has its first meeting. Debbie describes the differences between traditional development and acceptance test-driven development (ATDD). It's explained how ATDD fits into lean and agile.

The Triad and Its Units

Many books on agility refer to the developer team and the business team. Names often have a connotation. On a football field, two teams compete to see who can score more points and win the game. On a single football team, there is an offensive unit, a defensive unit, and a special teams unit. The offensive's unit job is to score points. The defensive's unit responsibility is to keep the other team from scoring. The special team unit has the goal of scoring points when it receives a kicked ball and preventing the other team from scoring when it kicks the ball. All three units must do their job to win the game.

Although each unit has a primary job, it doesn't stop there. If the offensive unit fumbles the football and the other team recovers, it does not simply stop playing and call for the defensive unit to come on the field. Instead, it plays defense until the end of the play.

The three basic units in a software project are the customer unit, the developer unit, and the testing unit.[1] The customer unit (which may include product owner, business analysts, and subject matter experts) determines the requirements, creates acceptance tests, and sets priorities. The developer unit implements the requirements and ensures the implementation meets the acceptance tests. The testing unit checks that an implementation does what it is supposed to do and does not do what it is not supposed to do. The testers help the customer unit develop acceptance tests, and the developer unit passes those tests. The triad works together to produce quality software.[2]

We start the story with Debbie, representing the developer unit, explaining to Cathy, the customer unit, two ways that teams approach software development. Tom, the testing unit, is sitting in the meeting of the triad (see Figure 2.1).

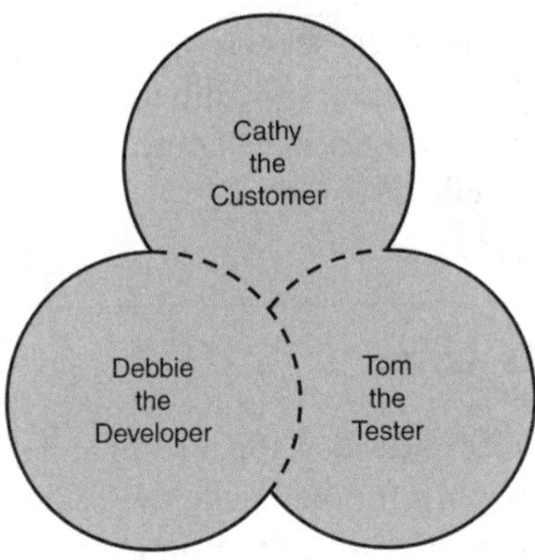

Figure 2.1 *The Triad*

1. As suggested in the previous chapter, some agile teams work more like a soccer team or a basketball team. Players have particular strengths, but everyone plays both defense and offense. The testing unit consists of players currently acting one way—focused on testing—but the same players may be part of the developer unit that acts another way—focused on implementation.
2. There are other players, such as the stakeholder who owns the charter (see Chapter 5, "The Example Project") and the users who use the system. Their roles will be introduced at appropriate times.

Post-Implementation Tests

Debbie and Tom meet with Cathy to explain how the development process works. Debbie begins with how the flow often works and compares it to how Debbie and Tom prefer to work.

Debbie introduces the chart shown in Figure 2.2.

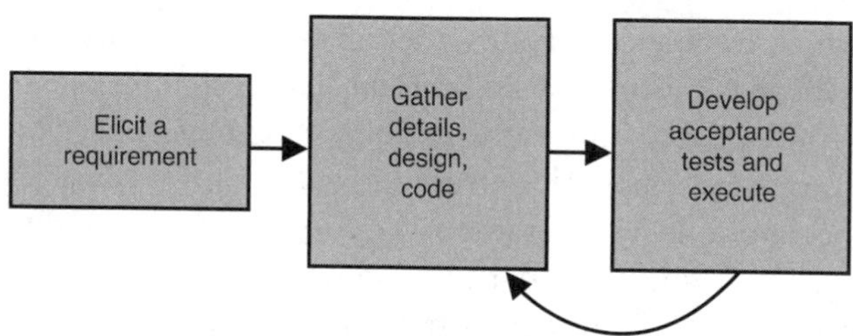

Figure 2.2 *Typical Development Flow*

"Cathy, this is how many development teams work to implement a requirement.[3] As a developer, I elicit a requirement from the customer. Then I gather detail on the requirement, followed by designing and coding an implementation. I turn over the program to a tester like Tom. He develops functional tests to check that the requirement passes. He works with the customer or his representative to create and run some acceptance tests."

"If the functional tests pass, as well as other tests, such as performance and usability, the system is ready to be deployed. Now if everything is perfect, the program passes through these stages in a straight line. But perfection only occurs in fairy tales. In reality, there are often misunderstandings. We don't always use the same words with the same meaning. You may say *always* when you really mean *usually*. Or I may hear *usually* and think it means *always*."

"Now when a misunderstanding is found, it needs to be corrected. If Tom finds that misunderstanding during testing, we have to figure out how to correct it. It could be that I simply made a mistake in coding. So you see a loopback shown by the line from test back to code in Figure 2.2. Tom tells me about the issue he discovered, and I correct it."

"It could be a misunderstanding that occurred while gathering details of a requirement. In that case, Tom and I would revisit the requirement. He might have interpreted one way and I might have interpreted another. We would check back with you to see which one of our interpretations was correct or whether you meant something else entirely different."

3. Particularly any team that does not use some form of test-driven development (TDD).

"This cycling back causes a delay in deploying the product, as well as extra cost in creating the product. So Tom and I like to operate in a different mode that uses quick feedback."

Quick Feedback Better Than Slow Feedback

Before describing Debbie and Tom's alternative process, let's look at the idea of feedback. Feedback involves using current output to influence future output. Feedback in software development is not quite the same as feedback in control systems. In control systems, values from the output are fed back into the input to regulate the output. In audio systems, the output sound from the speakers can accidentally get back into the input to the microphone. That positive feedback can cause an explosive sound to emit from the speakers. Instead, think of software feedback as a listener commenting that the sound from your stereo speakers is not the desired level. You adjust the amplifier volume to make the sound closer to what the listener likes.

Imagine you want to show off your new stereo to someone. You turn it on, but the listener says he cannot hear the music very well. You constantly increase the volume. If the listener gives you frequent feedback, you'll stop the increase just after you've increased past where he wanted it to be. So the volume will be pretty close to what he wants. You may home in even further by reducing the volume more slowly. If the listener does not give you frequent feedback, you will increase the volume well above what he wants and then decrease it well below. You will continually cycle between too loud and too quiet.

Quick Feedback on Mileage

Quick feedback promotes different behavior. Energy-efficient cars, such as the Toyota Prius and the Honda Insight, have instantaneous mileage displays. When you drive one of these cars, you find out quickly which actions decrease or increase mileage. For example, rapid acceleration shows up as really low mileage. Trying to beat the car next to you when the light turns green quickly indicates that you have used a lot of gas. Drivers of cars without mileage displays sometimes check their mileage every time they fill up the tank. But then it is hard to determine what actions during the previous tank-full caused either good or bad mileage. All that you can ascertain is that something during that period caused the mileage to vary.

Quick feedback means less delay. Quick feedback is good. The output will be closer to the desired outcome.

Preimplementation Tests

"So how are things going to be different working with you?," Cathy asks.

Debbie starts to describe another process. She shows Cathy the chart in Figure 2.3.

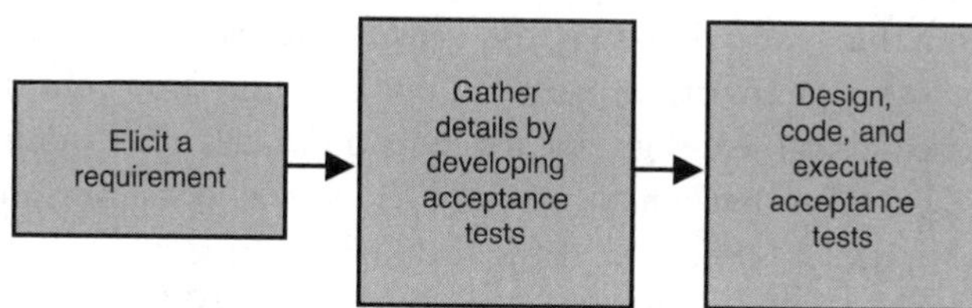

Figure 2.3 *ATDD Flow*

"Here's the process that Tom and I use. After we elicit a requirement from you, Cathy, we work together to create some acceptance tests for the requirement. These are specific examples of the requirement in action. When I'm coding, I'll use these tests to ensure that my implementation meets the tests. When it does, I'll turn it over to Tom for the other types of tests that are discussed later [in the next chapter]."

Tom chimes in. "This is a small application relative to some we've worked on in the past. Debbie's machine will be almost an exact duplicate of your computer where the application will be deployed. So when she turns the application over to me and I run it on the test system that exactly matches your computer, I don't expect any acceptance tests that we've created to fail."

"What this means," Debbie continues, "is that the three of us will be creating these tests together to make sure that we all have a clear understanding of what a requirement means. When a requirement is delivered, it will work as understood."

"I really don't know anything about testing," Cathy states. "So how will I help?"

Debbie replies, "The test creation starts with getting examples from you on how a requirement should work. Tom and I can take these examples and turn them into the actual tests."

"We will not be doing this up front for all the requirements. As you decide what the next requirement to work on is, we'll get together and work on the details. I know you have to work at the store and there is no room for us to set up our computers there. But because we're only a couple of miles away and there is a great bike path between our places, we'll ride over for these meetings. We've found that meeting face to face is much more effective than having a long conference call on the phone" [Cockburn01].

Cathy interjects, "I'm not always available. I have a lot of other work that Sam needs me to do."

Debbie answers, "I understand. We'll schedule the face-to-face meetings at your convenience. For things that are pretty standard in software, such as adding an item, Tom and I will make up the examples for the tests and then review them with you before I start implementing. If it's a quick question, we'll give you a call. The only thing we ask is that you get back to us relatively soon. We can often work on other pieces of the problem, but if the question regards something that is fundamental to the design, we'll need a quick answer. And we'll identify the difference between that which we need as soon as possible and that which can wait a little while. Of course, if the little while turns into a day or a week, your project will be delayed and there will be more costs."

Lean and Agile Principles

ATDD is based on some lean principles and some agile principles. The lean principles come from Mary and Tom Poppendieck [Poppendieck02], [Poppendieck03], [Poppendieck04].[4] The agile principles are listed in "The Agile Manifesto," which is a widely recognized statement on how to better develop software [Agile01].

The Poppendiecks developed principles of lean software development derived from lean manufacturing. One principle is to reduce waste in a process. Creating acceptance tests up front reduces waste by decreasing the loopbacks from testing back to coding.

Another principle is to build in integrity. Acceptance tests for each portion of the system help to ensure that the modules are high quality. The tests are run as each module is developed, not when the developers have completed the entire system.

The collaboration between the members of the triad helps amplify learning, which is another lean principle. The members learn from each other about the business domain and the development and testing issues.

The triad is one manifestation of the Agile Manifesto principle that "business people and developers must work together daily throughout the project." Although they may not be physically together, they will be working together continuously.

Another agile principle is that "working software is the primary measure of progress." With the acceptance tests, Debbie and Tom can deliver not only

4. See [Shalloway01] and [Larman01] for another explanation of lean principles.

working software, but software that delivers more precisely what Cathy is asking for.

Summary

- The triad consists of the three units—customer, developer, and tester—that collaborate to create high-quality software.
- Quick feedback is better than slow feedback.ATDD reduces unnecessary loopbacks.
- ATDD is lean and agile.

Chapter 3

Testing Strategy

"How do I test thee? Let me count the ways."

Elizabeth Barrett Browning (altered)

The different types of testing that occur during development are explained to give the context in which acceptance tests are developed. The tests that the customer provides are only one part of the testing process.

Types of Tests

Acceptance tests are one part of the testing strategy for a program. The easiest way to describe the full set of tests for an application is to use the testing matrix from Gerard Meszaros [Meszaros01]. The matrix in Figure 3.1 shows how acceptance tests fit into the overall picture.

Customer tests encompass the business facing functional tests that ensure the product is acceptable to the customer. These functional tests are the acceptance tests described in this book. The result of almost every acceptance test can be expressed in yes or no terms. Examples are, "When a customer places an order of $100, does the system give a 5% discount?" and, "Is the Edit button disabled if the account is inactive?"

As shown in lower right of the matrix, there are other requirements for a software system checked by the *property tests*. These include nonfunctional requirements (often called the *ilities* or quality attributes) such as scalability, reliability, security, and performance.[1] Some of the tests for these requirements can be expressed in questions with yes or no answers. For example, "If there are 100

1. Some people separate performance (and security for that matter) because it does not end in *ility*.

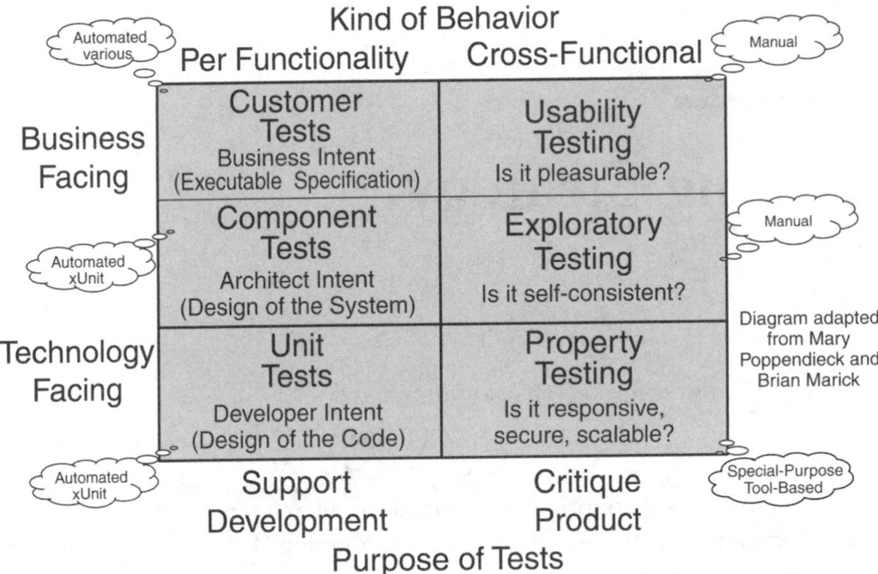

Figure 3.1 *The Testing Matrix (Source: Meszaros, Xunit Test Patterns: Refactoring Test Code, Fig 6.1 "Purpose of Tests" p. 51, © 2007 Pearson Education, Inc. Reproduced by permission of Pearson Education, Inc.)*

users on the system and they are placing orders at the same time, does the system respond to each one of them in less than 5 seconds?" However, for other quality attributes, the question can be asked, but the answer is unknowable, such as, "Is the system secure from all threats?" For the user to accept the system, the system needs to pass these nonfunctional tests. So the property tests are sometimes referred to as *nonfunctional acceptance tests.*

Usability tests are in a separate category. You might create some factual tests, such as, "Given a certain level of user, can he pay for an order in less than 30 seconds?" or, "Given 100 users ranking the system usability on a scale from 1 to 10, is the average greater than 8?" But often, usability is more subjective: "Does this screen feel right to me?" or, "Does this workflow match the way I do things?" Usability testing is strictly manual. No robot program can measure the usability of a system. Often the customer is of the mind, "I'm not sure what I'd like, but I'll know it when I see it." It's difficult to write a test for that [Constantine01], [Nielsen01], [Aston01].

Exploratory tests are tests whose flow is not described in advance [Pettichord01]. An exploratory tester does parallel test design, execution, result interpretation, and learning. Exploratory testing may disclose defects undiscovered by other forms of testing [Whittaker01], [Bach01].

The term has also been applied to a situation in which all team members—Tom, Cathy, and Debbie—take on the persona of a user and go through the system based on the needs and abilities of that user. Because a system has to be working to be explored, these tests cannot be created up front. But they can be performed whenever the program is in a working condition.

Unit tests are created by Debbie and other developers in conjunction with writing code. They aid in creating a design that is testable, a measure of high technical quality. Unit tests also serve as documentation for the way the internal code works.

Component tests verify that units and combinations of units work together to perform the desired operations. As we will see later, many of the unit and component tests are derived from the acceptance tests [Wiki03].

All types of testing are important to ensure delivery of a quality product.[2] This book discusses mainly acceptance tests—the functional tests that involve collaboration between the business customer, the developer, and the tester.

Where Tests Run

Acceptance tests, as defined in this book, can be run on multiple platforms at multiple times. An example of some of the platforms is shown in Figure 3.2. Debbie runs unit tests on her machine. She can also run many acceptance tests, particularly if they don't require external resources. For example, any business rule test can usually run on her machine. In some instances, she may create test doubles for external resources to avoid having tests depend on them. The topic of test doubles will be covered in Chapter 11, "System Boundary."

On a larger project, Debbie and the other developers would merge their code to a build or integration platform. The unit tests of all the developers would be run on this platform to make sure that the changes one developer makes in his code would not affect the changes that other developers make. The acceptance tests would be run on this platform if the external resources or their test doubles are available. In Sam's project, Debbie's machine acts as both the developer platform and the integration platform because she has no other developers on the project.

Once all tests pass on the build/integration platform, the application is deployed to the test platform. On this platform, the full external resources, such as a working database, are available. All types of tests can be run here. But often the unit tests are not run, particularly if the application is deployed as a whole and not rebuilt for the test platform.

Cathy, the customer, and other users try out the user interface to see how well it works. Tom can do some exploratory testing. If this were a system that

2. See [Crispin02] for a discussion of how to implement the other testing types.

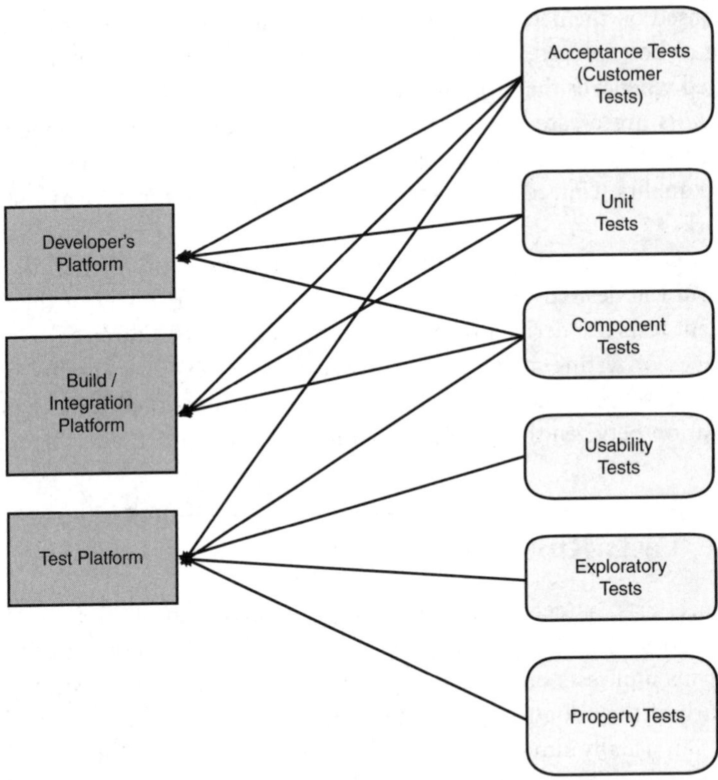

Figure 3.2 *Where Tests Run*

required it, the security testers and the performance testers could have their first go at the application.

Once the customer is satisfied with the outcome of all tests, the application is deployed to the production platform. There is still a possibility that bugs may show up. Users may do entirely unexpected things, or there may be some configuration that causes problems for the application. Debbie and Tom have a measure of quality that is the number of bugs in production. They are called *escaped bugs* because they escaped discovery from all other testing.

Test Facets

Figure 3.3 shows examples of positive and negative testing. Positive tests ensure that the program works as expected. Negative testing checks to see that the program does not create unexpected results. Acceptance tests that the customer thinks about are mostly in the "Specified Effect" box. The ones that Tom and

Debbie come up with are in the other three boxes. Tom, as the tester, has a particular focus on finding unexpected results.

	Expected Result	*Unexpected Result*
Valid Input	Specified effect	Unspecified effect
Invalid Input	Specified error handling	Any effects

Figure 3.3 *Positive and Negative Testing*

Control and Observation Points

Tests are often run from the external view of the system. Bret Pettichord talks about control points and observation points [Pettichord01]. A *control point* is the part of the system where the tester inputs values or commands to the system. The *observation point* is where the system response is checked to see that it is performing properly. Often the control point is the user interface and the output is observed on the user interface, a printed report, or a connection to an external platform. As seen in the next chapter, it is often easier to run many tests if you have control and observation points within the system.

New Test Is a New Requirement

Requirements and tests are linked. You can't have one without the other. They are like Abbott and Costello, Calvin and Hobbes, nuts and bolts, or another favorite duo. The tests clarify and amplify the requirements [Melnik01]. A test that fails shows that the system does not properly implement a requirement. A test that passes is a specification of how the system works. Any test created after the code is written is a new requirement or a new detail on an existing requirement.[3]

If Cathy comes across a new detail after Debbie has implemented the code, the triad needs to create a new test for that detail. For example, suppose there is an input field that doesn't have limits on what can go in it. Then Cathy realizes that there needs to be a limit. The triad would create tests to ensure that the limit is checked on input. The requirement that there is a limit and the tests that ensure it is checked are linked. Because the tests did not exist before Debbie finished the code, it is not a developer bug that the limit was not checked. It is

3. Thanks to Scott Bain and Amir Kolsky for the discussion where this idea occurred.

just a new requirement that needs to be implemented. Some people might call it an analysis bug or a missed requirement. Or you can simply say, "You can't think of everything" and call it a new requirement.

Summary

- Testing areas include
  - Acceptance tests that are business-facing functionality tests
  - Tests that check component and module functionality
  - Unit tests that developers use to drive the design
  - Usability, exploratory, and quality attribute (reliability, scalability, performance)
- Functionality tests should be run frequently on developer, build/integration, and test platforms.
- Tests and requirements are linked together.

Chapter 4

An Introductory Acceptance Test

"If you don't know where you're going, you will wind up somewhere else."

Yogi Berra

An example of an acceptance test is presented, along with four ways that you can execute an acceptance test.

A Sample Business Rule

Here is an example from a previous project where Debbie and Tom created tests in collaboration with the customer. The business representative, Betty, presented the two of them with a business rule for giving discounts that she had obtained from one of the stakeholders. The stakeholder wanted to give discounts to the firm's customers based on what type of customer they were. Debbie had already completed implementing a previous requirement that determined the customer type. Here's the rule that Betty gave them:

> If Customer Type is Good and Item Total is less than or equal to $10.00,
> Then do not give a discount,
> Otherwise, give a 1% discount.
>
> If Customer Type is Excellent,
> Then give a discount of 1% for any order.
>
> If Item Total is greater than $50.00,
> Then give a discount of 5%.

This rule may seem clear. It uses consistent terms, such as *Customer Type* and *Item Total.* Debbie and Tom had previously gotten from Betty the definitions of those terms [Evans01]. For example, Item Total did not include taxes or shipping. But even with that consistency, there was an issue. Tom and Debbie looked at the rule and tried to figure out what the discount percentage should be if a customer who is good had an order total greater than $50.00. So Betty, Debbie, and Tom made up a table of examples.[1]

Discount Calculation		
Item Total	**Customer Rating**	**Discount Percentage?**
$10.00	Good	0%
$10.01	Good	1%
$50.01	Good	1% ??
$.01	Excellent	1%
$50.00	Excellent	1%
$50.01	Excellent	5%

The answers in this table of examples are going to be used to test the implementation. The first two rows show that the limit between giving a good customer no discount or a 1% discount is $10.00. The "less than or equal to" in the business rule is pretty clear. The tests just ensure that the implementation produced that result. The ?? was put after the 1 in the third example because it was unclear to the triad whether that was the right value. To what type of customer did the last statement in the rule apply?

The fourth row indicates that the discount for an excellent customer starts at the smallest possible Item Total. The fifth and sixth entries show that the discount increases just after the $50.00 point.[2]

Betty took this table back to the stakeholder. He looked it over and said that the interpretation was correct. He did not want to give a 5% discount to good customers. So ?? from that result was removed from that cell. There was now a set of tests that could be applied to the system. The correct discount amount test is not just a single case but includes cases for all possible combinations.

Tom suggested other possibilities. For example, what if Item Total was less than $0.00? Tom asked Betty whether this would ever happen. She said it might

---

1. See Appendix D, "Tables Everywhere," for an example of putting the rule into a table.
2. There could be even more interpretations of this business rule, as reviewers pointed out. For example, if Customer Rating is any other type than Good or Excellent, what should the discount be?

be possible, because Item Total could include a rebate coupon that was greater than the total of the items. So Tom added the following possibilities.

Discount Calculation		
Item Total	Customer Rating	Discount Percentage?
$–.01	Good	0%
$–.01	Excellent	1% ??

Tom explained that it didn't seem right to apply a discount percentage that would actually increase the amount that the customer owed. Based on this example, Betty went back to the stakeholder and confirmed that the percentage should be 0% if Item Total is less than 0 for any customer. So the table became as follows.

Discount Calculation		
Item Total	Customer Rating	Discount Percentage?
$–.01	Good	0%
$–.01	Excellent	0%

These examples were the acceptance tests for the system. If Debbie implemented these correctly, Betty would be satisfied. Now it was a matter of how Debbie and Tom were going to use these tests to test the system.

Implementing the Acceptance Tests

Tom and Debbie needed to apply these tests to the implementation they were developing. There were at least four possible ways to do this. First, Tom could create a test script that operates manually at the user interface level. Second, Debbie could create a test user interface that allows her or Tom to check the appropriate discount percentages. Third, Debbie could perform the tests using a unit testing framework. Fourth, Tom and Debbie could implement the tests with an acceptance test framework. Following are examples of how they could use each of these possibilities.

Test Script

In this case, the program has a user interface that allows a customer to enter an order. The user interface flow is much like Amazon or other order sites. The user enters an order and a summary screen appears, such as the one in Figure 4.1.

Figure 4.1 *Order Interface*

What Tom would have to do is to create a script that either he or Debbie would follow to test each of the six cases in the Discount Calculation table. He might start by computing what the actual discount amount should be for each case. Unless the Order Summary screen shows this percentage, this value is the only output Tom can check to ensure the calculation is correct. Here is an addition to the table that shows the amounts he needs to look for.

Discount Calculation				
Item Total	Customer Rating	Discount Percentage?	Discount Amount?	Notes
$10.00	Good	0%	$0.00	
$10.01	Good	1%	$0.10	Discount rounded down
$50.01	Good	1%	$0.50	Discount rounded down
$.01	Excellent	1%	$0.00	Discount rounded down
$50.00	Excellent	1%	$0.50	
$50.01	Excellent	5%	$2.50	Discount rounded down

The script would go something like this:

1. Log on as a customer who has the rating listed in the table.
2. Start an order, and put items in it until the total is the specified amount in the Item Total column on the test.
3. Check that the discount on the Order Summary screen matches Discount Amount in the table.

Then the test would be repeated five more times to cover all six cases. Either Tom or Debbie would do this once the discount feature and order features are implemented. This test should be run for all possible combinations. That would have been more difficult if there were more discount percentages for more customer types. There's another possible way to run these tests.

Test User Interface

To simplify executing the tests, Debbie could set up a user interface that connects to the discount calculation module in her code. This interface would be used only during testing. But having it would cut down on the work involved in showing that the percentage was correctly determined. The interface might be a command-line interface (CLI) or a graphical user interface (GUI). For example, a CLI might be this:

```
RunDiscountCalculatorTest  <item_total> <customer_type>
```

And when it is run for each case, such as

```
RunDiscountCalculatorTest 10,00 Good
```

It would output the result

```
0
```

A GUI, such as what's shown in Figure 4.2, might be connected to the CLI.

Regardless of whether it is a GUI or CLI, the user interface has penetrated into the system. It exposes a test point within the system that allows easier testing. Here's an analogy showing the differences between this method and Tom's original test script. Suppose you want to build a car that accelerates quickly. You know you need an engine that can increase its speed rapidly. If you could only check the engine operation as part of the car, you would need to put the engine in the car and then take the car on a test drive. If you had a test point for the engine speed inside the car, you could check how fast the engine sped up without driving the car. You could measure it in the garage. You'd save a lot of

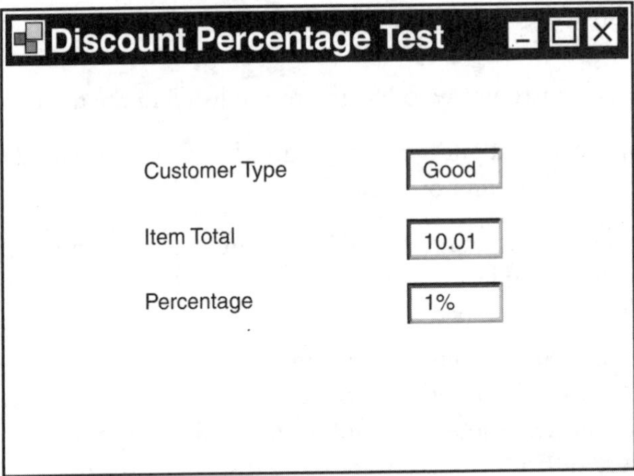

Figure 4.2 *User Interface for Testing*

time in on-the-road testing if the engine wasn't working properly. That doesn't mean you don't need to test the engine on the road. But if the engine isn't working by itself, you don't run the road test until the engine passes its own tests.

If you're not into cars, Figure 4.3 shows a context diagram. The Order Summary screen connects to the system through the standard user interface layer. The Discount Percentage user interface connects to some module inside the system. Let's call that module the Discount Calculator. By having a connection to the inside, a tester can check whether the internal behavior by itself is correct.

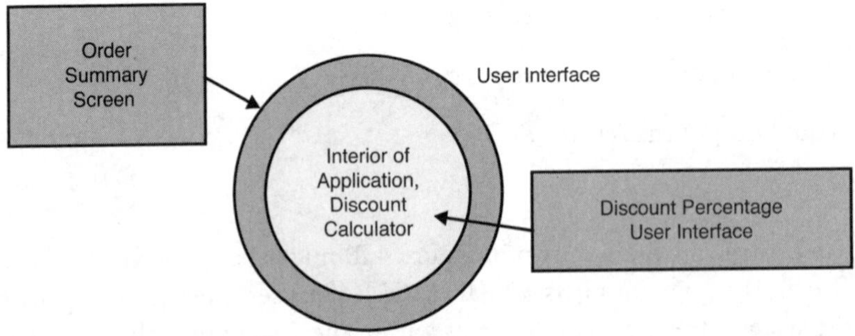

Figure 4.3 *Context Diagram*

xUnit Test

The next way to perform the testing is to write the tests for the Discount Calculator in a unit testing framework. The framework used is usually in the language that the program is written in. There is a generic framework called xUnit that has versions for many programming languages. Here's a sample of what these tests look like in Java using Junit [Beck01]. The test would look similar in TestNG [Beust01], but the order of the parameters would be reversed:

```
class DiscountCalculatorTest  {
   @Test
   public void shouldCalculateDiscountPercentageForCustomer() {
      DiscountCalculator dc = new DiscountCalculator();
      assertEquals(0, dc.computeDiscountPercentage(10.0,
         Customer.Good));
      assertEquals(1, dc.computeDiscountPercentage (10.01,
         Customer.Good));
      assertEquals(1, dc.computeDiscountPercentage (50.01,
         Customer.Good));
      assertEquals(1, dc.computeDiscountPercentage(.01,
         Customer.Excellent));
      assertEquals(1, dc.computeDiscountPercentage(50.0,
         Customer.Excellent));
      assertEquals(5, dc.computeDiscountPercentage(50.01,
         Customer.Excellent));
   }
}
```

Any time there is a change in the examples that Betty and the stakeholder use to explain the business rule, Debbie may want these tests to conform to the changed examples. That's a bit of waste. The next testing framework can eliminate that waste.

Automated Acceptance Test

Betty, Debbie, and Tom agreed that the examples in the table accurately reflected the requirements and there would be less waste if the table did not have to be converted into another form for testing. Several available acceptance test frameworks use tables. Some examples are in Appendix C, "Test Framework Examples." With these frameworks, you describe the tests with a table similar to the one for the example.

The following test table works in table-based frameworks, such as the FitNesse and Fit frameworks. A similar style table can be used in narrative-form frameworks, such as Cucumber.[3] The table looks practically like the one that Betty presented to the stakeholder.

---

3. Fit is the Framework for Integrated Tests, developed by Ward Cunningham [Cunningham01], [Cunningham02]. Fit was incorporated into FitNesse by Bob Martin [Martin01]. Cucumber can be found in [Chelimsky01].

Discount Calculation		
Item Total	Customer Rating	Discount Percentage()
$10.00	Good	0%
$10.01	Good	1%
$50.01	Good	1%
$.01	Excellent	1%
$50.00	Excellent	1%
$50.01	Excellent	5%

Now when the table is used as a test, the Fit/FitNesse framework executes code that connects to the Discount Calculator. It gives the Discount Calculator the values in Item Total and Customer Rating. The Discount Calculator returns the Discount Percentage. The framework compares the returned value to the value in the table. If it agrees, the column shows up in green. If it does not, it shows up in red. The colors cannot be seen in this black-and-white book. So light gray represents green and dark gray represents red. The first time the test was run, the following table was output.

Discount Calculation		
Item Total	Customer Rating	Discount Percentage()
$10.00	Good	0%
$10.01	Good	1%
$50.01	Good	Expected 1% Actual 5%
$.01	Excellent	1%
$50.00	Excellent	1%
$50.01	Excellent	5%

With the results shown in the table, it was apparent there was an error in the Discount Calculator. Once it was fixed, Betty saw the passing tests as confirmation that the calculation was working as desired.

An Overall Test

If the discount test is applied using one of the last three forms, there still needs to be a test using the order interface. This ensures that processing an order is correctly connected to the Discount Calculator. The script for an order would be run for a couple of instances. But unless there was a large risk factor involved, the script might just be executed for a few cases, such as the following.

Discount Calculation			
Item Total	**Customer Rating**	**Discount Percentage?**	**Discount Amount?**
$10.01	Good	1%	$0.10
$50.01	Excellent	5%	$2.50

Testing Process

The acceptance test is the original table that Betty, Tom, and Debbie developed to clarify the business rule. This acceptance test can be used at four different levels, as described earlier in this chapter. Because the acceptance test was customer supplied, all four levels are considered acceptance tests in this book. The last two forms are automated by their nature. The second form—an interface to the Discount Calculator—can be automated. The test for an order could also be automated with a little more effort. However, you should still check it manually as well.

Passing the acceptance tests is necessary but insufficient to ensure that the system meets the customer needs. Other tests, such as those for quality attributes and usability (described in Chapter 3, "Testing Strategy"), also need to be passed. See [Meszaros02] for more information.

Summary

- Examples of requirements clarify the requirements.
- The examples can be used as tests for the implementation of the requirements.
- Tests for business rules can be executed in at least these four ways:
    - Creation through the user interface of a transaction that invokes the business rule
    - Development of a user interface that directly invokes the business rule
    - A unit test implemented in a language's unit testing framework
    - An automated test that communicates with the business rule module

Chapter 5

The Example Project

"When you are inspired by some great purpose, some extraordinary project, all your thoughts break their bonds; your mind transcends limitations, your consciousness expands in every direction, and you find yourself in a new, great and wonderful world."

Patanjali

The team meets for a chartering session to develop the objectives for Sam's idea for a new system. The charter is the first step in the project (see Figure 5.1) and includes the objectives—the tests for the project as a whole. Then the team holds the initial requirements elicitation workshop that creates high-level requirements and high-level acceptance criteria.

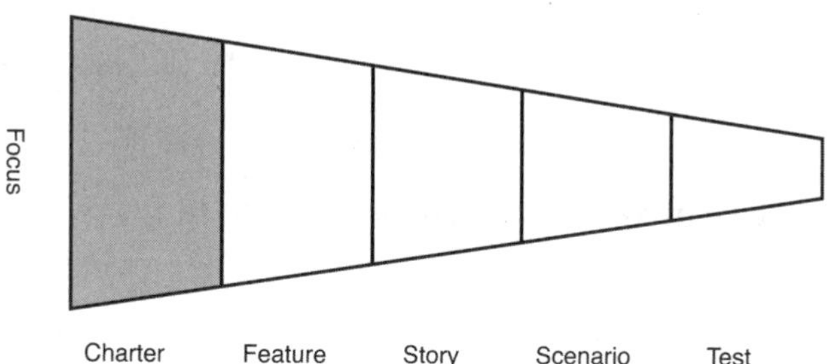

Figure 5.1 *Projects Start with the Charter*

The Charter

Sam rents a conference room for the initial project meeting. He is the sponsor of the project—in particular, the one who is paying for it. Cathy is the business customer. Sam's sister Mary and her husband Harry, who often work in the store, and Cary, who clerks in the store, are there as potential users. Debbie and Tom, representing the development and test units, participate as well.

The purpose of the meeting is to create a project charter. A charter can include many sections, such as vision, mission, scope, deliverables, objectives, and principles [Wiegers03] [Wiegers04]. The *vision* describes the end-state of the result of the project—why the project should be done. The *mission* involves the path that will be taken to get to the vision. The *scope* documents the boundaries of the project, including the key events that the project addresses. The *deliverables* are the tangible outputs. The *objectives* are measurable criteria for the success of the project that are visible by external observation. *Principles* are statement of values that a team uses to inform decision making. Other sections can include stakeholders (those affected by the project), project organization, plans for implementations, risks, and constraints.

Examples of a charter's vision, mission, principles, and objectives are shown in this chapter. Posting these sections of the charter on the project board helps keep everyone focused. The charter meeting involves more than just Sam and Cathy so that everyone can get an idea of the big picture, understand the issues involved, and agree that the project's objectives are feasible.

Sam starts by presenting his vision for the project. He wants to eliminate waste in the rental process and offer more services to customers. The discussion then starts revolving around objectives.

Objectives

Objectives should be SMART. SMART is an acronym that has many interpretations [Project01]. In the version here, SMART means

- **Specific**—Exactly what is going to be accomplished, or what is the specific outcome?
- **Measurable**—Can the outcome be measured?
- **Achievable**—Can the outcome reasonably be accomplished?
- **Relevant**—Does the outcome support the vision?
- **Time boxed**—How long will it take to achieve the objective?

Without detailing who-says-what-when, the sponsor, customer, and users (Sam, Cathy, Mary, Harry, and Cary) usually propose objectives. If Debbie and Tom (the developer/tester units) think that an objective is not achievable within the time box, the objective misses the "A" part of SMART. The measurement or the time box has to be changed so that the objective is agreed upon, or the objective has to be dropped. The meeting ends with everyone agreeing on the SMART objectives listed in the following sidebar.

Vision, Mission, Objective, and Principles of a Charter

Vision

- The rental process creates minimum waste and offers more services to customers.

Mission

- Create a custom software package.

Objectives

- Within two months after project initiation, clerks will spend 50% less time per transaction on both CD check-outs and returns.
- Within three months after project initiation, customers will be able to reserve CDs prior to renting them.

Principles

- Customer satisfaction is of primary importance.
- Clerk convenience is secondary.

Project Acceptance Tests

The objectives are the acceptance tests for the overall project.[1] The first objective requires that the current amount of time it takes to process a CD be measured.[2] In two months, the time will be measured again. If the second measurement is not 50% less than the first measurement, the test has failed and the objective has not been met. Did the project still produce business value by reducing the time? Yes. But it did not deliver the full business value, which is why the project was approved.

Even if the full effect was achieved, but not within the specified time box of two months, getting the business value was delayed. This delay reduces the return on investment (ROI) received from the project.

1. Objectives are also related to management tests. See [III01].
2. This could be more detailed, giving the exact events that make up the process time, such as from a customer handing the clerk the CD to the clerk handing the customer the rental contract.

A Simple Objective

A $200 million project had a simple objective: It was defined by the following:

- 70mpg

This was the objective for the Honda Insight: a new hybrid vehicle. The single focus drove the engineering design. When engineers needed to make a decision, they consulted the objective. Cutting weight is a large factor in increasing mileage. You might imagine the discussions:

"Seatbelts? Well, they weigh three pounds. Delete them." There were implicit constraints. The car had to be sellable at least.

"Air conditioning? It takes 2mpg. Skip it." The 2 miles per gallon would count against the mileage if air conditioning was factory installed. So the dealers had to install it.

The total capacity was 365 pounds. That is the total for two people and cargo.

The goal was not to sell a lot of cars, but to make the mileage objective.

And they did it.

P.S. Do you know what the charter objectives for your project are?

Objectives Should Be Measurable

A project at one company had the purpose of making its website more user friendly so that people would stay there longer, thus increasing the possibility that the people would buy more products and drive revenue. The company started with an objective that read something like this:

- Within six months, the site should be more user friendly.

The issue with this objective as it stands is that it is practically subjective. It needs to be stated in measureable terms. The measurement must be relevant to the goal. There are many ways to perform measurements, such as the time it takes for a user to perform certain operations. Detailed measurements can help determine why a particular program is or is not user friendly. But for purposes of a simple high-level measurement, you might use a survey, such as the System Usability Scale (a measure of 0 to

100) [Usability01]. Now the objective can reference a measureable result, such as this:

- Within six months, the website shall have an increase of 10 points on the System Usability Scale.

You can create a mini-charter for each release of a project. The mini-charter may include a vision and the objectives for that release. The time boxes for the objectives usually correspond to the release schedule. If an objective cannot be met during the release time box, it could be split into subobjectives, each of which is achievable within the schedule.

High-Level Requirements

A business must have capabilities to run. In Sam's case, the capabilities include keeping track of CDs and collecting payment for rentals. The capabilities today are implemented through manual features—a set of paper index cards and a cash register. The new system will have features that provide these capabilities. High-level requirements are usually gathered at the feature level (see Figure 5.2).

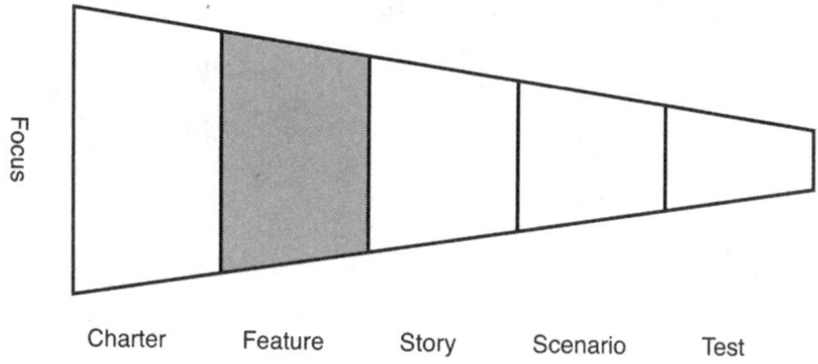

Figure 5.2 *After Charter, Elicit High-Level Requirements*[3]

Features

The entire team meets again for a high-level requirements elicitation workshop. Briefly, here is what goes on. Tom, who has had some facilitation training, manages the brainstorming workshop.[4] It is natural for him to facilitate because

3. This was adapted from a diagram by Jim Shore.
4. See [Gottesdiener01], [Gottesdiener02], [Gottesdiener03], [Tabaka01] for more details.

he does not have an investment in the outcome. For a few minutes, he has all the participants individually write down ideas for features, one per index card. Tom suggests that people not hold back on their thoughts. They should write down any ideas they can imagine that may pertain to the charter. Out-of-scope ideas will be eliminated later when the ideas are matched to the objectives of the charter.

The team members then place their cards on the table and match ideas that are almost the same. If there are natural groupings, they place the cards close to each other. The ideas that were grouped together show up beneath the overall idea. The results are as follows:

Feature List

- Check out and check in
- Reservation system for CDs
- CD catalog of all CDs so renters can select ones to rent or reserve
- For multiple stores, a way to return a CD to any store
- For multiple stores, a way to determine which stores have particular CDs
- Credit card charging to eliminate cash
- Hookup with a video rental store to offer combined reservations
- Have a party for customers who rent lots of CDs that month

The ideas need to be whittled down. The group came up with ideas related to Sam's expansion plans, not the current objectives. The customer unit needs to decide which features help achieve the objectives and thus should be part of the scope of the project. After some discussion, the group came up with the following features:

- Reservation system for CDs
- Check out and check in
- Credit card charging to eliminate cash

The remaining ideas are not tossed away. They are captured for revisiting once the selected features are implemented.

Feature Acceptance Criteria

Now that the features are selected, the entire team examines them to see what the high-level acceptance criteria are for each of them. As a tester, Tom has valuable input into this process. If the team cannot come up with a high-level idea of how to check that a feature is implemented correctly, the feature needs more definition. Working together, the team comes up with the following:

Feature Acceptance Criteria

Check out and check-in

- Check out a CD; make sure the details are correct and it's recorded as rented.
- Check in a CD; make sure that any late rental fees are computed and that it's recorded as returned.

Credit card charging to eliminate cash

- Check out a CD and see if a charge is recorded.
- Check in a CD and see if late rental fees are charged.

Reservation system for CDs

- Reserve a CD and see if a reserver is notified when a CD becomes available.

Now that the features are agreed upon, the developers and testers determine a high-level estimate for them to see if they can be implemented to achieve the objective within the specified time box[5] If not, the project needs review.

The team then plans the sequence and schedule for the features. The means for doing so depend on the development process. The developer/tester units could estimate the features and schedule them into iterations.[6] Or the items could be placed in a work queue and the developer/tester units could work on the highest item in that queue until it was finished.[7] Estimating, sequencing, and scheduling are covered in detail in other books, as [Shalloway01] and [Cohn01].

5. Some teams do a high-level business value estimate to determine a high-level ROI for each feature. This ROI can help in planning.
6. Such as in Scrum [Pichler01].
7. Such as in Kanban [Anderson01].

In this tale, Sam and Cathy agree that the features on the list should be developed in this order:[8]

1. Check out and check in
2. Credit card charging to eliminate cash
3. Reservation system for CDs

Summary

- A charter includes a project's vision, mission, objectives, and principles.
- Objectives should be specific, measurable, agreed upon, relevant, and time boxed.
- Objectives represent acceptance tests for the whole project.
- High-level requirements should support the objectives.
- High-level requirements have high-level acceptance criteria.

8. If they wanted to, they could determine the business value of each feature as shown in Appendix C, "Test Framework Examples," and use the rough return on investment as a consideration in determining the order of feature development.

Chapter 6

The User Story Technique

"It is better to take many small steps in the right direction than to make a great leap forward only to stumble backward."

Chinese Proverb

The triad (Cathy, Debbie, and Tom) meets to develop stories from a feature. Debbie explains roles in stories, their attributes, and their personas. She introduces a story card template. Tom shows how acceptance criteria can determine story size. The Independent, Negotiable, Valuable, Estimable, Small, and Testable (INVEST) criteria for stories is listed.

Stories

The features need to be broken down into smaller pieces, the next step shown in Figure 6.1. It is easier to devise specific acceptance tests for smaller pieces than for an entire feature. The focus of each story is narrower than the feature. One or two features are broken down into stories—just enough to fill the team's time until the next feature decomposition session.

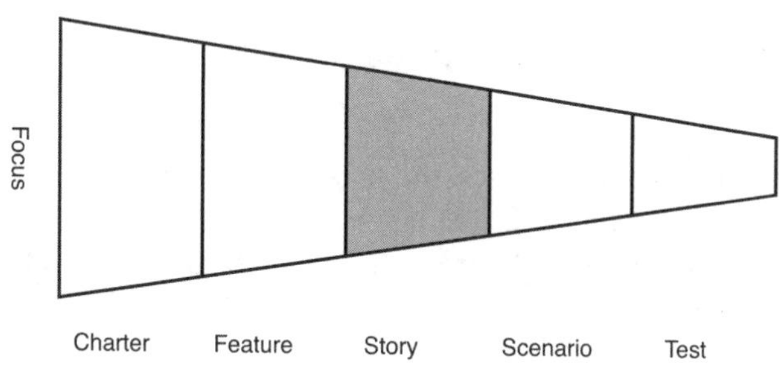

Figure 6.1 *After High-Level Requirement, Create Stories*

The team gets together again, this time without Sam. As the sponsor, he has agreed to and is happy with the features that are going to be implemented. He will come back as they are developed to see how things are going. Cathy will lead the effort to develop the stories, getting suggestions from the users (Cary, Mary, and Harry) along the way. Cathy has the necessary business and domain knowledge to create the stories. Debbie and Tom can work with Cathy to help her create the stories and to get a firsthand understanding of what the stories are all about.

The team is going to break down the first few features into stories. A *requirement story* is a small portion of a feature. Many of the requirement stories are called *user stories* because they involve something that a user wants to do with the system. Sometime a requirement story is just a constraint on the system, such as using open-source software to avoid license fees or writing the program in Java because that's the corporate standard. This type of story is often called a *constraint story*. The acceptance criteria for a constraint story are usually specified by the constraint.

Features into Stories

Debbie starts off, "Let's break down the features into stories. The features we are going to start with are"

- Check out and check in CDs.
- Enable credit card charging to eliminate cash.

"Tom and I use a story format that comes from *Extreme Programming* [Cohn02]. The form is"

As a <*role*>, I want to <*do something*> so that <*reason*>.

"The <*role*> represents the user, the <*do something*> is what the user is trying to accomplish, and the <*reason*> is why the user is doing it. The <*role*> and <*do something*> are the critical parts. The <*reason*> is often helpful, but it's not required. An example of this form is"

As the clerk, I want to check out a CD for a customer so that I can keep track of who has rented it.

Roles

Debbie continues, "Before we start on the user stories, we need to come up with some roles that are going to be involved in the stories. These roles are not necessarily specific people, but the 'hats' that people wear in the rental process and are important to uncover. When we gather the details for a story, we want to ensure that someone who plays that role is available for collaboration. When we do usability testing or exploratory testing, we take on a role to see how the system functions from that perspective."

"We use the same method that we did in coming up with features. Everybody brainstorms by themselves and writes down potential roles. We then put the cards on the table, match them up, and group them."

After thinking, writing, and grouping, Cathy, with the help of the rest of the team, came up with the following roles. Each role is clarified by listing its responsibilities.

Roles

Clerk—Checks out CD and checks them in

Inventory maintainer—Keeps track of overall CD inventory

Finance manager—Manages all monetary transactions, such as rental payments and late rental fees

Renter—Pays for CDs with cash or, in the future, with a credit card

Tom notes, "Cathy plays two of these roles: inventory maintainer and finance manager. The roles are separate because they have different interests and points of view, even though they are played by one person."[1]

Role Attributes

Debbie continues, "Now that we have the roles, it's useful to come up with attributes for them. These attributes give a better idea of how to design the system and how to test it for usability. For each role, you determine"

- **Frequency of use**—This is how often someone uses the system.
- **Domain expertise**—This is in the area that the system is designed for.

1. There are other roles to consider, such as system administration, operations, and help desk.

- **Computer expertise**—This is experience and comfort in using a computer.
- **General goals**—These are goals you desire, such as convenience and speed.

"Let's take the role of clerk. Is there anyone else other than Cary who works as a clerk? What are their backgrounds?," Debbie asks.

Cathy replies, "Harry and Mary. Cary works there every day and is a computer whiz. His dad Harry is a retired English professor who fills in every now and then. He gets all his information from the books in the stacks at the library rather than from the Internet. Mary still works as a French professor. Her computer skills are probably more in line with Harry's than with Cary's."

Debbie goes on, "To avoid giving them names loaded with connotations, let's call the two types full-time and part-time clerks."

Cathy replies, "Based on what I know about the three of them, I think the attributes look like this."

Role Attributes

Full-Time Clerk

- **Frequency of use**—Every day
- **Domain expertise**—Excellent
- **Computer expertise**—Excellent
- **General goals**—Speed (as few keystrokes as possible)

Part-Time Clerk

- **Frequency of use**—One day a week
- **Domain expertise**—Understands the general area
- **Computer expertise**—Low
- **General goals**—Lots of helpful reminders

Persona

Debbie continues, "We could create a persona for each of these sets of attributes. A *persona* is an imaginary person described with lots of details [Cooper01]. It helps me and Tom to envision an actual user, rather than just a dull set of attributes. It puts a human face on the user. Let's do one for the part-time clerk. We'll use a different name for the persona to keep it less related to a particular part-time clerk."

Here's what the triad came up with:

> ***Persona***
>
> Larry listens to classical music on CDs all the time. He comes in one day a week to help check in and check out CDs. He prides himself in doing that without making mistakes. He's not up to date with all current technology. He's not graphically oriented, so icons don't have much meaning for him. He wonders if the new system is going to be too complicated and whether he'll be able to use it without problems.

Debbie comments, "This persona gives me a good picture to keep in mind for which I'll be developing the user interface. Now let's start on the stories themselves."

Stories for Roles

Over the next few hours, Cathy takes the lead in developing the stories from the features. She winds up with the following on the whiteboard:[2]

> ***Stories***
>
> - As the clerk, I want to check out a CD for a customer.
> - As the clerk, I want to check in a CD for a customer.
> - As the inventory maintainer, I want to know where every CD is—in the store or rented.
> - As the finance manager, I want to know how many CDs are turned in late and what late charges apply.
> - As the finance manager, I want to submit a credit card charge every time a CD is rented so that the store does not have to handle cash.
> - As the finance manager, I want to know how much is being charged every day so that I can check the charges against bank deposits.

---

2. Some teams create stories for malicious roles. For example, "As a cheapskate renter, I want to check out a CD without paying for it." The system needs to prevent this story from occurring.

Story Acceptance Criteria

"As we create each story, we need to list its acceptance criteria.[3] The criteria will be expanded into specific acceptance tests just before the story is developed." The team comes up with the following tests. The titles are a short reference to the stories listed previously.

Story Acceptance Criteria

Check Out CD

- Check out a CD. Check to see that it is recorded as rented.

Check In CD

- Check in a CD. Check to see that it is recorded as returned.
- Check in a CD that is late. Check to see that it is noted as late.

Report Inventory

- Check out a few CDs. See if the report shows them as rented.
- Check in a few CDs. See if the report shows them as in the store.

Charge Rental

- Check in a CD. See if the rental charge is correct. See if the credit charge matches the rental charge. See if the charge is made to the credit card company. Check that the bank account receives money from the charge.

The team can record these stories using any appropriate technology, from cards on the wall to entries in a software system. In any case, at this point, the stories should be short—just a brief description. The details are gathered just prior to or during the story's implementation.

---

3. There is a risk that each story is individually correct, but together, they do not fully deliver the feature. Once the acceptance criteria for individual stories are created, the acceptance criteria for the feature may be updated. Those criteria can then be turned into specific acceptance tests. These tests may be harder to specify, but there will be fewer of them.

Story Estimates

Two estimates are often made for every story. These are the business value and the effort. The business value represents the relative worth of a story to the business. The effort estimate (often done in story points) includes all the work required to deliver the story, including implementing the code, testing it, and any other work involved. One way to estimate business value and effort is shown in Appendix B, "Estimating Business Value." Tracking the cumulative business value of delivered stories gives an idea of the project's progress. This keeps the entire team focused on delivering business value.

If a team uses iteration scheduling, the effort estimate can determine whether a story can fit into an iteration. If the team uses a work queue, the estimate indicates whether the items in the work queue are roughly the same size.

A rough return on investment can be calculated by dividing the business value by the effort. This can help the customer unit determine whether or when a particular story should be included in the project.

Acceptance Tests Determine Size

"That last story, Charge Rental, seems too big from the acceptance criteria," Tom suggested. "There are tests associated with the rental and tests associated with the credit card company. If we recognize that a story is too big at this point, we should break it down into smaller stories. Smaller stories are easier to develop and test. If we discover the number of specific acceptance tests is large when we detail the story, we may want to break it into two stories at that point."

"The Charge Rental story feels like it could be broken into at least two stories. One might be Compute Rental Charge and the other Submit Charge. The tests underneath each of these stories would be"

Compute Rental Charge

- Check in the CD. See if the rental charge is correct. See if the credit charge matches the rental charge.

Submit Charge

- Submit the charge to the credit card company. Check that the bank account receives money from the charge.

Tom continued, "In this case, Cathy, you may come up with acceptance tests for both of these stories because they are both business related. These two stories are related to Charge Rental. If you were estimating the business value [see Appendix B], these two stories may not have value because you can only submit a charge when both are complete. Charge Rental has a business value, and we get business value credit for it when it is complete."[4]

"When we get to the details, Debbie and I may find we need to break up stories into smaller ones that are technical. These stories are called *developer stories*. Debbie and I sometimes create them to cut down the size of the stories. Also, if we had multiple teams, we could break up one story into several stories that each team could work on in order to spread the work. It is the responsibility of the developer unit to create acceptance tests for developer stories" [see Chapter 16, "Developer Acceptance Tests"].

"Anytime stories are broken up, it's good to have the triad participate. Questions may arise in the breakup process that can yield answers which may lead to more understanding on everyone's part."

Customer Terms

Debbie announces, "Now we need to agree on common terminology. It seems that we are using the term *charge* in several ways. For example, *charge* can refer to both what you charge for a rental and a charge made on a credit card. This language duplication can be confusing later on. Cathy, we need to state the terms in business language, not computer language. So we can all agree on the terms, let's write a glossary. You're the lead on this, Cathy" [Evans01].

Cathy replies, "For what we've been talking about so far, here are the terms that Sam and I use."

Rental Fee—Amount due for a rental at check out

Late Fee—Amount due if the rental is late when it's checked in

Card Charge—Amount charged to a customer's credit card for any reason

"Now that we have the terms, we should use them consistently. So let's re-write the stories to use these words," Debbie said. "We'll take these two stories as an example."

---

4. Some teams credit business value to these smaller stories. It is either a separate estimate or a breakdown of the business value of the higher-level story.

Compute Rental Fee

Check in the CD. See if the rental fee is correct. Verify that the card charge matches the rental fee.

Process Card Charge

See if the card charge is made to the credit card company. Check that the bank account receives money from the card charge.

INVEST Criteria

The INVEST criteria for requirement stories was developed by Bill Wake [Wake02]. Stories should be compared to the criteria of independent, negotiable, valuable, estimable, small, and testable.

Independent means that each story can be completed by itself, without dependencies on other stories. Often a sequence of stories exists, such as the check-out and check-in stories. Some people term this sequence a *saga*. Although there is a relationship between the stories, check-out can be completed by itself, and later the check-in story can be done. But it could be harder to do the stories in reverse (check-in first and then check-out.)

Negotiable means that the triad has not made a hard and fast determination of exactly what is in the story. They will collaborate on that when they start working on the story.

Valuable means that the story has a business value to the customer. That's one reason the customer should put a business value on each story [see Appendix B]. If a story cannot be ascribed a business value, perhaps it should not be done. Any developer story that is created should relate to some story to which there is an assigned business value.

Estimable implies that the developer and tester can come up with some sort of rough estimate as to how long it will take to complete the story. If they lacked knowledge about the business domain or were implementing the story in some completely new technology, they might not be able to give an estimate. If the customer needed a rough estimate to justify spending money on the story, the developer would spend some time investigating the domain or the technology.

Small stories can be completed in a single iteration or in a reasonable cycle time. If a story cannot be completed in a single iteration, it's hard to track progress, and chances are it is too big a story to comprehend easily. Preferably, big stories (which some people call *epics*) are broken into smaller stories, each of which the customer can understand. Otherwise, the triad may need to break down the stories into developer stories to facilitate coding. For example, Charge

Rental was broken into Compute Rental Fee and Process Card Charge to make stories meet this criterion.

Testable means that the user can confirm that the story is done. Having acceptance tests makes a story testable, and passing those tests shows that the system meets the customer needs. As will be shown later, having acceptance tests that can be automated ensures that previous stories are not broken when new stories are implemented.

There may be other reasons to break a story into multiple stories, even if it meets these criteria. For example, not all the details of a story may need to be completed to deliver business value. So the details not currently required might be incorporated into a new story to be delivered later. Any member of the triad might think that some aspects of a story are riskier than normal. So the member might create a story to investigate those aspects early on in a project.

The triad spends a few minutes reviewing each story against the INVEST criteria. Then Debbie finishes, "I think we're ready to develop more details and specific acceptance tests for the first story."

Summary

- Requirement stories can be user stories or constraint stories.
- Every user story has a role and an action and usually a reason.
- Roles are the parts people play in a process, not individuals
- Stories should be written in the customer's language
- Stories should meet the INVEST criteria—independent, negotiable, valuable, estimable, small, and testable
- Each story should have acceptance criteria
- Acceptance criteria can help determine the size of stories.

Chapter 7

Collaborating on Scenarios

"What we've got here is a failure to communicate."

Captain, Road Prison 36, *Cool Hand Luke*

Debbie explains to Cathy how to create scenarios with use cases (see Figure 7.1). The triad constructs a use case for the user story about checking out a CD. Issues in collaboration are discussed.

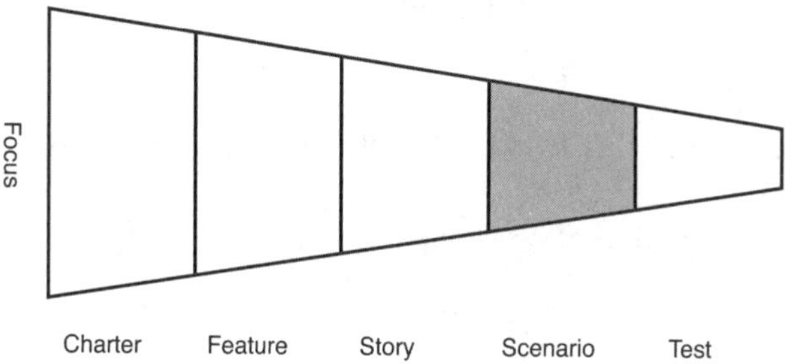

Figure 7.1 *Scenarios*

Use Cases from User Stories

Debbie explains to Cathy one way to discover the details of a user story. "We use a common technique called a use case.[1] The use case describes a sequence of actions and reactions between the user and the software. There are several

1. Another way is to use Event/Response, as shown in Chapter 15, "Events, Responses, and States."

formal templates for a use case, but Tom and I prefer a lightweight one. It's adapted from Alistair Coburn's book on use cases [Cockburn02]. Because the first story we're working on is Check Out CD, we'll create a use case for it. We do not create use cases for other stories until we need them. Otherwise, we could get stuck in what is called *analysis paralysis.*"

> Check Out CD
>
> As the clerk, I want to check out a CD for a customer so that I can keep track of who has rented it.

Debbie continues, "Often the use case is part of a workflow that either involves other use cases or actions that occur outside of the software system. Let's track the steps that occur when one of your customers rents a CD with the manual process. Cathy, can you describe the current flow for checking out a CD?"

"Sure," Cathy replies. She writes the steps on a whiteboard. After a few additions and corrections, the steps look like this:

> The customer selects a CD from the cases on the shelves. (The case just has the cover page).
>
> The customer brings the CD case to the clerk.
>
> The clerk gets the actual CD in another case from a shelf behind the counter.
>
> The customer presents his driver's license.
>
> The clerk pulls out the rental card from the CD case.
>
> The clerk writes down the customer's name and the current date on the rental card.
>
> The customer signs the rental card.
>
> The clerk files the rental card in a box on the counter and stores the CD case with the cover page on a back shelf.

Debbie starts, "The software system will not replace all these steps. A bigger system, like those red DVD rental kiosks, might, but not the system we're replacing. So we only need to concentrate on the steps involved with recording the rental itself. Based on your current workflow, what do you want the software to do?"

Cathy replies, "It seems like these are the steps:"

> The clerk enters the customer identification and CD identifier into the system.
>
> The system records the information.
>
> System prints a form that the customer signs

Simple Use Case

Debbie says, "These steps form the main course or the main scenario of a use case. Some people call this the happy path because it assumes that nothing goes wrong. The template for a simple use case looks like this:"

> *Simple Use Case Template*
>
> **Name**—Identifier to easily reference it by
>
> **Description**—Brief note
>
> **Actor**—Who initiates the use case
>
> **Pre-conditions**—What must be true before the use case is initiated
>
> **Post-conditions**—What is true if the use case successfully executes
>
> **Main course**—Steps that show the sequence of interactions

"The actor almost always plays the role of the user in the user story. The name of the use case can be the name of the user story. The brief description can be the same as the description on the user story. The pre-conditions describe the required state of the system prior to starting the main course. The post-conditions are how the state of the system has changed. They describe the results to check to ensure that the implementation successfully performed the use case. The pre-conditions represent the setup required to obtain those results. So, based on the story and the steps, the basic use case looks like this:"

Check Out Use Case

Name—Check out the CD.

Description—Check out a CD for a customer.

Actor—Clerk.

Pre-conditions—The customer has an identification. The CD has an identity.

Post-conditions—The CD is recorded as rented. The rental contract is printed.

Main Course:

1. The clerk enters the customer identification and CD identifier into the system.
2. The system records the information.
3. The system prints a contract that the customer signs.

Exceptions and Alternatives

Debbie states, "Now that we've identified the main course, we can add additional information to the use case. During the use case, conditions can occur that do not allow it to reach its post-conditions. We call these conditions *exceptions*. Exceptions can happen in almost any use case. For example, you could have a power failure or the computer could crash."

"We could deal with those sorts of exceptions with an overall response scheme, such as filling out the rental contract manually. Specific exceptions can occur during the main course. For example, it's possible that the customer identification is not recognized when the clerk enters it. Each exception forms a different scenario, which sometimes called an exception scenario. We identify this exception with an item that is numbered with the step in the main course where it could occur. We add a letter to denote it as an exception, rather than a main course step. So this might look like the following:"

Exceptions:

1a. Customer identification is not recognized.

"For many exceptions, the customer needs to determine the response. What should we have the clerk do?"

Cathy replies, "We could have the clerk enter the customer identification again. It could be that it was entered wrong."

Debbie continues, "So we make note of that action with the exception. We put that beneath the exception, like this:"

> Exceptions:
>
> 1a. Customer identification is not recognized.
> Repeat step 1.

"But suppose that this step is repeated and the customer identification is still not recognized. It could be that the customer identification is not very readable, or it could be a fake customer identification. It's not up to the developer to determine how to handle this exception. It's the business's responsibility. What should the system do?" Debbie asked.

Cathy replies, "I suppose the clerk could take down additional information from the customer and rent the CD anyway. We might lose a CD or two because of fake IDs, but we would avoid making real customers unhappy. I'll check with Sam, but for now, let's do that."

Debbie says, "Okay, so let's call these steps Record Customer ID and Check Out Manually. You can come up with the exact details later. Because it is a different exception, we give it a different letter. So the two exceptions that can occur during step 1 are"

> Exceptions:
>
> 1a. Customer identification is not recognized on first try.
> Repeat step 1.
>
> 1b. Customer identification is not recognized on second try.
> The clerk performs Record Customer ID and Check Out Manually.
> Use case exits.

Debbie asks, "Do you have business rules that apply to the rental process? Our definition of a business rule is something that is true, regardless of the technology."

"We do have one that is hard to enforce, given the way we do things now," Cathy replies. "Sam and I agreed that a customer should not be able to rent more than three CDs at any time. The rule limits our losses in case the customer skips out on us. It also keeps more CDs in stock for other customers."

Debbie responds, "So you want the check out abandoned in that case. If a use case is abandoned, the post-conditions are not met. Let's get that one down. Later on, you can change your mind, such as increasing the limit for a particularly responsible customer. But that would involve a little more coding."

> Exceptions:
>
> 1c. The customer violates the CD Rental Limit business rule.
> The clerk notifies the customer of the violation.
> The use case is abandoned.
>
> Business Rule:
>
> - CD Rental Limit
>   A customer can rent only three CDs at any one time.

"Each of these exceptions will be a scenario for which we create tests. One other facet of use cases is the alternative, which is another scenario. An alternative is a flow that allows the use case to be successful even if some condition occurs. For example, the printer might jam when printing the rental contract. In this case, the clerk could fill out the contract manually, if that's what you want, Cathy."

"I guess that's about the only thing that could be done. I'll have to make sure we still have some of the paper contracts left around." Cathy replied.

Debbie continues, "So we add an alternative to step 3:"

> Alternatives
>
> 3a. The printer jams.
> The clerk fills out the contract by hand.
> The use case exits.

"This use case is fairly straightforward. If there were several alternatives, we'd make up separate use cases to keep each one simple. We know from experience with testing that each alternative requires more tests. If the number of tests for an alternative seemed large, we definitely would split up the use case. If it took me a while to implement an exception or you could use the system without the exception being handled, we'd make up separate stories for either an individual or a group of exceptions. Those stories would be related to the one for the main use case."

Acceptance Tests

Debbie continues, "Now that we have the use case for this story, it's time to outline the tests to write against it. We need at least one test for the main course, each exception, and each alternative. Later, we will make up specific examples for each of these tests. The use case suggests these tests:"

Rent a CD—This is the main course.

One Bad Customer ID—Enter the customer ID wrong once.

Two Bad Customer IDs—Enter the customer ID wrong twice.

CD Rental Limit—A customer has three CDs and rents another one.

Printer Jam—Simulate a printer jam (maybe out of paper).

"As I mentioned before, the pre-conditions convert to the setup for these tests, and the post-conditions are the expected results. If there is an exception and the use case is abandoned, we should see something other than the post-condition, because the use case did not completely execute. Tom will be talking about the tests more in little bit" [see Chapter 8, "Test Anatomy"].

"If a business rule such as CD Rental Limit is complicated, you would have tests that exercise just the business rule. The test scenarios for the use case would exercise two conditions: when the business rule passes and when it fails. If there was a particular risky aspect to the business rule, we might create more test cases for the scenario."

Documentation

"In general, use cases," Debbie states, "are more than just our joint understanding of how things should work. They also document the computer part of the workflow. If you create a user's manual for the clerks, you could just put the use case into the manual. Or you could rephrase it so that it reads better for a non-computer savvy person. Each use case captures all the issues for a particular operation so it is a document that is worth making correct."

Story Map

Another way to generate scenarios is with a story map [Patton01] [Hussman01]. You can use this technique to break down features into stories. Or, in reverse, the technique can take tasks that people perform and relate them to each other.

The tasks can be generated with a brainstorming session on high-level requirements, as shown in Chapter 5, "The Example Project." The tasks that are written on cards are then collaboratively formed into a map.

On the map, the sequence from left to right shows the time relationship between activities (groups of related tasks). The columns show tasks related to the activity. Some are essential tasks (such as the happy path in a use case). Other tasks can be alternatives, exceptions, or details.

The map can display a workflow, where each activity is a step in that workflow, as shown in Figure 7.2. Underneath each step are the stories associated with that step. To get through the flow, you need to have an implementation of at least one story associated with each step. You can place the highest priority story at the top in each column. When you have a tested implementation for each of these, you then have an implementation for the entire activity you can test.

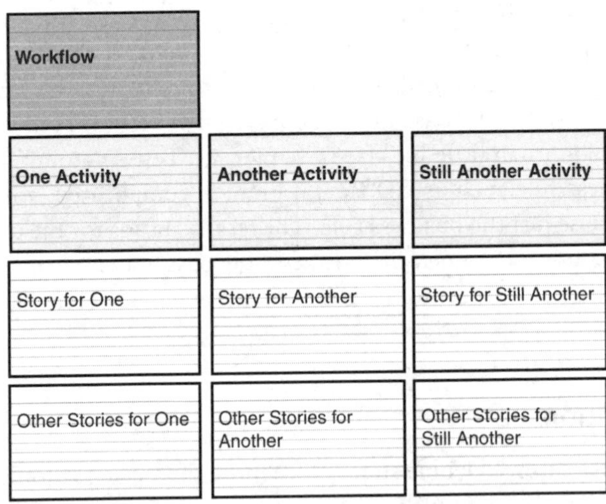

Figure 7.2 *Story Map Template*

The Check Out story, along with the subsequent Check In story, could have a map, as shown in Figure 7.3.

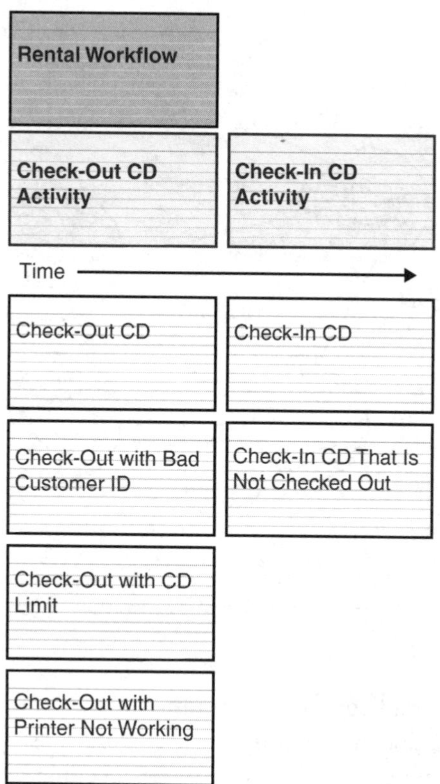

Figure 7.3 *Rental Story Map*

Conceptual Flow

Cathy, the customer who Tom and Debbie are working with, understands how the system will work even without seeing a user interface. But if the interface was unclear, prototype user interfaces and a conceptual flow could be created to visualize the steps. For example, the conceptual flow for check-out might look like Figure 7.4.

The user interface prototype is a means for understanding the customer's requirements. If the customer needs to see the flow in action, demonstrate it with as few business rules as possible and no database storage. Use test doubles, as shown in Chapter 11, "System Boundary," to simulate any required actions or data.

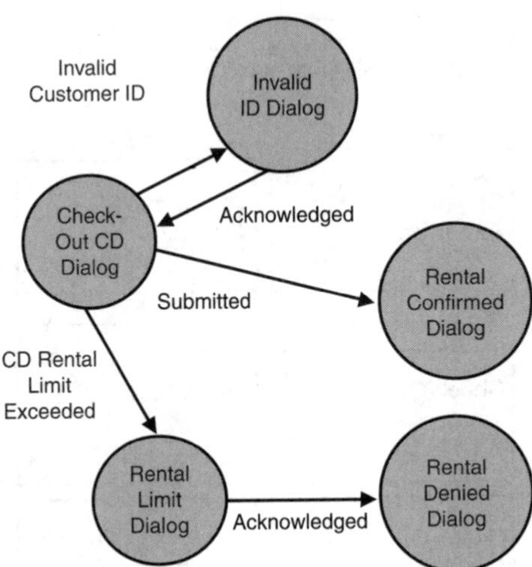

Figure 7.4 *Conceptual Flow*

Communication

In development, the triad communicates more through face-to-face interactions than through written documentation. The user stories, use cases, and acceptance tests are developed interactively. Face-to-face meetings with a whiteboard to record and display ideas are the most effective form of communication [Cockburn02]. If the triad members are separate, having a video meeting with a shared desktop is an alternative.[2] Let's take a bird's-eye view of how Tom, Debbie, and Cathy interact in these face-to-face meetings.

All three perform active listening [Mindtools01]. In *active listening*, they listen to understand. If they understand, they acknowledge their understanding with an "I follow you" gesture—a nod or a verbal affirmation. They focus on what the speaker is saying, not what they are going to say next. If they need clarification, they ask for it, such as "Give me an example."

When recording ideas on the whiteboard, Tom, Debbie, and Cathy practice what is termed *active writing*. Recording on a whiteboard instead of on paper provides instant feedback. When a person is recording ideas, the speaker waits until each idea is recorded before proceeding to the next. That keeps the pace reasonable. If an idea is not recorded clearly, the group can immediately suggest a correction. Ideas are clarified in person and recorded with a common understanding.

2. You can use video conferencing sites such as ooVoo.com or Skype.com.

When documenting ideas, the three recognize that each person may have a preferred way of receiving information. Some like textual descriptions in either prose format or outline form. Others would rather view diagrams and charts than text. If necessary, information is recorded in both formats so that both preferences can be honored.

When Tom, Debbie, and Cathy are brainstorming or describing ideas, they realize that each person can have different responses. Some people get their energy from verbal discussions with other people (extroverts), whereas others process their ideas internally (introverts) [Wiki05]. So the triad has mechanisms for allowing both to interact. They have times when people think individually and write down thoughts as well as times when people discuss thoughts as a group.

They understand that some people like to see the big picture without getting into details (intuition), whereas others want to see the details (sensing). So they have both brief requirements (such as user stories) and detailed requirements (such as use cases). They recognize that progress usually can be made without first gathering all the details. But they acknowledge sometimes that work needs to stop if an important detail is unknown.

They realize that clarity is important, so they develop a common terminology. The developers and testers accept that the terms and definitions come from the business customer. The customer understands that the ambiguous terms they use may have to be renamed to provide clarity.

Communication Is More Than Words

Communication, even when you understand it, can be difficult. We each have our own preconceived notions as to what is clear and what is correct. I was working with a colleague on developing a PowerPoint presentation for a conference. We had gone through the slides together and had a good working understanding of what we were going to present.

A little before the presentation, I got a printed copy of the slides from him. They were printed four to a page: two rows and two columns. I looked at the printout and exclaimed that he had rearranged the slides. He looked at the printout and said that he had not.

Here's a question for you: If the first slide is in the upper-left portion of the page and the fourth slide is in the bottom-right portion, where should the second and third slides be located?

If you said the second should be upper-right and the third should be lower-left, then you would have been as surprised as I was. If you said the reverse, you would have had no issue with the printout.

Communication is about more than just words. It's about how you organize those words.

Summary

- A use case describes the scenarios in a user story.
- A use case states the pre-conditions, post-conditions, and main course or main scenario.
- A use case may have scenarios with exceptions that do not allow it to successfully complete.
- A use case may have scenarios with alternative ways to achieve the post-condition.
- If a use case is large, the exceptions and alternatives may become user stories.
- Use case scenarios suggest acceptance tests.
- Collaboration requires an understanding of the differences in how people create and process information.

Chapter 8

Test Anatomy

"Whoever named it necking was a poor judge of anatomy."

Groucho Marx

Tests for scenarios are now developed (see Figure 8.1). The basic structure of tests—given, when, then—is explained. Examples are shown in tables and text.

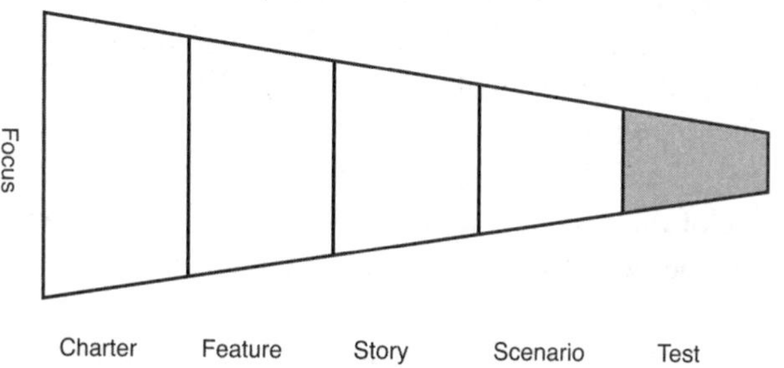

Figure 8.1 *Creating Tests*

Triad Creates Tests

All three members of the triad create tests. The customer usually leads with examples for the basic workflow tests, and the developers and testers come up with ones from their training and experience. Testers are responsible for ensuring that there is a set of tests that is as complete as practical. For example, Tom might envision more tests that can be run for the use case in the previous chapter:

Check Out Rented CD—Customer attempts to rent a CD that is already rented.

CD ID Not Recognized—The system does not recognize the CD ID.

Ideally, the triad should come up with all tests prior to Debbie starting to implement the story. But sometimes, they may discover a test during implementation or later. During exploratory testing, Tom or the team may discover missed conditions or other issues that suggest new tests. If the need to create tests post-implementation occurs frequently, the team should investigate the root cause.

Test Context

A system's operation is defined by its inputs and its outputs, as shown in Figure 8.2. This is a context diagram. What is external to a system is outside the circle. These externalities define the context in which the system operates. An input or sequence of inputs should result in a determinable output. For example, if the clerk inputs a rental for a particular customer and a particular CD, the output should be a rental contract. If the clerk inputs another rental for the same CD without its being checked in, he should get an error.

The response of the system is different the second time someone tries to rent the CD, because the system has stored (that is, made persistent) the rental information for the first check-out.

A system can store the rental data internally or externally. If it stores the data internally, it changes the internal state of the system. If it stores the data externally, the data is simply another output and input to the system.

For Sam's system, the data will be treated as internally persistent. Renting a CD the second time causes a different output because the state of the system is different. Part of a test involves specifying what the current state of the system is.

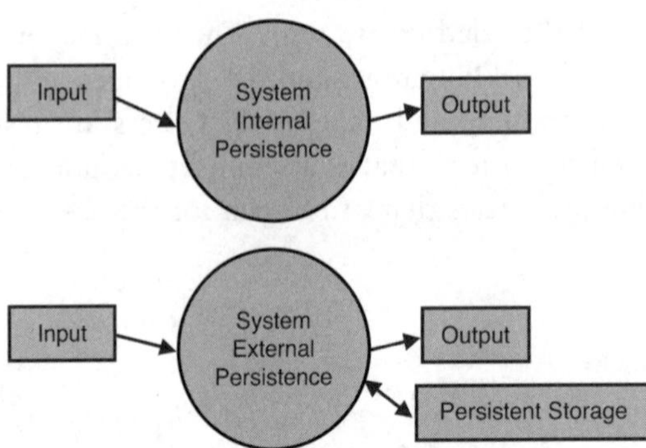

Figure 8.2 *Context Diagram*

Test Structure

There is a basic flow to a test, shown in Figure 8.3. The test starts with setting up the state of the system. Then a trigger occurs—an event or action is made to happen. The test has an expected outcome of that event—a change in the state of the system or an output from the system. The test compares that expected outcome to the actual outcome of the system under test. If the two are equal, the test succeeds; otherwise, it fails. The flow is often shown in text like this:

Given <setup>

When <event or action>

Then <expected outcome>

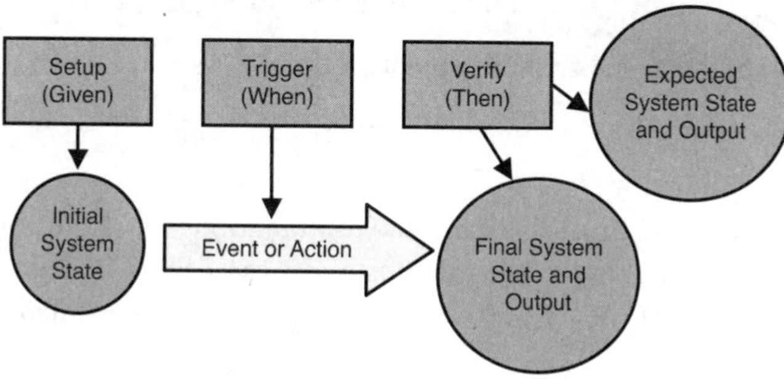

Figure 8.3 *Test Flow*

For simple calculations, like the discount in Chapter 4, "An Introductory Acceptance Test," the action is just calling some module to perform a calculation. So the form could look like this:

Given <inputs>

When <computation occurs>

Then <expected results>

The computations looked like this.

Discount Calculation		
Item Total	**Customer Rating**	**Discount Percentage?**
$10.00	Good	0%
$10.01	Good	1%
$50.01	Good	1%
$.01	Excellent	1%
$50.00	Excellent	1%
$50.01	Excellent	5%

So a single test case could be as follows:

Given Item Total of $10.00 and a Customer Rating of Good

When computing the discount percentage

Then the output should be 0%

In the discount example, there are six combinations of values for the input. Each combination (or row in the table) is a test case. For something like a calculation, the group of these test cases can be referred to as a *calculation test* or a *business rule test*.

The flow for the tests for Check Out CD would be something like this:

Given (Setup)

  Customer has ID (initial system state)

  CD has ID (initial system state)

  CD is not currently rented (initial system state)

When (Trigger)

  Clerk checks out CD (action)

Then (Verify)

  CD recorded as rented (final system state)

  Rental contract printed (output)

There can be multiple ways to flow through a use case. Each exception or alternative in a use case is called a *scenario*, because there is a different flow. For each scenario, a different test scenario is needed that has a different setup or a different action. A *test case* is a test scenario with the actual data. The term *acceptance test*, as used in this book, may refer to a single test case or a group of test cases for either calculations or scenarios.

Business rule tests are usually not as complicated as test scenarios. The business rules often have no initial state setup, and the verification is simply comparing a single result to the expected result.

Because a test scenario is more complicated, you should not duplicate it just for a different business rule case. Separately testing the business rule can reduce the number of test scenarios that need to be written.

When writing a test, use the same domain language you use to write up the stories. The consistency reduces misunderstandings. If you discover during the test writing that the terms are ambiguous, go back and fix the glossary and the stories.

To complete a test case, the case needs values that are setup, input, and output. These values can be specified in tables or in text, whichever way the customer prefers.

Customers who have experience with spreadsheets may like having the values in tables because that is more familiar. Tables come in many forms. Three common ones are the calculation table, the data table, and the action table.

Calculation Table

The table structure used in the previous discount calculation example in Chapter 4 followed this form.

Title			
Input Name 1	**Input Name 2**	**Result Name?**	**Notes**
Value for input 1	Value for input 2	Expected output	Anything that describes scenario
Another value for input 1	Another value for input 2	Another expected output	

This structure is used primarily for calculations.[1] A question mark (?) appears after names that represent outputs. Following is an example of this table with only one input and one output.

1. The structure is sometimes used for actions, such as recording that a CD is rented, particularly for lots of test cases for the same action. There is another structure used specifically for actions, which will be described shortly.

CD Rentals	
CD ID	**Rented?**
CD2	No
CD3	Yes

The name of the input is CD ID, and the name of the result is Rented. The value for the input is CD2, and the expected output is No.

Another example of this table is the one that was used for discounts. The two input names are Item Total and Customer Rating. The result is Discount Percentage. The input values are $10.00 and Good, and the expected output is 0%.

Discount Calculation		
Item Total	**Customer Rating**	**Discount Percentage?**
$10.00	Good	0%

Data Table

Another table structure declares that information in the system exists (or should exist). Part of the name of the table can indicate that it is a data table rather than a calculation table.

Title	
Value Name 1	**Value Name 2**
Value for 1	Value for 2
Another value for 1	Another value for 2

Here's an example for customer data. This shows that there should be a customer whose name is James and whose customer ID is 007 and a customer named Maxwell whose customer ID is 86.

Customer Data	
Name	**ID**
James	007
Maxwell	86

The columns represent different fields in a data record, and each row represents a data record. But the table does not have to correspond to any specific database table. It can represent any collection of the data items. It is the user's view of how the data elements are related, regardless of how they are stored. If the table is used for the setup part of a test, the data is put into the collection, if it does not already exist. If the table is used as expected values, the test fails if the data items do not exist in the collection or have different values.

There is a variation of the data table that shows only rows that meet certain criteria. The criteria are specified after the name. For example, if you only want to see customers whose names begin with J, you could have the following.

Customer Data	Name Begins with="'J"
Name	ID
James	007

Action Table

The third table structure is an action table. The easiest way to describe the table is that it works like a dialog box, although it can be used for other purposes. If a team member needs to visualize a system through a user interface, an action table can often stand in for a dialog box.

The table starts with a title that represents a procedure or the name of a dialog box. The first column has one of three verbs: *enter*, *press*, and *check*. Each verb has an object that it uses. *Enter* enters data into an entry field; *press* initiates a process, such as a Submit button on a dialog box; *check* sees if a result is equal to an expected value.

Action Name		
Enter	Value Name 1	Value for 1
Enter	Value Name 2	Value for 2
Press	Submit	
Check	Value Name 3	Expected value for 3

Following is an example for Check Out CD.

Check Out CD		
Enter	Customer ID	007
Enter	CD ID	CD2
Press	Submit	
Check	Rented	True

Some people are horizontally oriented. Others are vertically oriented. The action table can be represented horizontally. If there is a repeated set of actions, using the previous layouts requires repeating the value names. So sometimes a table that looks like a calculation table is used for actions. For example, if a customer checked out two CDs, it could look like this.

Check Out CD		
Customer ID	CD ID	Rented?
007	CD2	True
007	CD1	True

Tests with Example Values

Tom starts off, "Let's put some data into the test structure. Cathy, can you give me an example of a rental?"

Cathy puts up some values on the whiteboard. After the triad discusses them, they come up with this test:

Check Out CD

Given Customer has ID
and CD has ID
and CD is not currently rented

Customer Data	
Name	ID
James	007

CD Data		
ID	Title	Rented
CD2	Beatles Greatest Hits	No

When a clerk checks out a CD:

Check Out CD		
Enter	Customer ID	007
Enter	CD ID	CD2
Press	Submit	

Then the CD is recorded as rented and a rental contract is printed:

CD Data			
ID	Title	Rented	Customer ID
CD2	Beatles Greatest Hits	Yes	007

Rental Contract			
Customer ID	Customer Name	CD ID	CD Title
007	James	CD2	Beatles Greatest Hits

Tom says, "The rental contract shows the information that will be printed on the form, but not all the surrounding text. This way, you can be sure that the correct information is on the contract. Later on, you can decide with Sam how the rental contract should be worded."

Requirements Revised

"Now that you can see how the test is structured, does it look like anything is missing?," Tom asked.

"Yes," Cathy replied. "The tables definitely make things more apparent. Every CD has a rental period. If the customer returns the CD after the end of the rental period, we charge him a late fee. The rental contract should have the date of the end of the rental period. We also want the rental fee itself on this contract, but I think we covered that in another story."

"Okay," said Tom. "Let's revise the tables to include this rental period. Let me make sure of something. To get the date for the rental period end date, you add the rental period to the start date. Is that right?"

"Sure," said Cathy.

"Okay, so let's make up a quick table to check out both the calculation and our terminology," Tom stated. The triad came up with this.

Calculate Rental End			
Start Date	Rental Period (Days)	Rental Due?	Notes
1/21/2011	2	1/23/2011	
2/28/2012	3	3/2/2012	Leap Year
12/31/2010	4	1/4/2011	New Year

Cathy says, "It looks like Tom came up with some odd cases. Thinking about leap years is not something I would normally consider."

Tom continues, "So you want the rental due date on the rental contract. I guess we should keep it with the CD as well so we know when it's due. I just have a feeling from the bigger picture—the Inventory Report story—that it would be a good idea. Because that story is coming up soon, it's okay to consider it now as part of our big picture scope. "

Acceptance Test Revised

Tom continues, "So given that we have that simple calculation correct, what our tests need to do is set the current date. We do not want to have to change our test just because the date has changed. I'll show how we set a date here and talk about it more when we discuss test doubles [see Chapter 11, "User Story Breakup"]. So the test could now read:"

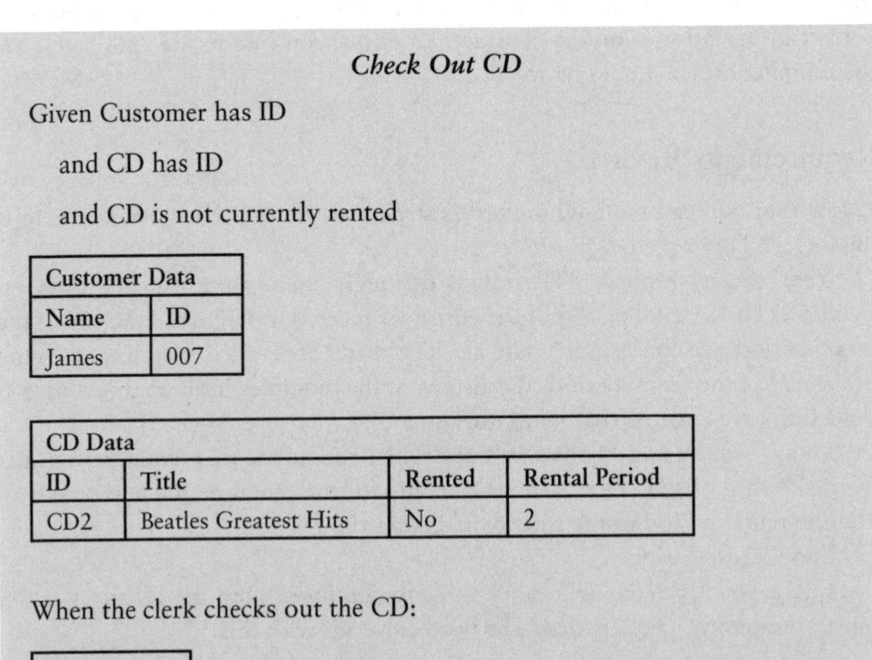

Check Out CD

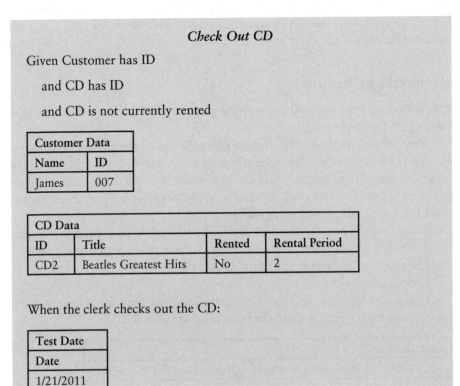

Given Customer has ID

and CD has ID

and CD is not currently rented

Customer Data	
Name	ID
James	007

CD Data			
ID	Title	Rented	Rental Period
CD2	Beatles Greatest Hits	No	2

When the clerk checks out the CD:

Test Date
Date
1/21/2011

Check Out CD		
Enter	Customer ID	007
Enter	CD ID	CD2
Press	Submit	

Then the CD is recorded as rented and a rental contract is printed:

CD Data				
ID	**Title**	**Rented**	**Customer ID**	**Rental Due**
CD2	Beatles Greatest Hits	Yes	007	1/23/2011

Rental Contract				
Customer ID	**Customer Name**	**CD ID**	**CD Title**	**Rental Due**
007	James	CD2	Beatles Greatest Hits	1/23/2011

The example tables have been presented with formatting that distinguishes between the column headers and the data. The formatting is not mandatory. When coming up with these on the whiteboard, headers are not bolded. Teams take pictures of the whiteboard, transcribe the information into tables, and have the customers review them to make sure no errors crept in.

Test with Values in Text

Some triads use what looks like regular text to specify the tests. So they might write something that looks like this:

Given

Customer "James" with ID 007
and CD with ID CD2, title "Beatles Greatest Hits,"
a rental period of 2 days,
and is not currently rented:

When

The clerk checks out the CD with ID CD2
to customer with ID 007 on 1/21/2011

Then

CD with ID CD2 is recorded as rented
and rental is contract printed with customer ID 007, customer name "James," CD ID CD2, CD title "Beatles Greatest Hits,"
and rental due on 1/23/2011

There is a table form that is halfway between the text and a table [Martin02]. The entry field names and the values are in a single row. An example of this layout for the When part of the test looks like this.

Check Out	CD with ID	CD2	to Customer with ID	007	On	1/21/2011

The examples of tests in this book are presented with tables. It is usually easier to translate a table into narrative text than it is to do the reverse. For business rules, such as discount percentage, that have multiple test cases, it is usually less repetitive to express these cases in a table, rather than in free text. The names and column headers, which represent the domain language [see Chapter 24, "Context and Domain Language"], are separate from the values. This can make it easier to check for consistency.

When and Where Tests Are Run

The acceptance test for the Check Out CD test can be on multiple levels. It can be run as a user acceptance test through the user interface. It can also be tested though the middle tier by simulating the input from the user interface.[2] Or a unit test can be written to ensure that the rented value is changed to Yes when the check out occurs.

2. See [Koskela02] for other ways to run acceptance tests.

Summary

- The structure of a test is
  - Given <setup>
  - When <action or event>
  - Then <expected results>
- For calculation tests, the structure is
  - Given <input>
  - When <computation occurs>
  - Then <expected results>
- Following are three types of tables:
  - Calculation—Gives result for particular input
  - Data—Gives data that should exist (or be created if necessary)
  - Action—Performs some action

Chapter 9

Scenario Tests

"I did then what I knew how to do. Now that I know better, I do better."
Maya Angelou

The triad creates tests for the exceptions in a use case. Tom explains the levels at which the tests are run. Debbie shows how early implementation can give quick feedback on meeting the charter's objectives.

Tests for Exception Scenarios

Cathy starts off, "We've finished the test for the main course of the Check Out CD use case. I suppose we should do tests for the other scenarios, because we're focused on that use case. Where should we start?"

Tom replies, "If you had limited time, Debbie and I would create tests for the exceptions and alternatives and then review them with you. You've already told us how the system should respond to many of the exceptions and given us an example for the main course. But because you have the time and interest, let's create a test for the scenario Check Out Rented CD. The customer attempts to rent a CD that is already rented. The change is in the setup. What do you want to see as a result?"

Cathy replies, "I think the clerk should see an error message."

Tom states, "So the test looks like the following:"

CD Already Rented

Given a CD that has already been rented:

CD Data			
ID	Title	Rented	Rental Period
CD2	Beatles Greatest Hits	Yes	2

Customer Data	
Name	ID
Maxwell	86

When a customer attempts to rent the CD, an error message is displayed.

Check Out CD		
Enter	Customer ID	86
Enter	CD ID	CD2
Press	Submit	
Check	Error Message	CD_Already_Rented

Tom continues, "You can see that the customer data is the same. We could put the Customer Data table into a common location and reference it from the other tests. There is a trade-off between using a common setup and redoing the setup for every test. We'll talk about that later [see Chapter 31, "Test Setup"]. The difference in the setup in this case is that the CD is already rented. The difference in the result, which we put as the final step in the action, is that an error is produced. The Check in the last table verifies that the error message is reported as CD_Already_Rented. This name could be what is output, or it could represent text that is determined later. No contract is printed out since the error occurred."

"Another test scenario is CD Rental Limit. This is when a customer who has three CDs rented tries to rent another one. We need to setup the situation where a customer has rented three CDs. Without repeating the Customer Data, the setup looks like this:"

Given a customer who has rented the CD limit of three:

CD Data	Customer ID = 007		
ID	Title	Rented	Rental Due
CD2	Beatles Greatest Hits	Yes	1/23/2011
CD3	Lucy Michelle Hits	Yes	1/24/2011
CD4	Janet Jackson Hits	Yes	1/25/2011

"We included one additional aspect in this setup. It's customer ID = 007. This table reflects the rentals for which the customer ID is 007 or James. That way, we do not have to duplicate the 007 in every row for the Customer ID column. Also, if the CD data in the system has rentals for customers other than 007, this table only reflects those for 007. Now, you might notice that Rented is Yes for every row. So we could move that up to the first line.

CD Limit Reached

Given a customer who has rented the CD limit of three:

CD Data	Rented = Yes	Customer ID = 007
ID	Title	Rental Due
CD2	Beatles Greatest Hits	1/23/2011
CD3	Lucy Michelle Hits	1/24/2011
CD4	Janet Jackson Hits	1/25/2011

When James attempts to rent another CD, an error message is displayed.

Checkout CD		
Enter	Customer ID	007
Enter	CD ID	CD5
Press	Submit	
Check	Error Message	CD_Rental_Limit_Exceeded

"In this case, the error message is different from the previous test. To check that the CD limit was applied correctly, we should make up a test where two CDs are currently rented. If this story was critical, I might try more conditions.

For example, I could try to rent lots of CDs and make sure that the error occurs on every attempt after the third CD."

"The given part of this test could be simplified. In this case, the title of the CD and the rental due dates are not needed by the test. So it could be shown as the following:"

CD Data	Rented = Yes	Customer ID = 007
ID		
CD2		
CD3		
CD4		

"This test scenario might be further condensed into a single table, such as this one:"

CD Limit Reached

Given a customer who has rented a number of CDs, is he allowed to rent another one?

CD Limit Business Rule	
Current Rentals for Customer	Allowed?
CD2, CD3	Yes
CD2, CD3, CD4	No

Tom continues, "This is a simple business rule test. You can test it by connecting to the module that implements the rule. Then you need to create a test that ensures the business rule is correctly connected to the check-out process. That test would look like the uncondensed one."

A Couple More Scenarios

In a financial application, one customer wanted the tester to add an additional test scenario. In the application, the net worth of the corporation was computed every day. The net worth calculation depended on the current Federal Reserve inter-bank rate. The developer asked what rate to use if the inter-bank rate was unavailable due to a server or network issue. The customer replied that he wanted a way to input the rate manually.

The tester then asked what the rate should be if the Federal Reserve goes broke and has no rate. The customer answered, "Then I think we'll have a few other things to worry about in that case. Without the Federal Reserve, our net worth would be zero."

Tests for Business Rules

Cathy states, "I think I've gotten the idea now. Sam and I were thinking of another business rule. We won't let a customer rent another CD if he has one that is late. So, based on your examples, here's what I think the test should look like:"

Current Late Rental When Renting

Given a customer who has a rental that has not been returned by the due date:

Test Date
Date
1/24/2011

CD Data	Rented = Yes	Customer ID = 007
ID		Rental Due
CD2		1/23/2011

When he attempts to rent another CD, notify him that he has a late rental and he cannot rent the CD.

Check Out CD		
Enter	Customer ID	007
Enter	CD ID	CD3
Press	Submit	
Check	Error Message	Customer_Has_Late_Rental

Cross-Story Issues

Tom notes, "It's possible that both the CD Limit and the Late Rental conditions occur at the same time. For example:"

CD Limit Reached and Late Rental

Given a customer who has a rental that has not been returned by the due date:

Test Date
Date
1/24/2011

and who has reached the CD limit of three:

CD Data	Rented = Yes	Customer ID = 007
ID	Rental Due	
CD2	1/23/2011	
CD3	1/24/2011	
CD4	1/25/2011	

When the customer attempts to rent another CD, an error message is displayed.

Checkout CD		
Enter	Customer ID	007
Enter	CD ID	CD5
Press	Submit	
Check	Error Message	CD_Rental_Limit_Exceeded

Cathy interrupts, "I can see from the test what the issue is. Should the system report Customer_Has_Late_Rental or CD_Rental_Limit_Exceeded? In this case, even if the customer returns the two CDs that are not late, he cannot rent a CD. So I'd have the system report as Customer_Has_Late_Rental. When the customer return the late CD, the CD limit will not be reached."

Tom resumes, "This is an example of cross-story issues. As best as we try, some stories have issues with other stories. Many times, we can identify these in advance. At other times, we may not discover the issues until later."

Unit Tests Are Not Enough

Several companies make highly available disk storage systems. As part of the system, there is a monitoring module that checks to see if each disk has problems (see Figure 9.1). One measurement it uses is the response time for a disk. If a disk does not return requested data in a certain amount of time, such as 1 second, the monitor reports a failure. Tests are run to ensure that the monitor operates properly.

A second requirement has been added to make the system green. To save power, a power saver monitor turns a disk off if it is not accessed for a certain amount of time. The tests for that requirement also passed.

Testing the individual pieces is insufficient to verify the entire system. When the new feature was tested in an integrated environment, the disk monitor signaled failures at random times. The power saver was turning off disks when they had not been accessed in the recent past. The next time a powered-down disk was accessed, it sometimes took more than a second to respond, because it had to be powered up. So the disk monitor reported an error. When the operator checked the disk, it was perfectly fine.

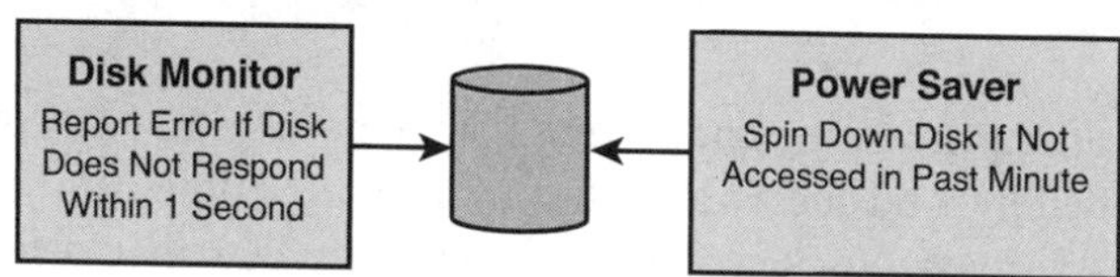

Figure 9.1 *Cross-Story Interaction*

Don't Automate Everything

Tom starts off, "Cvathy, we've created a couple of exceptions for entering a bad customer ID." Debbie could program this into the system. She could track the number of times a bad customer ID was entered and put up an appropriate error message. I'd have to write some tests to ensure that was coded correctly." Cathy replies, "It seems like this exception could be handled by manual instructions to the clerk. It could be:"

> If the system responds with a bad customer ID, try re-entering the ID. If you try the ID a second time and it does not work, make a copy of the customer's driver's license and manually fill out a rental contract for the customer to sign.

Tom continues, "Then we just have to write a test for one bad customer ID."

Bad Customer ID

Given that we have all valid customers in our customer data:

Customer Data	
Name	ID
James	007
Maxwell	86

When a customer ID is entered that is not valid, inform the clerk.

Check Out CD		
Enter	Customer ID	99
Enter	CD ID	CD3
Press	Submit	
Check	Error Message	Customer_ID_Invalid

"The cost of implementing and testing for the number of bad entries is probably not justified by a business value. But that's your call. Part of our job is not just to deliver software to you, but to deliver software that delivers business value."

Multi-Level Tests

Tom starts off, "The tests we created can be used on multiple levels within the system. For example, the CD Check Out Test can be applied at the user interface level or the middle tier (see Figure 9.2). If we apply the test at the middle tier, we check that the functionality works in Debbie's code. Once we design the user interface, we test that the user interface is coupled properly to the correct functionality in the middle tier."

"As a side note, running the test at the middle-tier level ensures that business rules are not coded in the user interface. This makes a clean separation of responsibilities between the two levels."

"We may run some tests just against the middle tier, such as Calculate Rental End [see Chapter 8, "Test Anatomy"]. To clarify the context, I created a diagram (see Figure 9.3). The results of that calculation show up in an output in the rental contract. I've added an additional screen, CD Data Screen, to allow viewing of CD data for setup and expected outcomes. We will use this additional screen just during testing, not in the deployed system. It is not a good idea to keep test-related functionality in production. It can cause security problems and other issues."

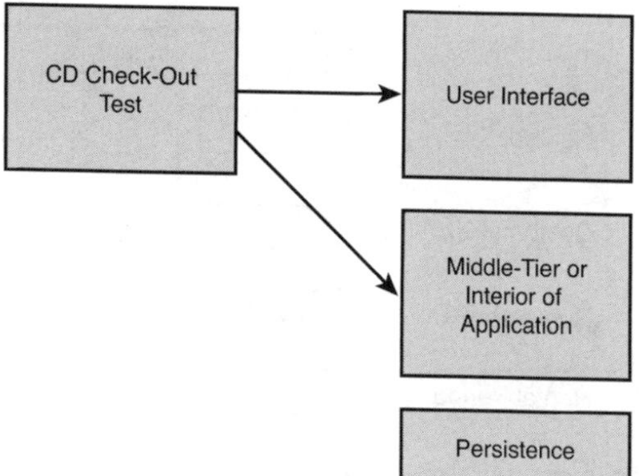

Figure 9.2 *Multi-Level Tests*

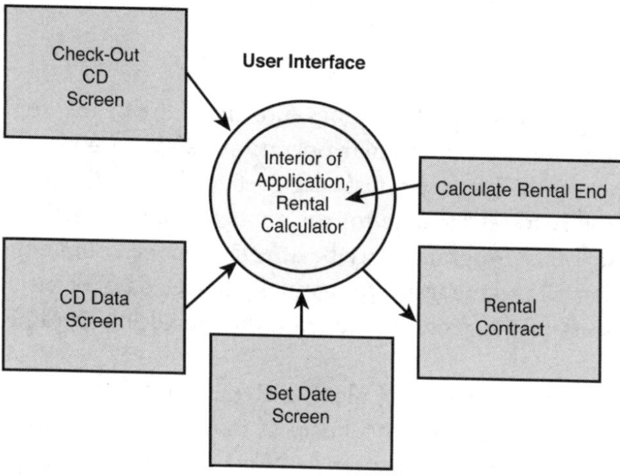

Figure 9.3 *Tests for Different Layers*

Cathy states, "If this screen shows all the data on a CD, we could use it on a regular basis. It made me think of a situation where the clerk might want to know whether a particular CD was rented. Let's make it into a requirement. What will it look like?"

Tom displays the screen in Figure 9.4.

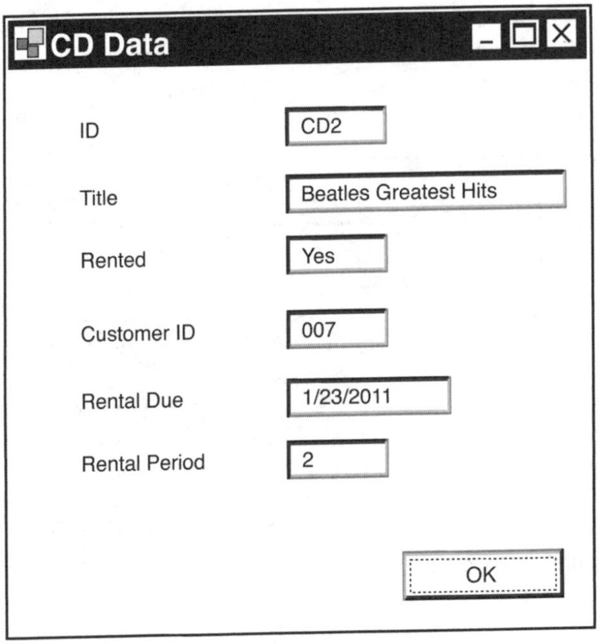

CD Data

ID CD2

Title Beatles Greatest Hits

Rented Yes

Customer ID 007

Rental Due 1/23/2011

Rental Period 2

OK

Figure 9.4 *The CD Screen*

"The Calculate Rental End test goes into the heart of the application. You probably would not use it in regular operations, so we are not going to create a user interface for it. Just use a test that goes to the middle tier. However, we do need the ability to set the date for the application, not for the entire computer. Otherwise, other programs may be affected. So we could either have a Set Date screen that allows the tester to manually set the date, or we could have an input at the start of the program (called a command-line parameter) that sets the date."

"Another reason that we run Calculate Rental End to the middle tier is that we can run many test cases on this business rule without the user interface. As we talked about earlier [see Chapter 4, "An Introductory Acceptance Test"], tests run directly to the middle tier allow execution of lots of test cases without getting carpal tunnel syndrome."

"All the test scenarios from the use case should be run through the user interface. But sometimes the business rules are so numerous that it could take a long time to create test scenarios. For example, if there were hundreds of discount levels, creating an order to test every one of them would be onerous. In cases like that, if Debbie, you, and I agree that there is little risk for a particular aspect of a story, it makes more sense for us to concentrate our time elsewhere. We will run at least one case for each scenario that causes the user interface to generate a different display, such as an error message."

User Interface Tests

Tom starts off, "If you need a more visual representation of how the user interface works, we could work together to create a prototype. We might come up with something like this display [see Figure 9.5]. We could get preliminary feedback from you and the clerks. After Debbie implements the first version of the user interface and tests it against the acceptance tests, you and the clerks can start using it. The interface may change dramatically based on your comments. For example, the order and position of the two input fields might change. Or we might not have a Submit button on the check-out screen. When both fields are filled in, the rest of the rental process would commence."

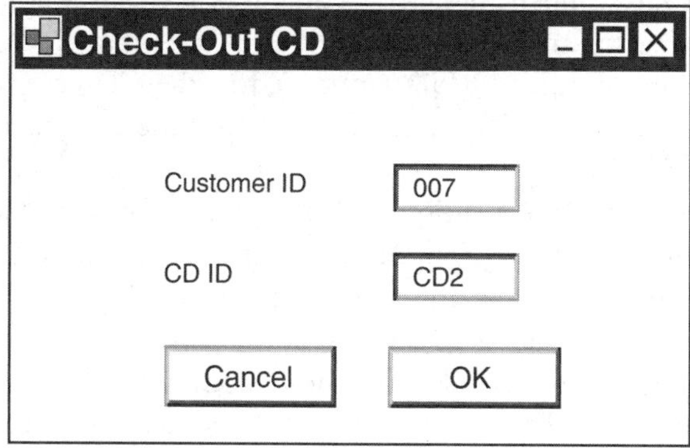

Figure 9.5 *Check-Out Screen*

"For each of the error messages that appeared during the Check Out tests (such as Customer_Has_Late_Rental), Debbie will create an indication on the display. The message could appear on the entry screen or in a separate dialog box. The error could create a loud beep or just a quiet ding." Cary, Mary, and Harry will tell Debbie what they want. We will talk later [see Chapter 14, "Separate View from Model"] about ways to capture tests for displays."

Check the Objectives

Tom continues, "Once we have a user interface for the Check Out CD story, we can see how the check-out time compares to the objective stated in the project charter. Remember that the measure is to achieve 50% less time [see Chapter 5, "The Example Project"]. We are going to start with the easiest way to implement the check-out screen. The benefit of this approach is that it requires no hardware. However, it does take more clerk time and introduces the possibility of errors, even if appropriate check digits are incorporated in the IDs. If we meet the objective, we are done."

"If we come shy of the 50%, we have a system that is faster than before. You and Sam can decide whether there is a business reason for spending more money to reach the 50% measure. If there is little financial justification, you may want to revise the objective."

"If the measured time is far off, we could investigate ways to cut it down. We could add a handheld barcode scanner for either or both IDs. A customer might forget to bring his customer card with a bar code, so we might have to figure the potential time savings for just scanning the CD. And we need to take into account unreadable bar codes. If the handheld scanner isn't fast enough, we could look at an in-counter scanner."

"If the bar code scanner doesn't look like it will be fast enough, well, Debbie has been dying for an opportunity to try out those new radio frequency ID (RFID) microchips. With an RFID embedded in the CD case and one in the customer identification card, you could check out the customer as he walked past the clerk's desk."

Debbie's responds to the mention of RFID, "I'm pretty sure that's overkill for this size operation. But when Sam ramps up the marketing for this place after the software is developed, it might be a thing to try."

Tom resumes, "If we had a larger system to measure, we might record a log file that monitors the speed and correctness of entries. The time delay due to errors or slowness could be converted to dollars based on some conversion ratio. Unfortunately, the negatives caused by the delay or customer impatience are harder to measure. When the dollars that are lost due to delay justify the cost of additional hardware, we can upgrade the system."

Summary

- Create a test for each exception and alternative in a use case.
- Do not automate everything.
- Run tests at multiple levels.
- Create a working system early to check against objectives.

Chapter 10

User Story Breakup

"Life affords no higher pleasure than that of surmounting difficulties, passing from one step of success to another, forming new wishes and seeing them gratified."

Samuel Johnson

The triad meets to discuss another story. Cathy discovers how stories can emerge from the details. Tom shows some boundary tests.

Acceptance Tests Help Break Up Stories

Cathy begins, "I tried out the Check-Out story on Tom's computer. Obviously, you need to add more customers and CDs, but at this point, it looks okay to me. So what's next?"

Debbie replies, "I worked with Cary on the user interface screen. Mary and Larry need to try it to see if it's usable for them. We could do the Check-In story next, but it's along the same lines as Check-Out. To save your time, Tom and I created some tests, and we'll review them with you. The Charge Rentals story is related to Check-In, so let's do that now. The story is":

> **Charge Rentals**—As the finance manager, I want to submit a credit card charge every time a CD is rented so that the store does not have to handle cash.

Debbie states, "When we initially discussed the story, we thought about breaking it into two stories with these acceptance criteria."

Acceptance Criteria

Compute Rental Fee

- Check-in the CD. See if the rental charge is correct. See if the credit charge matches the rental charge.

Submit Charge

- See if a charge is made to the credit card company. Check that the bank account receives money from the charge.

"I'd keep these as two separate stories, based on the tests. The tests for the first one relate to computing the correct charge. The tests for the second one revolve around transactions and interfaces with third parties.

Business Rule Tests

Debbie continues, "Cathy, could you explain the details for the computer rental fee?"

Cathy answers, "Sure. Sam and I created three categories of CDs: Regular, Hot Stuff, and Golden Oldie. We have different rental rates for each category. They are as follows."

CD Rental Rates
Regular: $2/2 days plus $1/each extra day
Golden Oldie: $1/3 days plus $.50/each extra day
Hot Stuff: $4/1 day plus $6/each extra day

Debbie requests, "To make it clearer, I'd like to put the values for these rates in a table." Cathy replies, "Sounds fine to me."

Debbie asks, "We need some names for the column headers for those values like $2 and 2 days. What do you call them?"

Cathy replies, "Sam and I just talk about rates. But I can understand that you need more clarity. So I'll call the rates Rental Rate, which is the base rate for the Rental Period Days, and Extra Day Rate, which is for days over the Rental Period Days."

Debbie shows the following.

Rental Rates			
CD Category	Rental Rate	Rental Period Days	Extra Day Rate
Regular	$2	2	$1
Golden Oldie	$1	3	$.50
Hot Stuff	$4	1	$6

Cathy replies, "This is the way it works now. I know we discussed a late fee in our original talks. Sam and I agreed we should just make a single charge when the CD is returned, rather than two separate charges."

Debbie asks, "Do these rates ever change?"

Cathy answers, "Not too often. But I obviously would like the ability to change these rates."

Debbie comments, "Let's make up another story for that. As you can see, there are often new stories that emerge when we get to the details. The story could be this one."

> As the finance manager, I need to modify the rental rates.

Debbie continues, "We'll get everything done for this current set of rates. I have the big-picture idea that the rates will change. When I program this story, I'll code it so that the effort to add modifiability won't be a big deal. If it would take a lot of work to make the code easy to change, I'd code what I needed now and make the alterations later. When I eventually add modifiability, I'll know that my alterations did not affect the original story, because there will be all the acceptance tests we are going to develop around this story."

Tom says, "So let's make up some tests." He writes the following on the whiteboard.

Rental Fees			
CD Category	Rental Days	Rental Fee?	Notes
Regular	2	$2	
Regular	3	$3	1 extra day
Hot Stuff	2	$10	1 extra day

Cathy replies, "That doesn't seem like enough. You don't have an example for Golden Oldie."

"We can add one," Tom responds. "We're going to have a test for the rate table you proposed. So we'll have already made sure that the Rental Period Days and so forth are correct for Hot Stuff. The test cases in the table show that we can compute the Rental Fee correctly for a normal and an extra day rental. If we had 50 different CD categories, repeating the same calculation for each one would be redundant. We don't want to over-test a low-risk situation, such as a simple calculation. If we had all 50 calculations in this table and you changed the formula, we'd have to change all 50 results."

"There could be a reason for adding Golden Oldie. The test case would show that our calculation worked for cents. So the new row looks like this."

Rental Fees			
CD Category	**Rental Days**	**Rental Fee?**	**Notes**
Golden Oldie	4	$1.50	Shows cents in the rental fee calculation

Tom continues, "If the values for Rental Rates are fixed, we need a test that checks that the values are correct in the application. In essence, it would make sure they matched the values in the Rental Fees table. If values are modifiable, we need a test to ensure that when you change a value, the new value is stored correctly."

"The application can check when you change rates that the new values are in a reasonable range, such as a Rental Rate greater than $.99 and less than $10. However, if you entered an incorrect Rental Rate, for example $1 for Hot Stuff instead of $4, that rate would seem reasonable to the application and it would be stored. Trying to prevent an input error like that can be difficult and often is practically impossible."

"I'd like to ask about some more test cases. I always think about the boundary conditions, so let me see if I've interpreted your rule correctly."

Rental Fees			
CD Category	**Rental Days**	**Rental Fee?**	**Notes**
Regular	1	$2	Short rental
Regular	100	$100	Long rental
Regular	0	$2	Really short rental

"Wow!" exclaims Cathy. "You really do have an active mind. I never even thought about those last two test cases. That one charging someone $100 for a rental seems right according to your calculations. But that doesn't seem right for the business. I think we need to cap the amount of the Rental Fee to the price of the CD. It will take a little bit of time for Sam and I to get together to determine how that should work—whether a rental that goes on for a number of days is automatically terminated and the CD is sold to the customer or whether we give the renter a call or so forth. I think there may be a couple of new stories:"

> As the finance manager, I want to limit the fee for a rental.
> As the inventory maintainer, I want to be able to handle a rental that goes on for a long time.

Cathy continues, "So what do you mean by that test for 0 Rental Days? We never rent anything for 0 days. We wouldn't make any money doing that."

Tom replies, "It's unclear to me how you determine rental days. Is it a 24-hour period? What if someone checks out the CD and then immediately returns it? How long is that?"

Cathy smiles, "You are really being picky. I guess I need to be more precise so that you can give me exactly what I want. If a rental is returned by 11:59:59 p.m. on a particular day, we count that as being returned on that day. We charge the Rental Rate for anything that is returned on or before the Rental Due Date. So it doesn't matter if a customer returns it on the same day. It's still charged the full Rental Rate."

Tom answers, "I might make up a table that gives examples of what you just said. But I can't see ambiguity, like when I worked on an application for one place where they were using time periods based on minutes."

Cathy asks, "How did that create a problem?"

Tom answers, "This was a case of where they needed to calculate days, hours, and minutes. I came up with the following table."

Calculate Time Period							
Start Date	Start Time	End Date	End Time	Days?	Hours?	Minutes?	Notes
1/21/2008	12:01 AM	1/22/2008	2:04 AM	1	2	3	
2/28/2008	12:01 AM	3/1/2008	3:05 AM	2	3	4	Leap year
11/2/2008	1:59 AM	11/2/2008	1:01 AM	0	0	–58	Do you know why?

"What's that last one?" Cathy inquires. "You can't have an end time that is before the start time."

Tom answers, "It's when daylight savings time ends. There is a small window between 1 a.m. and 2 a.m. If the start falls within this window and the stop occurs within one hour of setting the clock back, it's possible to get negative time. Even if you have a start before this window and a stop after this window, you get one less hour than exists in reality."

"Okay, so what did you do?" Cathy asks.

Tom responds, "The customer said he didn't want us to spend the time figuring out how to handle it. The situation would occur so rarely that it's not worth trying to solve it. So we just limited the number of minutes not to be less than zero."

Debbie says, "Testers tend to think of edge conditions, like what Tom showed. Often, these edge conditions relate to decisions that businesses have to make. So it makes sense to bring up these conditions as part of a requirements discussion."

A Story with a Business Rule

Debbie starts off, "Let's see how the business rule calculations fit into a check-in scenario. I had a preliminary acceptance test for Check-In. Let's add the Rental Fee calculation to it."

The triad works together to create this test.

Check-In CD

Given that a CD is rented to a customer:

Customer Data	
Name	ID
James	007

CD Data					
ID	Title	Rented	CD Category	Customer ID	Rental Due
CD3	Janet Jackson Number Ones	Yes	Regular	007	1/23/2011

When the clerk checks in the CD:

Test Date
Date
1/24/2011

Check-in CD		
Enter	CD ID	CD3
Press	Submit	

Then the CD is recorded as not rented, and the correct rental fee is computed.

CD Data					
ID	Title	Rented	CD Category	Customer ID	Rental Due
CD3	Janet Jackson Number Ones	No	Regular		

Rental Fee				
Customer ID	Name	Title	Returned	Rental Fee?
007	James	Janet Jackson Number Ones	1/24/2011	$3

Debbie continues, "We don't have to run through all the combinations that we tested in the rental fee computation. One will do. We could do a second one to ensure that the check-in flow is correctly tied to the rental fee computation and it wasn't just luck that we happened to get the right rental free. If Cathy wanted a different outcome between an on-time check-in and a late check-in, such as sending an e-mail for every late check-in, we would come up with two test cases. We should also create test cases for exceptions, such as trying to check-in a CD that hasn't been rented or an ID that does not exist in the CD data. These cases essentially follow the same form as the Check-Out test cases."

Summary

- Creating acceptance tests can yield additional ideas.
- Break acceptance tests into ones for business rules and ones for scenarios.
  - Business rule tests verify all combinations.
  - Scenario tests each instance where a business rule produces a different outcome.
- Determine the edge cases and how the system should respond.

Chapter 11

System Boundary

> *"You cannot always control what goes on outside. But you can always control what goes on inside."*
>
> Wayne Dyer

The triad works on stories that involve interfaces to external systems. Tom explicates on test doubles and mocks.

External Interfaces

Debbie starts off, "Now that we've determined correctly how much to charge the customer, let's move on to the Submit Charge story. I see the high-level tests for this were as follows."

> Submit Charge
>
> - Submit the charge to the credit card company. Check that the bank account receives money from the charge.

"Cathy, would you explain how charging works," Debbie asked.

Cathy answers. "I've talked with my bank and the credit-card processing company. The rental system needs to send a charge to the credit-card processor, like our current charge card reader does. The processor returns a message that the charge is accepted or declined. At the end of the day, the processor makes a bank transfer for all the charges during a day less any charge-backs and the processing fee. Don't get me started on the size of that processing fee. Anyway, I can go online and see the transfers that were made during the previous days.

If I need to, I can get a listing of all the charges that were made from the credit-card processor. I can also confirm with my bank to see that the transfer was received."

Debbie draws a diagram (see Figure 11.1). She says, "This is my understanding of what you said. Am I right?"

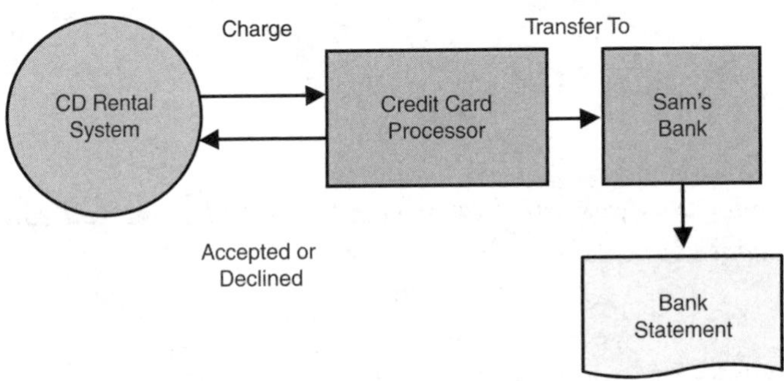

Figure 11.1 *Credit-Card Charge Processing*

"That looks good to me," Cathy replies.

Tom states, "Do you have in mind some acceptance tests for this workflow?"

"Yes," Cathy replies. "It seems like there are two acceptance tests. The first is to verify that the credit-card processor got all the transactions that the rental system said it sent. And the second makes sure the bank got all the transfers that the processor said it sent. So the first one would be this."

Card Processor Charges Matches Rental Charges

Given a list of credit-card charges that the rental system sent for a day:

Credit-Card Charges from Rental System			Day = 1/21/2011
Card Number	Customer Name	Amount	Time
4005550000000019	James	$2	10:53 a.m.
4111111111111111	Maxwell	$10	10:59 a.m.

When I request a list of charges for the day from the credit-card processor:

Request Rental Charges from Processor		
Enter	Date	1/21/2011
Press	Submit	

Then the charges should match the list from the rental system.

Credit-Card Charges from Processor			Day = 1/21/2011
Card Number	Customer Name	Amount	Time
4005550000000019	James	$2	10:53 a.m.
4111111111111111	Maxwell	$10	10:59 a.m.

Cathy continues, "As finance manager, I've gotten this report of credit-card charges many times, but I've only been concerned with the dollar numbers. The three of us should see if you two need to know about anything else on the report. For example, there is a column for transaction ID on the report. That might be useful."

Tom replies, "That would be great. We could run this test as an acceptance test for the system. In that case, we would do a manual comparison of the two lists, and we could incorporate the comparison into part of daily process. If we did that, Debbie could create a way to compare the information you downloaded to the list that the rental system generates. We could create a story to do that. Have you ever had a problem with a charge not showing up?"

Cathy answers, "There may have been one or two, but it's never been an issue that crossed my mind. The effort of calling up the credit-card processor to check on a $2 charge isn't really worth it. So I think we can put that story on hold."

"Oh, I forgot," Cathy exclaimed. "What about charge-backs? How should we handle those?"

Debbie replied, "We can give it to you in whatever form is easiest for you to match up. If the transactions from the credit-card processor are listed separately as charges and charge-backs, we'll give you two lists. If they are listed on one list, say sorted by the time, we'll give you one list. Our job is to create a system that makes it easy for you to do your job."

Tom queries, "Cathy, is there another test you apply to the flow?"

Cathy replies, "There should be one to verify that a transfer was made each day and that the bank received it. This step follows after the first one. So the test would be this."

Charges Agree with Transfer

Given the charges processed by the credit-card processor:

Credit-Card Charges from Processor			Day = 1/21/2011
Card Number	Customer Name	Amount	Time
4005550000000019	James	$2	10:53 a.m.
4111111111111111	Maxwell	$10	10:59 a.m.

When the bank statement is checked the next day for transfers made:

Request Transfers from Bank		
Enter	Day	1/21/2011
Press	Submit	

Then there should be a transfer for the total of the charges less the processing fee.

Transfers Received by Bank	Day = 1/21/2011	
From	Amount	Notes
Credit-Card Processor	$10.80	10% fee

Cathy continues, "I do this every now and then for a whole set of days. In the past few years, I've never seen a transfer for the amount absent from the bank statement. There was one time it was off by a day, so there were two transfers on the same day. I'll continue to do so for the present. We can put off automating this process until later."

Cathy concludes, "This whole idea of charging our customers automatically instead of handling cash is appealing. Of course, we may lose a few customers who don't want to have their rentals appear on their credit-card statements. I know of one whose spouse would become really angry, to put it mildly, if the amount of money spent on CD rentals became known. But the savings in the clerk's time in collecting money and balancing a cash drawer, my time in taking deposits to the bank, and the insurance costs of not having money on the premises will more than make up for any lost rentals. Please get going on Submit Charge pronto."

More Details

Debbie says, "I think we've got the big picture for this story. Let's take a look at more details. From the results of the Check-In story [Chapter 10, "User Story Breakup"], we have a rentals fee to be charged for a particular day. This fee becomes the input for the next step: Submit a charge to the credit-card processor. An additional test for Check-In appears as follows."

Charge Submitted During Check-In

Given that the customer has a credit-card number and has a CD rented:

Customer Data		
Name	ID	Credit-Card Number
James	007	4005550000000019

CD Data					
ID	Title	Rented	CD Category	Customer ID	Rental Due
CD3	Janet Jackson Number Ones	Yes	Regular	007	1/23/2011

When the CD is returned and the rental fee computed:

Test Date
Date
1/23/2011

Check-In CD		
Enter	CD ID	CD3
Press	Submit	

Rental Fee					
Customer ID	Name	Title	Rental Fee	Return Day	Return Time
007	James	Janet Jackson Number Ones	$2	1/23/2011	10:53 a.m.

Then submit a charge to the credit-card processor at that time.

Credit-Card Charge				
Card Number	Customer Name	Amount	Date	Time
4005550000000019	James	$2	1/23/2011	10:53 a.m.

External Interface Tests

Debbie starts off, "So far, we can create the values for a card charge and confirm that the charge is received by the credit-card processor. However, there is still one missing piece: having the rental system actually submit the charge. Cathy, can you go through the possibilities from the business side? How do you submit a card charge now?"

Cathy replies, "The clerk enters the amount and swipes the card. Either a card charge is confirmed, or it is declined. Based on how we've been expressing tests, I can see two cases."

Given a valid credit-card charge:
When the charge is submitted to the credit-card processor.
Then a charge accepted status is received.

Given an invalid credit-card charge:
When the charge is submitted to the credit-card processor.
Then a charge declined status is received.

"With the manual system, if a charge is declined, the clerk asks for another card. I guess that will be harder to do with this application. I'll think about what to do for the second condition and get back to you on that."

Debbie says, "That's fine. It'll take a little time to get the information I need from the credit processor."

Component Tests

After a while, the triad meets again. Debbie starts off, "The credit-card processor has coding standards and protocols on how to submit a charge and what messages are transmitted between a merchant's system and a retailer's system. Once I understood some of the issues, I determined I needed a component that would handle the charge submission. I created component tests that my code needed to pass. Using your cases, they are as follows."

Given a valid credit-card charge:

Card Charge									
Customer Name	Street Address	City	State	ZIP	Charge Identifier	CC Issuer	CC Number	Expires	Amount
James	36500 Some-where Street	Anchor Point	AK	99556	Sam CD Rental Return 1-23-2011	Visa	4005550 00000 0019	01/2020	$1.00

When the charge is submitted to the credit-card processor:

- (Contact website and submit properly formatted charge.)

Then the charge is accepted

- and a message is received with this data.

Transaction Receipt			
Transaction ID	Amount	Charge Identification	Result
123456789012345	$1	Sam CD Rental Return 1-23-2011	Accepted

"I made up one for charge declined: The input information includes a credit number that should be declined."

Invalid Card Response Is Charge Declined

Given a invalid credit-card charge:

Card Charge									
Customer Name	Street Address	City	State	ZIP	Charge Identifier	CC Issuer	CC Number	Expires	Amount
James	36500 Some-where Street	Anchor Point	AK	99556	Sam CD Rental Return 1-23-2011	Visa	411111 11111 11111	1/2020	$1.00

When the charge is submitted to the credit-card processor:

- (Contact website and submit a properly formatted charge.)

Then the charge is declined.

- and a message is received with this data.

Transaction Receipt				
Transaction ID	**Amount**	**Charge Identification**	**Result**	**Reason**
123456789012346	$1	Sam CD Rental Return 1-23-2011	Declined	Card not on file

"Now how all this information is formatted and transmitted is technical and detailed. I'll be using test-driven development with unit tests to design the code that passes this component test. As you can see, the tests have a lot of detail for the card charge. The reason I'm showing them to you is they bring up business questions. A simple one is how do you want to phrase the Charge Identification that appears on the customer's statement?"

Cathy replies, "That looks okay to me. What else?"

Debbie continues, "I found that there are a lot of reasons a card can be rejected. Many of the rejections are for reasons such as the expiration date being in a bad format. These types of issues I will handle in the component. They are standard programming concerns. But I've come up with some results that call for a business decision. I may come across a few more when I get into the details."

Declined Reasons
Card number not on file
Contact the financial institution
Expired credit card

Debbie says, "You need to decide what should be done in each of these cases."

Cathy works through the options and comes up with the following actions.

Credit-Card Charge Declined Actions		
Reasons	**Action**	**Notes**
Card number not on file	Inform the customer. Get information for another card.	Generate a dialog box on check-in. Generate an e-mail to Cathy.

continues

Credit-Card Charge Declined Actions, Continued		
Reasons	**Action**	**Notes**
Contact the financial institution	Do not inform the customer. Make person look up at security camera. Put up a message to call the police.	Card may be stolen.
Expired credit card	Inform the customer. Get information for another card.	Generate a dialog box. Generate an e-mail to Cathy.

Debbie continues, "Tom and I will come up with tests that generate all these results to make sure the action occurs. Details will need to be gathered on the wording of the dialog boxes and e-mail messages. But those are display concerns, not business rule issues."

Tom asks, "Debbie, what happens if the network goes down in the middle of processing a credit-card transaction? You and I both know that periodically the Internet seems to come to a grinding halt, which is the equivalent of going down."

Debbie replies, "I'll just queue up the charges and submit them when it does come back up. I'll add a component test to make sure that is what happens."

Tom answers, "What if it doesn't come up for full day?"

Debbie counters, "I can send them when it does. But the date of the charge will not match the date of the return. Cathy, will that work for you?"

Cathy replies, "We faced the same problem when the phone line was down. The clerks had to write down the credit-card numbers and submit them the next day. We did have one customer who knew the line was down, so he used an invalid card. But you can only do so much. Submitting them when you can sounds fine to me."

Test Doubles and Mocks

Cathy has a burning question. "How are you going to run all these tests? Are you going to use your credit-card number? How can you make sure that a credit card is rejected for a particular reason?"

Debbie answers, "One way to do it is to use Tom's cards. He's maxed out on some of them. But the banks might get after Tom for trying to use those credit cards. So we will use what many developers call a *test double* [Meszaros01]. A test double is something that stands in for a real system when tests are being run. It comes from the idea of a double who stands in for the real actor when shooting a movie."

"A test double encompasses a couple of other concepts that you might hear Tom and me or other developers throw around. They are mock [Hillside01], stub, and fake. [Craig01]. The mock term comes from Alice in Wonderland by Lewis Carroll. You may remember the line:"

"Once," said the Mock Turtle at last, with a deep sigh, "I was a real Turtle."

Debbie continues, "I'm not going to get into the differences and details between these three terms. That's something that developers love to discuss on blogs. The key is that using test doubles makes a system easier to test. The credit-card processor provides a test double. Instead of connecting to the real credit-card system, you connect to the test double that's provided. The test double accepts credit-card charges and returns confirmations just like the real system."

"To get the test double to return different results, you send it different combinations of values. For example, with your processor, you send a charge for the credit-card number 4111111111111111. This causes a charge to be declined."

"If there wasn't already a test double, I would write one myself. In fact, whenever there is some external interface to a system, I usually create a test double. In this case, as long as I can have all the different results sent back to me, I don't need my own test double. I haven't checked, but I'm sure there is some number I can send that would create a result that puts up a dialog to call the police. If not, I'll bet one of Tom's cards would do that."

"To test the complete system, we do need to make some credit-card charges all the way from the return of a CD through seeing it on the credit charges processed list. We'll use your card for a good one and use an invalid number to see if things are rejected."

What Is Real?

A system in production—"the real world"—interacts with many things outside itself. It may ask an external service for information or to do a calculation or perform an action. Events may occur at random times and in random sequences that require a response from the system. In production, there is usually no control over these external interactions. But in testing, control is needed so that the same test case can be performed over and over again and still get the same expected result.

An external service may provide the same information every time it is requested. (In programmers' terms, it is *idempotent.*) Even so, the developer may want to create a test double for it so the tests run faster. The context of our system is shown in Figure 11.2.

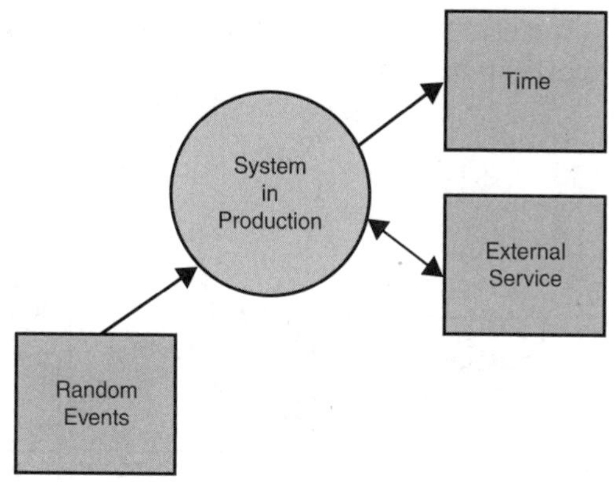

Figure 11.2 *System Context*

You often need control of time to get tests to run the same way. The test double that the credit-card processor provides allows for repeatable tests. If there were random events that the system had to respond to, a test double for them would be created.

As an example, suppose several clerks were doing check-outs and check-ins at the same time. The developer could simulate a sequence of check-outs and check-ins. A test double would generate a series of actions like the following sequence to see if the implantation could handle it.

Rental Sequence				
Operation	**CD ID**	**Customer ID**	**Date**	**Time**
Check-out	CD7	99	1/21/2011	11:01:01.001 p.m.
Check-out	CD4	99	1/21/2011	11:01:01.002 p.m.
Check-out	CD5	007	1/21/2011	11:01:01.003 p.m.
Check-out	CD2	86	1/21/2011	11:01:01.004 p.m.
Check-in	CD7		1/21/2011	11:01:03.005 p.m.
Check-out	CD3	007	1/21/2011	11:01:03.006 p.m.
Check-in	CD4		1/21/2011	11:01:03.007 p.m.

Story Map of Activities

As described in Chapter 7, "Collaborating on Scenarios," a story map can organize various stories into activities. For the stories so far, the map could look like the following (see Figure 11.3). As soon as the top story for each activity is completed, the entire workflow from check-in through seeing the entry in the card processor's report can be executed.

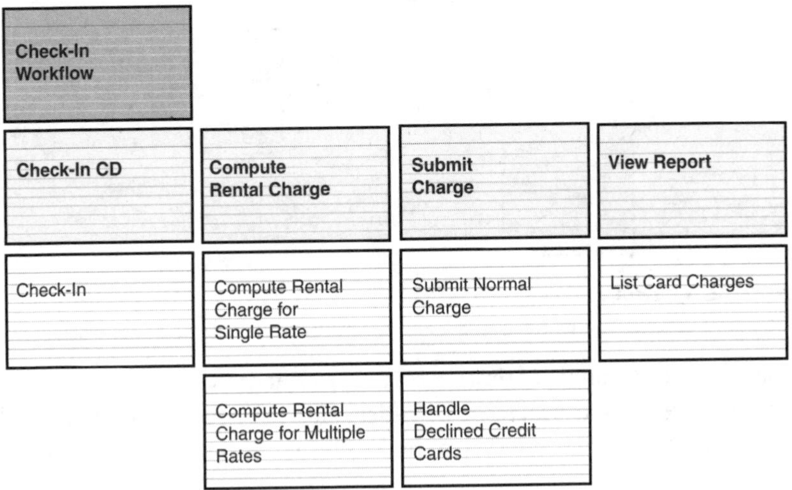

Figure 11.3 *Check-In Story Map*

Summary

- Create acceptance tests for external interfaces.
- Developers can create component tests for internal processing functionality.
- Details from lower levels may generate questions that need customer answers.
- Use test doubles or mocks for external interfaces to simplify testing.
- Create story maps to organize stories into workflows.

Chapter 12

Development Review

"May you have the hindsight to know where you have been, the foresight to know where you are going, and the insight to know when you have gone too far."

Anonymous

The triad demonstrates to Sam the current state of the system. Debbie and Tom recount other stories that have been completed and tests that have been run.

The Rest of the Story

The triad meets with Sam. Cathy begins, "Sam, as sponsor, I'd like to update you on the current status of the system. I've shown you some of the user interfaces and tests as we've gone along. I've worked together with Debbie and Tom on the acceptance tests for Check-Out, Check-In, and Credit-Card Charging. I reviewed the other stories and acceptance tests they came up with. I'll let Debbie tell you more about them."

Debbie begins, "Because the system deals with customers and CDs, we needed a way to add, update, and delete customers and CDs. We had to add customers and CDs to test check-in and check-out. But we didn't go into the stories themselves."

"Adding, deleting, and updating data is so common that Tom and I know it needs to be done. We just create stories for those actions and let the customer schedule them. If the customer has the time, we work through the details with him. Otherwise, we just review the tests with him."

"For adding a customer, we checked the business-related decisions with Cathy. For example, you want to ensure that a customer isn't accidentally added twice. So we asked Cathy for a business rule to determine if you have two customers who are duplicates. She said the rule should look for the same credit-card number. This duplicate rule is also used when updating a customer."

"Another action was to a delete a customer. Cathy said not to completely delete customers, but to deactivate them since they may still have outstanding rentals. She said she wanted to keep a record of previous customers so it would be possible to welcome them back or have on file that you don't want them back.[1] We asked for similar rules for adding, editing, and deleting CDs."

The acceptance tests Cathy approved were run through both the middle tier and the user interface. Talking about the user brings up the usability issues that Tom will talk about."

Usability Testing

Tom starts, "Debbie described acceptance tests for functionality. There are also usability tests; quality attribute tests, such as security and performance; and exploratory tests [Chapter 3, "Testing Strategy"]."

"Debbie and I worked with Cary, Harry, and Mary on the usability of the check-out and check-in screens. Harry is color blind, so he couldn't distinguish that messages displayed in red and green had different meanings. So we added textual indicators to the messages to clarify whether they meant "This is a problem" or "This is okay." Mary doesn't want to use her glasses to read the screen, so we increased the size of the font. These examples represent issues that we often find in usability testing."

"We talked to a couple of your customers to see if the rental contract was readable. The wording that your lawyer approved seemed a bit obfuscated." Sam interjects, "I think talking about lawyers and obfuscation is redundant." Tom replies, "Agreed. And so did the customers. So we worked on a simple language contract, which is still undergoing review by the lawyer" [ABA01].

Separating State from Display

Tom continues, "We'll talk more about the concept of separating display from state later [Chapter 14, "Separate View from Model"], but because we're talking about what the user sees, I think it's appropriate to introduce the idea now. A while back [Chapter 9, "Scenario Tests"], we presented to Cathy the idea of separating the form of input from the internal logic. For example, whether the input is from typing, the scan of a barcode, or the reading of an RFID tag, the middle-tier tests should not be affected. This separation makes for less test maintenance."

---

1. A full deletion of a customer would require that all references to a customer (rentals, card charge history, and so on) be deleted to maintain what is called *referential integrity* [IBM01].

"A similar issue applies to separating a state from the way it is displayed. As you can see for tests for check-out, we listed the error messages as CD_Rental_Limit_Exceeded. For example:"

Check-Out CD		
Enter	Customer ID	007
Enter	CD ID	CD5
Press	Submit	
Check	Error Message	CD_Rental_Limit_Exceeded

Tom resumes, "Debbie coded this test with a reference to an identifier, such as CD_Rental _Limit_Exceeded. When Cathy decided what should appear on the screen, we put that into a separate table, as follows."

Error Message	
Identifier	Text
CD_Rental_Limit_Exceeded	The customer has exceeded the CD rental limit. Sam has set the limit at 3. Please gently inform the customer of the limit.

Tom continues, "These two tables allow for separation of testing. One test verifies that the system produces the right state. The other test confirms that, given the state, the output is as is desired. It also allows testing the system even when the final wording has not been approved."

"Because the contract wording has not yet been agreed upon, the test for the Rental Contract [Chapter 8, "Test Anatomy"] just verifies that the data on the contract is correct. Now we have a separate test for the printed contract:"

Given data for a rental contract:

Rental Contract				
Customer ID	Customer Name	CD ID	CD Title	Rental Due
007	James	CD2	Beatles Greatest Hits	1/23/2011

And this template:

Rental Contract Template
The customer named <Customer Name> with the ID <Customer ID>, hereafter referred to as the Renter, ha rented the CD identified by <CD ID> with the title "<CD Title>," hereafter referred to as the Rented CD, from Sam's Lawn Mower Repair and CD Rental Store, hereafter referred to as the Rentee. The Renter promises to return the Rented CD to the Rentee by <Rental due>. If said Renter exceeds ... blah...blah...blah.

When the contract is printed, it should appear as this:

Rental Contract Printout
The customer named James with the ID 007, hereafter referred to as the Renter, has rented the CD identified by CD2 with the title "Beatle's Greatest Hits," hereafter referred to as the Rented CD, from Sam's Lawn Mower Repair and CD Rental Store, hereafter referred to as the Rentee. The Renter promises to return the Rented CD to the Rentee by 1/23/2011. If said Renter exceeds ... blah...blah...blah.

Debbie injects, "When the lawyer approves the wording, we need to change this test."

Quality Attribute Tests

Tom resumes, "I often do extensive performance testing on stories. Just as with the other acceptance tests, I make up a table for the desired behavior. For example, if Sam is expecting to have many checkout people other than Cary, Harry, and Mary on the system simultaneously, I would make up a table such as what follows. As the stories are developed, they are checked to see if they meet the performance measures."

Check-Out Performance	
Number of Simultaneous Check-Outs	**Response Time Maximum (Seconds)**
1	.1
10	.2
100	.3

Tom continues, "Security is an important area for testing. You need to ensure both physical security of the system and software security. You don't want a customer to go behind the counter and check-in a CD that he really isn't checking in. We have name/password security on the screens, but based on usage patterns, you may need to change the means and timing for that verification. You could have a logon at the beginning of the day or before every rental. You could have software verification, or you could have employee cards."

"Because you are keeping credit-card information, Debbie discovered that you need to abide by the PCI Data Security Standard. So we'll need tests to ensure that each of the requirements in that standard is met" [Security01].

"Security is such a broad issue that I can't really get into much more detail in a limited amount of time. Suffice it to say that I can test a system to see if there are known security issues, but I can't test to make sure that it is absolutely secure. Security is not about letting people do things; it's about making sure they can't do things. It's easier to test the former than the latter."

"The entire team can try exploratory testing [Chapter 3] on the system. Each member takes on the role of a different persona. Each performs the operations related to that persona and sees how the system feels. Issues may be discovered that do not come out in our predetermined tests. Because the system is in a runnable state and we'll keep it that way as we add features, exploratory testing can continue throughout the project."

Workflow Tests

Debbie starts, "Just because we have tests for each story does not mean that the system is fully tested. We need to have a test for an entire workflow. The workflow can correspond to a story map [see Chapter 11, "System Boundary"] or a set of story maps. The workflow test verifies that there are no issues between related stories and that the entire flow is usable. Here's an example of a workflow test (see Figure 12.1). If the workflow was really complicated, we might have multiple workflow tests that go along alternative paths."

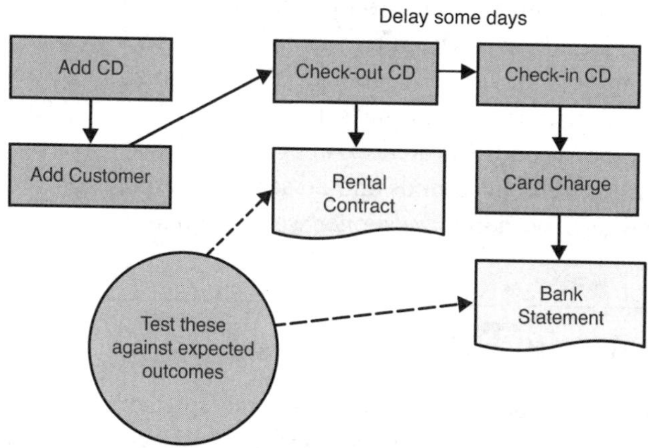

Figure 12.1 *Workflow Test*

Debbie resumes, "Because this test involves many facets of the check-in process, it can break for a variety of reasons and may have to be maintained frequently. For example, if the wording of the rental contract changed, the rental rates changed, or other things changed, the test would have to be rewritten or it would fail. So we only want the essential workflow tests."

Deployment Plans

Sam speaks up, "Cathy has been keeping me in the loop about your discussions. So let me ask the bottom-line question: How quickly can you get the system into operation? Other than the stuff you've already outlined, what else do you need to do?"

Debbie replies, "We already have a way to get customers and CDs into the system. We don't have all the data. If we had a spreadsheet with all the data, we could input it into the system."

Sam states, "I'll have Cary, Harry, and Mary start inputting all that information. What else?"

Debbie answers, "You'll need a transition plan to go from the old system to the new one. You could start with doing rentals both ways for a little while, or doing all new rentals in the new system, or doing rentals in the new system for just a few customers."

Sam says, "Let's work on that in a little while. Is that it?"

Debbie replies, "Anything else you can think of, Tom?" Tom responds, "I think that's it."

Sam states, "Then let's go for it. The sooner this starts to happen, the quicker we can start renting more CDs with the same number of people and thus make the money to pay you for all your hard work."

Cathy injects, "I think it's time to look back at the objectives. The one we're dealing with right now is "Within two months, CD check-outs and returns will be processed in 50% less time." From what I've seen so far, it looks like that will be met. The manual system measurement was 1 minute, 40 seconds for a check-out and 55 seconds for a check-in. The preliminary measurements using the user interface were 46 seconds and 26 seconds, respectively. But as you say, the sooner we get it working, the sooner we'll find out."

From Charter to Deliverable

The triad (Cathy, Debbie, and Tom); Sam the sponsor; and the users Cary, Harry, and Mary have gone from the initial project charter through the first deliverable. Along the way, acceptance criteria have been created as objectives in the charter through the high-level features and stories. The criteria have been expressed as specific tests. Cathy now understands the importance of helping to create acceptance tests. Debbie and Tom have learned about the business domain. The more they comprehend the domain, the more effective the triad will be in producing quality software.

Summary

- It is insufficient to have just acceptance tests that revolve around the functionality of a system.
- Acceptance criteria need to be established for usability, security, performance, and other quality attributes.
- Workflow tests catch inter-story issues.
- Developing in deployable chunks allows for quicker cost recovery.

PART II

Details

This part explores the details of acceptance testing and discusses other ways to create scenarios for testing.

Chapter 13

Simplification by Separation

"Life is like an onion: You peel it off one layer at a time, and sometimes you weep."

Carl Sandburg

The triad discusses a new story from their sponsor, Sam, to let people reserve CDs online. The story illustrates how separation of issues allows the creation of simpler tests.

Complex Business Rules

Cathy starts off, "Sam has an idea for a website. The website connects back to the charter, because we want to give our customers the ability to reserve a CD. Sam has come up with two ideas. He wants to allow customers to reserve CDs on the web, and he wants them to be able to search CDs. We haven't worked out the details on the second story. But Sam has already decided on the first."

"He has worked out a pretty elaborate business rule for whether a customer should be allowed to reserve a CD. He created a table, because he's been following along with our discussions. The table looks like the one that follows."

Debbie interrupts, "That table looks complicated, but I've seen some business rules that look like it."

Cathy replies, "I think Sam can be a little complex sometimes. He wants the decision for allowing someone to reserve to be based on a number of criteria. The criteria includes the number of times the customer rented in the past month and the cumulative number of rentals since becoming a customer and the number of late returns for the past month and beginning rentals. Sam also has a few people who are his favorites; he wants them to be allowed to reserve unless they have a really bad rental history."

Allowed to Reserve Business Rule			
Monthly Rentals	**Cumulative Rentals**	**Sam's Favorite Customer**	**Allowed to Reserve?**
If Rentals Past Month > 30 and Late Rentals Past Month <= 1	If Cumulative Rentals > 100 and Late Cumulative Rentals <= 2	Does Not Apply	Yes
Does Not Apply	Does Not Apply	Yes	Yes
If Rentals Past Month > 30 and Late Rentals Past Month <= 3	If Cumulative Rentals > 300 and Late Cumulative Rentals < 10	Unknown	Yes
If Rentals Past Month > 20 and Late Rentals Past Month <= 3	If Cumulative Rentals > 200 and Late Cumulative Rentals < 5	No	No
Does Not Apply	Anything Else	Does Not Apply	No

Simplify by Separating

Cathy asks, "So what do we do with this?"

Tom replies, "With all these comparisons and complex conditions, this is a hard table to understand. We can break it into smaller tables, if Sam lets us or you let us, in lieu of Sam being here. As David Parnas states [Parnas01], tables can clarify the requirements. And smaller tables can add more clarification."

Cathy responds, "It's as clear as mud to me. So let's break it up."

Tom says, "Let's start with the Monthly Rentals column. We can separate the values into separate fields and put the comparisons in single cells. I like to make up names for the result of each comparison. My suggestion is to call the results Monthly Rental Levels, or MRLevels to keep it short. If there were meaningful names we could assign to each result, we might name them MRExcellent, MRGood, and so forth. But in this case, let's just label them with letters. The table for Monthly Rental Levels looks like this."

Monthly Rentals Level Calculation		
Rentals in Past Month	**Late Rentals in Past Month**	**Monthly Rental Level**
>30	<= 1	MRLevelA
>30	<= 3	MRLevelB
>20	<= 3	MRLevelC

Cathy says, "I know we'll need some tests for these Monthly Rental Levels." The triad works together and creates the following.

Monthly Rental Level Tests		
Rentals in Past Month	**Late Rentals in Past Month**	**Monthly Rental Level**
30	1	MRLevelA
30	2	MRLevelB
31	1	MRLevelA
31	2	MRLevelB
31	3	MRLevelB
32	4	??
20	3	??
21	3	MRLevelC

Cathy says, "I'm not sure what the results should be for those two rows with the ??."

Tom replies, "By breaking the original table into smaller tables, we can see whether we have left out anything. Creating some tests for just the Monthly Rental rule shows that some possibilities have not been covered. Perhaps these possibilities may never occur during production. But at least we've identified them and Debbie can be sure to make allowance for them in the implementation. She could at least record that they occurred, put up a dialog box, or do whatever is appropriate."

Debbie interjects, "It seems like there should be a MRLevelD as the default level if none of the conditions are met. That would make it easier to keep track of those possibilities when they occur."

Tom resumes, "We can do the same thing for the Cumulative Rentals. To save time, here's a quick outline."[1]

Cumulative Rentals Level Rule	
Condition	**Level**
If Cumulative Rentals > 100 and Late Cumulative Rentals <= 2	CRLevelA
If Cumulative Rentals > 300 and Late Cumulative Rentals < 10	CRLevelB
If Cumulative Rentals > 200 and Late Cumulative Rentals < 5	CRLevelC
Anything Else	CRLevelD

1. Creating the tests for the Cumulative Rentals Level is left as an exercise for the reader.

The Simplified Rule

Tom continues, "With these individual tables taking care of the details for Monthly Rentals and Cumulative Rentals, our revised table now looks like this."

Allowed To Reserve Business Rule (Revised)			
Monthly Rentals Level	**Cumulative Rentals Level**	**Sam's Favorite Customer**	**Allowed to Reserve?**
MRLevelA	CRLevelA	Does Not Apply	Yes
Does Not Apply	Does Not Apply	Yes	Yes
MRLevelB	CRLevelB	Unknown	Yes
MRLevelC	CRLevelC	No	No
Does Not Apply	CRLevelD	Does Not Apply	No

Cathy asks, "Have we covered all the cases? It seems like there are some missing ones."

Tom replies, "You're right. It's clearer now what all the cases are. There are several combinations of MRLevels, CRLevels, and Sam's Favorite Customer that do not appear in the table. Here are a few."

Allowed to Reserve Business Rule—Missing Cases			
Monthly Rentals Level	**Cumulative Rentals Level**	**Sam's Favorite Customer**	**Allowed to Reserve?**
MRLevelA	CRLevelB	No	No??
MRLevelA	CRLevelB	Unknown	No?

"We need to ask Sam whether the answer is yes or no in these cases. He could simply say that the answer is no in all other cases. That would make Debbie's life easier, as well as mine. In any event, you and he need to approve these new tables as being the way to represent the business rule. As you can see, separating rentals into separate tables decreases the amount of information that needs to be absorbed for each table and makes the tests cleaner."

Rental History

To allow reservations based on Sam's business rule, the system needs to keep track of the rentals for each customer. The system could keep separate information on each rental. At this point, Cathy does not need the history. All she needs is a count of rentals for the month and the total number of rentals. So for each customer, there might be the following."

Reservation Allowed Based on Rental History

Given this rental history:

Customer Data						
Customer ID	Name	Rentals in Past Month	Late Rentals in Past Month	Cumulative Rentals	Late Cumulative Rentals	Sam's Favorite
007	James	100	3	300	30	Yes
86	Maxwell	200	1	400	30	No

Determine if a reservation is allowed.

Reservation Allowed	
Customer ID	Allowed?
007	Yes
86	No

When Tom tests the overall system including the user interface, he'll look up both 007 and 86 and see whether the reservation is allowed.[2] There also should be a test ensuring that the system calculates rental history correctly, such as this.

Compute Rental Counts

Given this rental history:

Rental History Data	Customer ID = 86	
CD ID	Rental Due	Rental Returned
CD3	1/21/2011	1/21/2011
CD5	1/23/2011	1/23/2011
CD7	1/23/2011	1/24/2011
CD2	2/11/2011	2/12/2011
CD4	2/13/2011	2/13/2011
CD6	2/13/2011	2/14/2011
CD7	2/14/2011	2/14/2011

2. If there was already a system in production with real data, Tom might try to find two customers: one who is allowed to reserve according to the rule, and one who is not. This could expose any data-dependent issues.

And a day in the next month:

Test Date
Date
3/1/2011

The monthly and cumulative rental counts should be as follows.

Rental Summary					
Customer ID	Name	Rentals in Past Month?	Late Rentals in Past Month?	Cumulative Rentals?	Late Cumulative Rentals?
86	Maxwell	4	2	7	3

The test does not imply whether a rental history is kept. If it is, the history could be used for other features that are scheduled to be developed soon. All that is needed now is to change the numbers whenever a check-in occurs. When the check-in happens, the number of rentals is incremented by one. If the rental is late, the number of late rentals is incremented by one. Once a month, the system clears out the rental count for the past month.[3]

It might be easier to keep a history. The check-in process would add the data for a rental to the history. The Rental Summary calculation would find all the rentals for a customer and calculate the counts. In either case, the test is independent of the way the calculation is performed.

Summary

- Simplify business rules by separating them in component parts.
- Create tests for the component parts.
- Use the simpler components to determine missing logic.

3. Alternatively, the system could increment the Late Rentals count when a CD was not returned by the Rental Due date. This would be a time-base event, as described in Chapter 15, "Events, Responses, and States."

Chapter 14

Separate View from Model

"To each his own. (Suum Cuique)"

Cicero

Tests can be made more maintainable by separating what appears to the user from the logic in the underlying business model.

Decouple the User Interface

For the CD Reservation story in the previous chapter, the business rule (the model) for determining whether a customer is allowed to reserve CDs was documented, and tests were written for it. This reservation tests go to some module inside the system, as shown in Figure 14.1. The triad did not talk about how the reservation-allowed condition is displayed (the view), and they did not make up tests for the user interface.

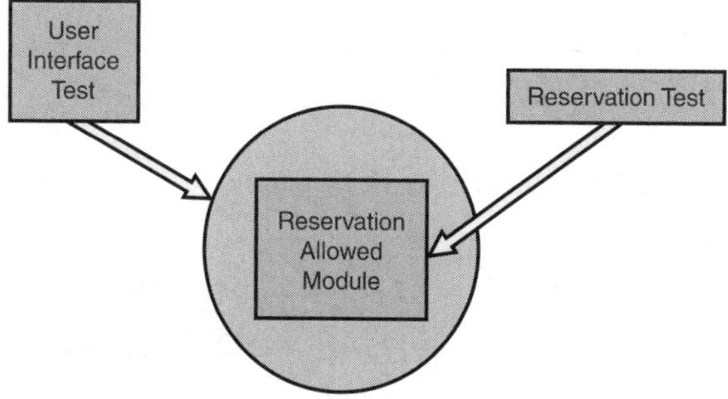

Figure 14.1 *User Interface and Logic Tests*

There are at least three ways that the application could show how a customer was not allowed to reserve a CD:

- The application could hide the Reserve option.
- It could disable the Reserve option.
- It could have the Reserve option go to a dialog box that informs the customer that he is not allowed to reserve.

Here are the three ways displayed in tables.

Display for Reservation Allowed	
Allowed	**Reserve Button Displayed?**
Yes	Yes
No	No

Or

Display for Reservation Allowed	
Allowed	**Reserve Button Enabled?**
Yes	Yes
No	No

Or

Display for Reservation Allowed	
Allowed	**Reserve Button Goes To?**
Yes	Make Reservation dialog box
No	Sorry No Reservation dialog box

Each variation can be described with a specific test, as shown here.

Display for Reserve Allowed or Disallowed

Given that these customers are either allowed or disallowed to reserve:

Reservation Allowed		
Customer ID	**Allowed**	**Name**
007	Yes	James
86	No	Maxwell

Display the Reserve button if the customer is allowed to reserve (see Figure 14.2).

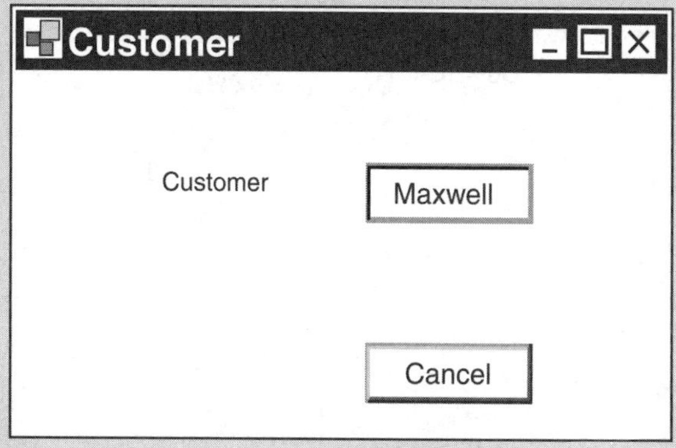

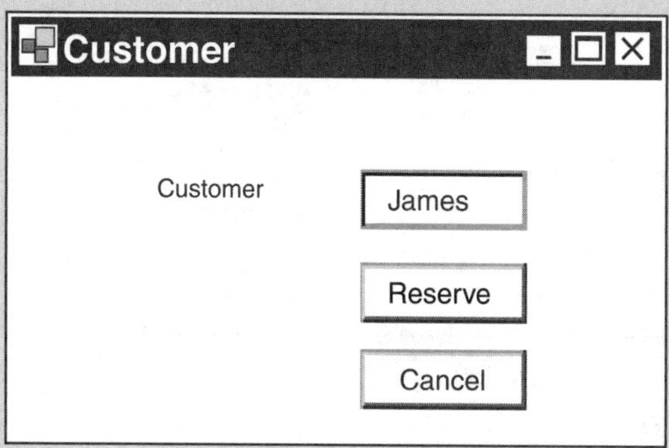

Figure 14.2 *Reserve Button Displayed or Not Displayed*

Or

Enable the Reserve button if the customer is allowed to reserve (see Figure 14.3).

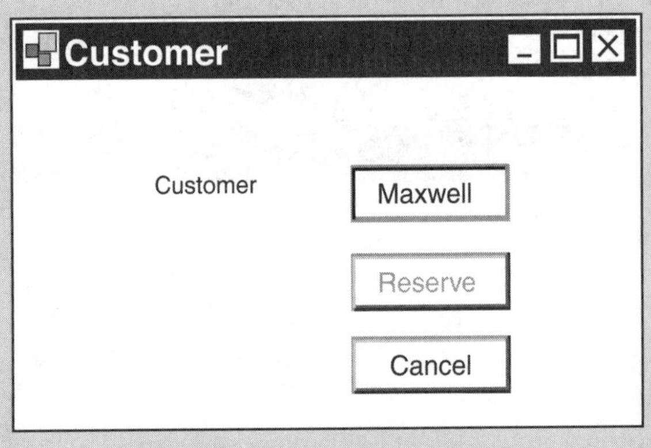

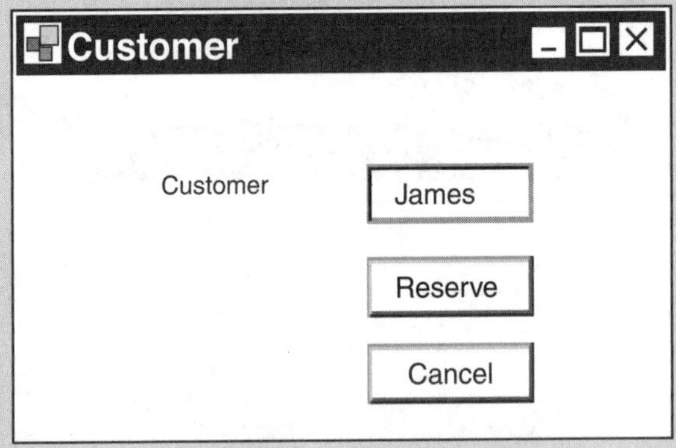

Figure 14.3 *Reserve Button Enabled or Disabled*

Or

Display the Customer Allowed to Reserve option and put up a different dialog box. If the customer is not allowed to reserve, display a No Reserve dialog box. If the customer is allowed to reserve, display a Reservation dialog box (see Figure 14.4).

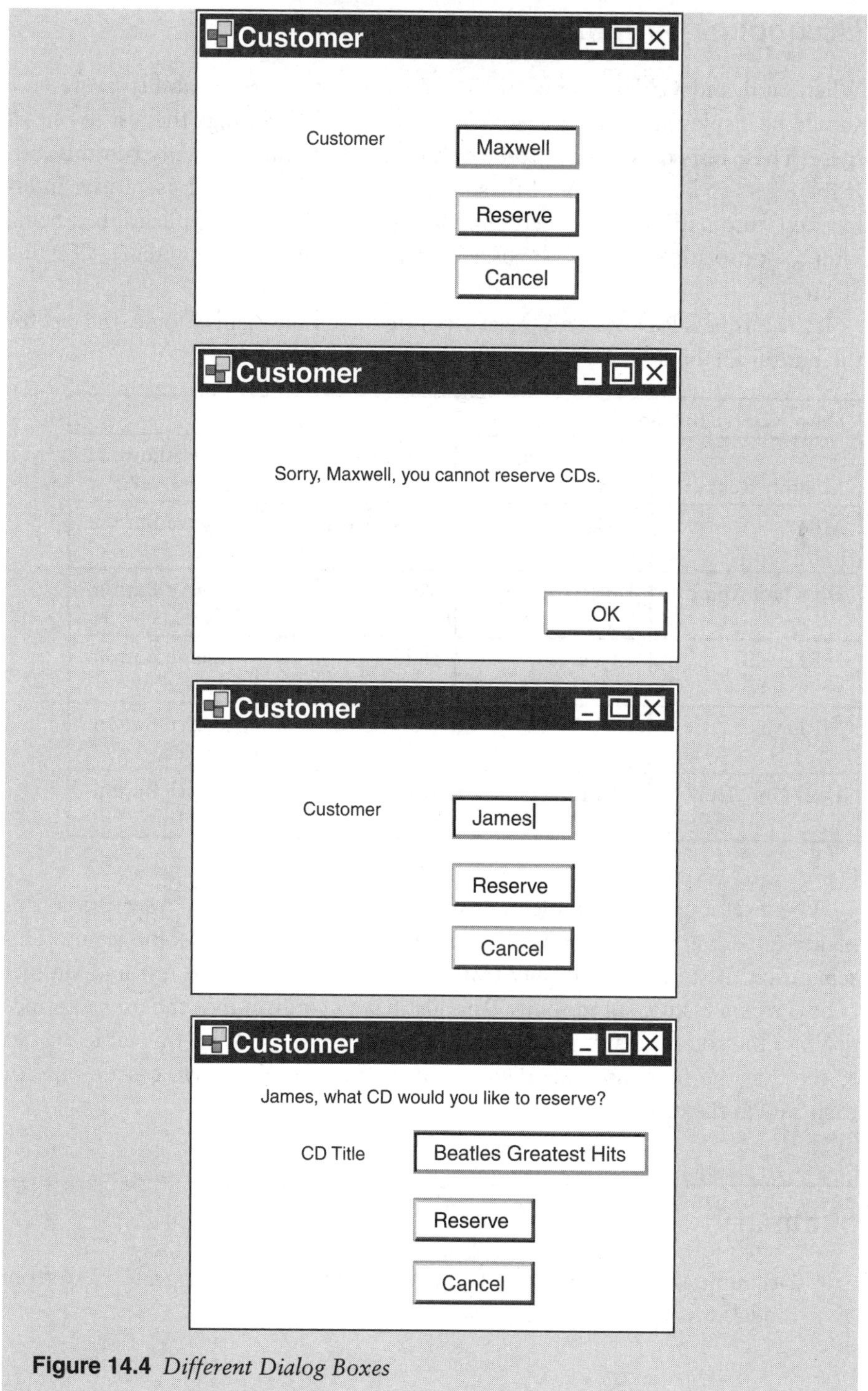

Figure 14.4 *Different Dialog Boxes*

Decoupling Simplifies Testing

When Sam and Cathy change their minds about how the ability to reserve should be displayed, all Debbie and Tom have to do is change the test to one of these. These tests do not have to be automatic. Tom can manually run this test. If there gets to be too many of these manual tests, Tom could use a user interface test automation tool. The tool could be used when the application is being built to automatically verify the user interface, as shown in Chapter 3, "Testing Strategy."

If the business logic had not been separated from the display logic, the test for the button Enabled/Disabled option might be as follows.

Show Reserve Button			
Monthly Rentals	**Cumulative Rentals**	**Sam's Favorite Customer**	**Show Allowed to Reserve?**
MRLevelA	CRLevelA	Does Not Apply	Reserve Button Enabled
Does Not Apply	Does Not Apply	Yes	Reserve Button Enabled
MRLevelB	CRLevelB	Unknown	Reserve Button Enabled
MRLevelC	CRLevelC	No	Reserve Button Enabled
Does Not Apply	CRLevelD	Does Not Apply	Reserve Button Disabled

Whenever a change is made in how to display the allowable reservation, this bigger table has to be changed. Mistakes might be made at some point. This separation of state from display translates both into easier to test and simpler code. From a testing standpoint, Tom just has to confirm that the user interface displays the correct result in two cases—for 007 and 86. With this table, he has to see that the user interface displays the correct result in five cases—one for each row in the table.

Summary

- Decouple the user interface from the business logic (separate view from model) to simplify testing.

Chapter 15

Events, Responses, and States

"I just dropped in to see what condition my condition is in."

Mickey Newbury, "Just Dropped In"

This chapter explains the event-response way of capturing requirements and testing the state transitions caused by events.

Events and an Event Table

The CD rental process is driven mostly by user actions. So employing use cases was a natural fit for eliciting requirements. There are other ways to discover requirements. A popular technique is the *event table*. It defines events that occur and determines how the system should respond. An event could be something that a user initiated or something that a piece of hardware signaled. It could also be a particular time, such as the first of the month, or a time interval, such as every hour. The response of the system could be a visible output or a change in the internal state.

The triad brainstorms to come up with events to see if any issues have been missed. They come up with the following:

Events for CD Rental	
Event	**Notes**
Customer rents CD	Human initiated
Customer returns CD	Human initiated
First of the month	Specific time
Base rental period ends	Period of time
Bank statement arrives	External event

continues

Events for CD Rental, Continued	
Event	**Notes**
Customer enters store	Human initiated
Chicken Little announces the sky is falling	External event
Customer reports CD is lost	Human initiated
Inventory Maintainer cannot find CD	External event
Counter Clerk drops CD, and it breaks	External event
Counter Clerk sees CD is dirty	External event

The triad now needs to come up with how the system should respond to all these events. Cathy decides on the business response to events. Other events may trigger internal actions. After a certain period, the triad winds up with the following:

Events and Responses for CD Rental		
Event	**Response**	**Notes**
Customer rents CD	Record CD as rented Print rental contract	Human initiated
Customer returns CD	Record CD as returned Charge for rental	Human initiated
First of the month	Print inventory report	Specific time
Rental period ends	Notify customer of end of rental	Period of time
Bank statement arrives	Nothing	External event
Customer enters store	Nothing	Human initiated
Chicken Little announces the sky is falling	Nothing	External event
Customer reports CD is lost	Record as lost Charge for CD	Human initiated
Inventory Maintainer cannot find CD	Record as lost	External event
Counter Clerk drops CD, and it breaks	Record as broken	External event
Counter Clerk sees CD is dirty	Set aside to clean	External event

Anything that does not require a response from the system is out of scope. For example, the bank statement arriving does not have a response from the system, although Cathy will have a response. Many of the human-initiated events are turned into use cases. Some of the external events, such as dropping a CD, are also turned into a simple story. Making up a use case might be overkill, because there are not many details associated with them.

A test should be created for every one of the events, even the simple ones. The tests clarify exactly what the system response should be. For example, dropping a CD might have a test something like this:

Dropping a CD

Given a CD in the inventory:

CD		
ID	Status	Rented
CD5	Okay	No

When it is broken by the Counter Clerk or Inventory Maintainer, record the event:

Record Broken CD		
Enter	CD ID	CD5
Press	Submit	

Then the CD status should change:

CD		
ID	Status	Rented
CD5	Broken	No

The number of tests might suggest a different approach for the conditions. For example, all losses could be grouped into a small number of categories, such as things that are irreversible, such as a broken CD, and things that are possibly reversible, such as a dirty CD or a missing one. (A missing one might be found sometime.)

States and State Transitions

Entities such as CDs take on different states or conditions. The CD transitions from one state to another due to an event, such as the ones shown in the event-response table. Documenting the states and the transitions is a collaborative effort, just as for the event-response table. The outcome of the effort is a list of the states and a map of the transitions.

Based on the events, more discussion, and some simplification, the triad agrees on the following states:

CD States	
State	**Meaning**
Ready to Rent	In inventory, ready for renting
Rented	Customer has it on rental
Irreversible Loss	For example, broken or badly scratched
Reversible Issue	For example, dirty, cracked case
Missing	Not rented, but not found in inventory
Lost	Customer reports CD is lost

The transitions can be documented in two ways. The first is a state diagram. In Figure 15.1, the states are shown in circles, and transitions are shown as lines with labels. Each state may have associated data. For example, the rented state can have the date the CD was rented and the customer it was rented to. The large black circle on the left is called the initial state. It points to which state is the first one. The small black circle on the right is the final terminal state. There are no transitions from the final state.

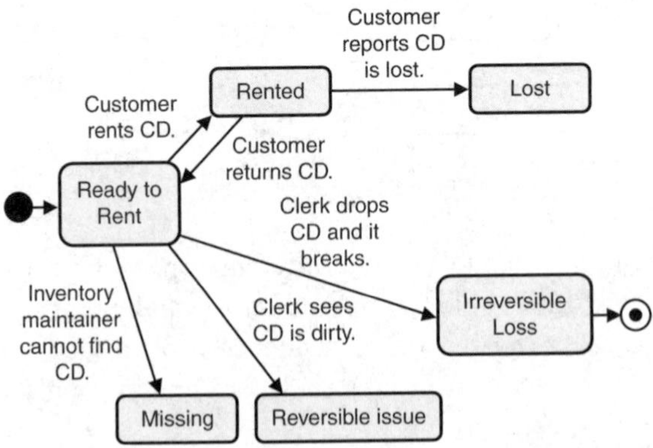

Figure 15.1 *State Diagram*

Alternatively, the states and events can be specified in a table. Initially this may display the same information as parts of the event/response table, such as these:

CD States and Events						
States/Events	Customer Rents CD	Customer Returns CD	Inventory Maintainer Cannot Find CD	Counter Clerk Drops CD, and It Breaks	Customer Reports CD Is Lost	Counter Clerk Sees CD Is Dirty
Ready to Rent	Rented		Missing	Irrevers-ible Loss		Reversible Issue
Rented		Ready to Rent			Lost	
Irreversible Loss						
Reversible Issue						
Missing						
Lost						

The state diagram does not show an event that causes an Irreversible Loss for the terminal state. No events are shown that cause the CD to transition out of states such as Missing or Reversible Issue. After some discussion, the triad comes with these additional events. The entire table is not repeated, because it would exceed the width of the page.

CD States and Events				
States/Events	Customer Reports CD Is Found	CD Prepared for Rental (Cleaned)	Monthly Inventory Report Created	CD Is Found by Clerk
Irreversible Loss			Remove CD from system Terminal	
Reversible Issue		Ready to Rent		
Missing				Ready to Rent
Lost	Rented			

With the state-event table, blank cells are easily identified. A blank cell represents that an event should not occur for a particular state or, if it does, it should not cause the state to change. Examine all blank cells to ensure that all the bases are covered—that is, all possible state transitions due to events are identified. A blank cell can be filled in once it's examined with some indicator, such as N/A for not applicable to show that the state/event combination has been considered and that the event should cause no response when the CD is in that state.

The primary purpose of the state table is to show transitions. Other responses and state data such as the date rented can be put into this state table. For example, the action of Remove CD from System is shown in the state/event combination of Irreversible Loss/Monthly Inventory Report Created.

There should be a test for every state transition. Some of the transitions are already covered by other tests. The ones for check-out and check-in already cover the transitions between Ready to Rent and Rented. Other transitions may show additional user stories that need to be implemented, such as a Prepare CD for Rental. The tests for these stories would show the transition from Reversible Issue to Ready to Rent.

Internal State or External Response

Here is another example of event, state, and response. Every external event causes a system to produce an externally visible response, change its internal state (such as persistent data), or both. An internal state change alters an externally visible response in the future. For example, suppose the system keeps the addresses of customers. The address of a customer can be changed, as shown in Figure 15.2.

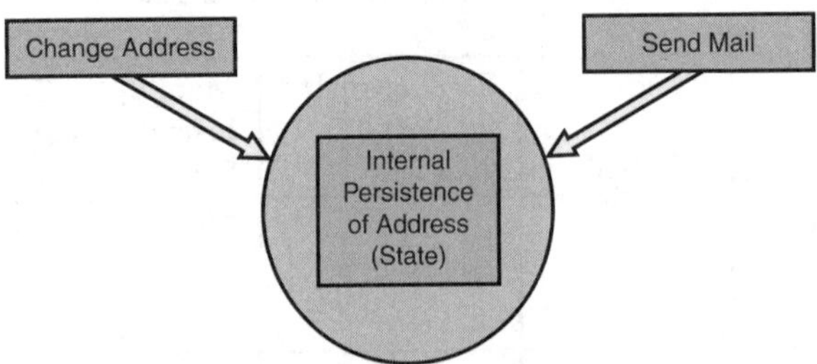

Figure 15.2 *Internal State*

Event/Response	
Event	Address changed
Response	Address change confirmation
Internal State Change	Address updated

In the future, when the system sends mail, the new address will be used:

Event/Response	
Event	Send mail
Response	Send to current address of customer

An acceptance test for an internal state change could confirm that the state has been changed. Or it could be combined with another test that shows the result of that changed state. So the Change Address—Send Mail test would flow together.

Alternatively, if the address is kept in a repository that is external to the system (see Figure 15.3), the update is part of the response.

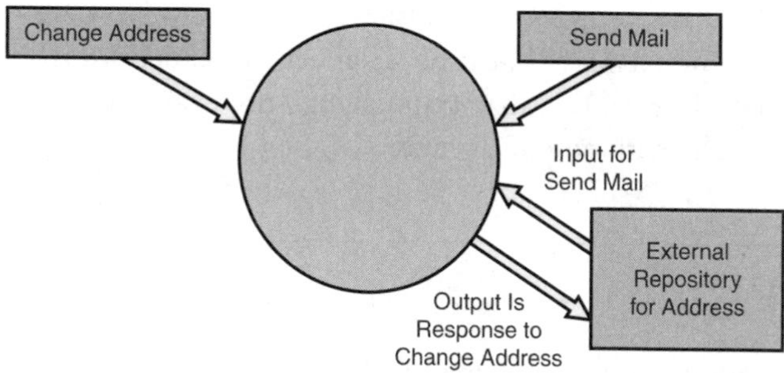

Figure 15.3 *External State*

Event/Response	
Event	Address changed
Response	Address change confirmation
Output	New address output to external repository
Internal State Change	None

In this case, an output is expected. The acceptance test can verify this output to another system, just as was done with the credit charge in Chapter 11, "System Boundary." In creating a response to an event, a system may use data that comes from the external world. That data may affect the response. In this case, the input data in the repository changes the response. For testing, developers may create a test double to simulate the input data from the external repository. With the external data, the response to send mail is as follows:

Event/Response	
Event	Send mail
Response	Input address from external repository Send mail to that address

Transient or Persistent States

A state change may be transient or persistent. A transient state change exists for a short period. For example, an address could be changed just for a single order or for all the orders made during a web session. A persistent change would change the address permanently, or at least until it was changed again.

A Zen Question

If the internal state changes, but it never affects anything directly or indirectly seen in the outside world, is that state change necessary? Does a tree make a sound when it falls with no one around?

Summary

- Event/response tables are a complementary way of eliciting requirements.
- Every event/response combination should be covered by an acceptance test.
- A state table documents the events that cause the state of an entity to change.
- Every state/event combination should be covered by an acceptance test.
- State tables and event/response tables may show the same information, but they are organized with a different emphasis.

Chapter 16

Developer Acceptance Tests

"What is good for the goose is good for the gander."

Anonymous

The triad has developed acceptance tests for stories that Cathy created. When a developer needs a component from another developer, the requester should create acceptance tests for that component.

Component Acceptance Tests

Acceptance tests are not generated by just the customer unit. Many software development organizations have groups that develop common modules or components for other groups. The requesting group needs to supply acceptance tests for those modules.

Field Display Tests

For example, specialized developers often create custom user interface components. User interface developers use these components in web pages. Let's look at a couple of common components. One is a text box that accepts a formatted string, such as a phone number or an e-mail address. The other is a tabular style–component that allows sorting by the values in columns. The tests may look like specifications or vice versa.

Cathy wants a field on the display for entering a phone number. Obviously, you should check the data entered into the field for validity. The format differs between nations; so to keep it simple, the example shows a U.S. phone number. The N in the table means a number or a digit.

Formatted Field			
Field Type	Example	Format	Validation
U.S. phone number	1-919-555-1212	1-NNN-NNN-NNNN	Area code must be valid

Here are some of the tests Debbie might create for a U.S. phone number field.[1]

U.S. Phone Number Component Tests		
Value	Valid?	Notes
1-919-555-1212	Y	
1-000-555-1212	N	Bad_area_code

Suppose Don is the developer who is going to create this component. The first thing Debbie needs to do is give an acceptance test for what it should look like. For example, will it display the dashes immediately or as a person types the digits? Let's suppose the former. Debbie creates an image of what the component should look like in Figure 16.1. The image is part of the acceptance test, but one you have to verify manually. You also need to check the color and font.[2]

Figure 16.1 *State Diagram*

Debbie also needs to specify to Don what should occur if the phone number is incorrectly formatted. Should the component just return a failure code? Or should the component produce an output as a beep or error message? Since the phone number box will be used repeatedly on every form that requires one, this decision may need to be made by a corporate user interface standards group. Suppose Cathy wants the error to be displayed when the user finishes an entry in the field. So Debbie constructs a table that describes how the error should appear.

---

1. Creating additional tests for phone numbers is left as an exercise for the reader.

2. A test process could include a step in which the customer approves the image that an application generates. That image could be used in a test to ensure that it did not change.

U.S. Phone Number Errors		
Error	**Display Message?**	**Notes**
Bad_area_code	"You entered an invalid area code"	All errors should be displayed to the right of the entry field on leaving the field

Debbie needs to show Don what component should be output when the value is submitted. This table shows that the dashes should be included in the output value. Another possibility is that the dashes should be eliminated.

U.S. Phone Number Output		
Field ID	**Field Entry**	**Output?**
"HomePhone"	1-919-555-1212	"HomePhone=1-919-555-1212"

Don creates a form with a Phone Number field on it and a Submit button. He then demonstrates to Debbie that the component passes the tests for both a valid and an invalid entry. Next, he shows that the field sends the correct information when the Submit button is pressed. He also devises a form with three entry fields—one prior to the Phone Number field and one after it—and a Submit button. He demonstrates that the field works with other entry fields by allowing the user to tab to the next and previous entries.

This component is a user interface component, so there will be some manual tests to ensure that it is acceptable to a human being. You can create automated tests to check that the component continues to work even if you change its underlying implementation.

Tabular Display Tests

Here's a display component that is more complicated. A user interface often contains a table of items. The table component might allow the user to sort the table by the values in each column, or it may have links within the table. Cathy or Debbie needs to determine what should be displayed if there are no values in the data to be shown in the table and what to do if the number of values is large.

Here are some potential inputs to a table display. It doesn't matter whether these values come from a program component, such as a Java class, or a database query. That's a matter of connecting up the table to the appropriate code. The first input is a simple set of data.

Table Data		
Name	Date	Amount
James	2/21/2011	$5.00
Maxwell	1/23/2011	$.01
Agent	12/12/2011	$10.00

Debbie needs to show Don how this data should appear on the screen. Suppose that Cathy wants to have shaded column heads and shading on every other row (see Figure 16.2). The output specification is concerned only with appearance, not how the display is generated.[3]

Name	Date	Amount
James	2/21/2011	$5.00
Maxwell	1/23/2011	$.01
Agent	12/12/2011	$10.00

Figure 16.2 *Table Display*

Debbie and Don need to clarify the contract for the table display component. Should it be Debbie's job to ensure that the component never gets passed an empty table or a really big table, or should it be the component's responsibility to handle these cases? If the latter, Debbie needs to create some tests for these two conditions.

Empty Table Display

Given the following data:

Table Data		
Name	Date	Amount

The following should appear on the screen (see Figure 16.3).

---

3. It could be generated by Hypertext Markup Language (HTML) attributes, Cascading Style Sheets (CSS) styles, or some other set of acronyms. However, a constraint might be that it uses the same framework as the rest of the system.

Name	Date	Amount
No matching records		

Figure 16.3 *Table Display for Empty List*

She also creates tests for a larger number. Suppose the table should only display 20 rows at a time. There would be a test that shows what happens if there are more rows to display. For example:

One Greater Than Screen Size Display

Given the following data:

Table Data		
Name	Date	Amount
James	2/21/2011	$5.00
Maxwell	1/23/2011	$.01
Agent	12/12/2011	$10.00
Plus 18 more rows...		

The display should look like Figure 16.4.

Name	Date	Amount
James	2/21/2011	$5.00
Maxwell	1/23/2011	$.01
Agent	12/12/2011	$10.00
Plus 17 more rows...		

Previous 20 | Next 20 | 1-20 of 21

Figure 16.4 *Table Display for Numerous Entries*

Tom might come up with a few more tests. He might want to see what happens if there are exactly 40 or some large number such as 10,000,000. Debbie and Don might then decide that the component does not need to handle more than a reasonable number of components, such as 1,000.

Instead of the buttons at the bottom to see the other items, the table could display 20 items but have a scrollbar if there are more. There would then be a test that provided 1,000 items of data to see how fast the component could scroll.

The table data might have links associated with it. Suppose that clicking on the name was supposed to go to a particular page associated with the data. The links would be in the supplied data, and the test would look like this.

Table with Links

Given the following data:

Table Data			
Name	Date	Amount	Link
James	2/21/2011	$5.00	James.html
Maxwell	1/23/2011	$.01	Maxwell.html
Agent	12/12/2011	$10.00	Agent.html

The display should appear as Figure 16.5.

Name	Date	Amount
James	2/21/2011	$ 5.00
Maxwell	1/23/2011	$ .01
Agent	1/12/2011	$10.00

Figure 16.5 *Table Display with Links*

And clicking on a name should go to the link.

Click On	
Name	Go to Page?
James	James.html
Maxwell	Maxwell.html
Agent	Agent.html

The table might offer a sorting feature. When the user clicks on a column header, the rows should be sorted by the values in that column. Debbie gives tests to Don to demonstrate what she means. The tests could include more rows than fit on the screen to show that sorting is on the entire set of data, not just the rows displayed on the screen. With just a few rows, here's a test for the Date column.

Sorted Table Display

Given the following display (see Figure 16.6):

Name	Date	Amount
James	2/21/2011	$ 5.00
Maxwell	1/23/2011	$ .01
Agent	1/12/2011	$10.00

Figure 16.6 *Table Display Unsorted*

When the user clicks on the Date column header, the rows should be sorted by date, with the earliest date first (see Figure 16.7).

Name	Date	Amount
Maxwell	1/23/2011	$ .01
James	2/21/2011	$ 5.00
Agent	12/12/2011	$10.00

Figure 16.7 *Table Display Sorted*

There are a lot of other considerations in the sorting. For example, what if two values match? Which should come first? Or if the user clicks a second time on a column header, should it reverse the sort?[4]

Summary

- Developers should supply acceptance tests for components created by other developers.
- Acceptance tests for display components should include combinations of inputs that result in different display appearance or response.
- Acceptance tests for user interface components may be manual.

4. Creating requirements and tests for the details of sorting a table is left as an exercise for the reader.

Chapter 17

Decouple with Interfaces

Wizard of Oz: "Pay no attention to that man behind the curtain."

The Wizard of Oz

Developers can create acceptance tests for service implementations. The tests can be both for accuracy and for performance.

Tests for a Service Provider

Cathy wants the ZIP code to be checked for customer contact addresses. Debbie needs a service for the verification of a ZIP code for an address; she is not going to code the service herself, but obtain it from another group. Dave is another developer who is going to provide that service. As a backup plan in case Dave cannot implement the service, Debbie may purchase it from an external vendor.

As the requester, Debbie needs to create acceptance tests for the service that Dave will use to test his implementation. The tests should be independent of the service provider. Ideally, she should not have to rewrite any of her production code if the service provider is changed, so she creates an application programming interface (API) that Dave should implement [Pugh01]. If she uses another service provider, she will adapt its interface to this API. The tests that she writes as well as her production application are coded to the API.

The Interface

Debbie creates an API that describes what she wants the ZIP code verification interface to look like:

```
interface ZipCodeLookup {
   ZipCode lookupZipCode( String streetAddress,
       String City, StateID state ) throws ZipCodeNotFound
   }
```

"ZipCode" is a data class that contains the ZIP code. The lookupZipCode() method needs to indicate an error if the ZIP code cannot be found. From a programmer's point of view, if the ZIP code was not findable, the method could return the value of null or throw an exception that contained further information. The "StateID" is a data class that contains a reference to a valid U.S. state or territory.

There are other things that Debbie may need, such as the ability to get the city and state that correspond to a ZIP code. If so, she would add that to the interface.

Debbie provides the following table as an example of the tests she is going to run against the interface.

ZIP Code Lookup			
Street Address	**City**	**State**	**ZIP Code?**
1 East Oak Street	Chicago	IL	60611
101 Penny Lane	Danville	VT	05828
1 No Place	Nowhere	OK	NotFound

Dave may create an implementation that uses a subscription to the United States Postal Service (USPS) web-service, a corporately-owned address validation program, or some other system. If Debbie needs a quick way to do an end-to-end test, she might create a browser-simulator version that interacts with the usps.com website and provides the answers found on that site. If she needs a way to have a quick unit test for her code that uses this service, she might create a "test double" (see Chapter 11 "System Boundary") for ZipCodeLookup. The test double might only return a small set of ZIP codes, such as the set listed in this table.

The "StateID" data class listed in the interface specification needs to be defined. Debbie can use a table to do that. She could include just the states or all USPS recognized abbreviations.

StateID	
Full Name	**Abbreviation**
North Carolina	NC
Massachusetts	MA
... and more	

The ZIP Code Lookup tests do not have to include states that are not in this table.

Quality Attribute Tests

Debbie can provide quality attribute tests for an interface implementation. The initial test checks that the interface is working properly. She may also be concerned with the performance of the implementation. If it takes a long time to look up a ZIP code, then the user experience will suffer. So she can specify the amount of time in a test. The time limits may differ based on the type of result (success or failure) and the particulars of the data being passed to the service.

ZIP Code Lookup				
Street Address	City	State	ZIP Code?	Time?
1 East Oak Street	Chicago	IL	60611	.01
101 Penny Lane	Danville	VT	05828	.01
1 No Place	Nowhere	OK	NotFound	.2

For a data-lookup style service, such as the ZIP code, Debbie could also make up acceptance criteria for the completeness and accuracy of the data. The criteria can be specified in a table such as:

ZIP Code Lookup Qualities	
Completeness	Accuracy of What Is Available
99.999%	99.9999%

Determining whether an implementation meets these criteria is a difficult task and beyond the scope of this book. However if you have two implementations of a service, you can at least cross-check them.

Comparing Implementations

In the case of ZIP Code Lookup, Debbie may be able to obtain two implementations of the interface. She may not know in advance what the correct results are. All she knows is that the results of the two implementations need to match. This is often the case when you have an existing system and you are rewriting the system to use another technology. The external behavior of the new system must match the existing system. So you first run one implementation and store the results. This forms the acceptable values (the oracle [Bach01]) for the new system. Then you run the second implementation and compare the results to those found in the first implementation.

There are at least two ways to do this. The first way involves using variables. It's introduced here to show how a test can reuse results from earlier in a test. The second way eliminates some redundancy.

Using tables to represent this comparison involves creating some type of variable. A variable is used to store the results of one action for use in a later action. You need to be able have a way to show when a value is stored in the variable and when it is retrieved. For the purposes of demonstration, we'll use a → symbol to show a value is stored into a variable and a → symbol to show the value is retrieved from the variable.[1] Debbie creates the following table for the first implementation of the interface.

ZIP Code Lookup		**Implementation = Dave's**	
Street Address	**City**	**State**	**ZIP Code?**
1 East Oak Street	Chicago	IL	→eastoakzip
101 Penny Lane	Danville	VT	→pennylanezip
1 No Place	Nowhere	OK	→noplacezip

The ZIP codes are stored in variables named eastoakzip, pennylanezip, and noplacezip. Debbie then makes the next table for the second implementation.

ZIP Code Lookup		**Implementation = USPS**	
Street Address	**City**	**State**	**ZIP Code?**
1 East Oak Street	Chicago	IL	←eastoakzip
101 Penny Lane	Danville	VT	←pennylanezip
1 No Place	Nowhere	OK	←noplacezip

The ZIP codes returned by this implementation are compared to values stored in eastoakzip, pennylanezip, and noplacezip. If a value does not match, an error is indicated. If an error appears, Debbie cannot be sure which implementation was wrong without further investigation.

If the number of comparisons was large, Debbie might use a second way to compare the ZIP codes that eliminates some redundancy. Rather than use a table to list the individual data items, she might create a module that does the comparison internally. So all she would list are the input values. If a mismatch occurs between the two implementations, the two answers can be shown in the ZIP Code column as follows:

---

1. The methodology and symbols used for storing and retrieving values vary in each test framework.

ZIP Code Lookup Comparison		Implementation = Dave's Implementation = USPS		
Street Address	City	State	Dave's ZIP Code?	USPS ZIP Code?
1 East Oak Street	Chicago	IL	60611	60612
101 Penny Lane	Danville	VT		
1 No Place	Nowhere	OK		

Comparing Implementations

Using and comparing two or more implementations is a common design solution, particularly in critical systems. For example, in space flight, three computers calculate the required flight operations, such as when to turn on the rocket booster. The results of the three are compared. If all three computers report the same results, the operation commences. If two agree and one doesn't, the majority usually wins and the report is, "Houston, we have a problem that we can deal with for the moment." If all of them disagree, the flight reports, "Houston, we have a big problem."

Separating User Interface from Service

Debbie has not specified how the state in the address is going to appear in the user interface. She knows that separating the business rules from the display makes for easier testing, as shown in Chapter 14, "Separate View from Model." There are at least four ways the state could appear on the user interface:

- A text box that accepts two-character abbreviations for the state
- A text box that accepts the full name for the state
- A drop-down list that contains the two-character abbreviations for each state
- A drop-down list that contains the full name for each state[2]

These are four display manifestations of the same requirement; they are not four different requirements. They differ in the user experience. In the drop-down

2. As a resident of North Carolina, I highly prefer the two-character drop-down list. Can you figure out why?

version, users cannot enter an incorrect state, but they may have to type more.[3] The selection of one is based on user quality feedback.

In any event, the field for the ZIP code should only allow either five or nine digits to be entered. These are the two valid lengths for U.S. ZIP codes. Allowing other characters or lengths would cause unnecessary calls to the ZIP Code Lookup.

If Debbie had a field that allowed the user to enter a ZIP code, she would check that ZIP code against the one returned by ZIP Code Lookup. How she displays a mismatch is based on the desired user experience. The mismatch might show up in a dialog box, as a line at the top of the dialog box, as a message next to the ZIP code, or as a different colored ZIP code.

Separation of Concerns

The preceding example is being pretty U.S centric. Debbie might need to do postal code matching for all the countries in the world. To keep things simple, she could have a master table of all the countries that breaks out to tables of tests for each country.

Country Breakout			
Country	**ISO Code**	**Input With**	**Validate With**
U.S.A.	US	US Address Form	ZIPCodeLookup
Canada	CA	CA Address Form	CAAddressValidator
	...and many more		

Reusable Business Rules

A business rule is something that is true regardless of the technology employed (paper, computer, and so on). The rule that a ZIP code be valid for an address is true regardless of whether the envelope is printed on a laser printer or handwritten. Implementations of business rules should be exposed so that they can be used in multiple places, not just the middle tier.

For example, the user interface may require business rule checking to allow errors to be identified in a more user-friendly manner. The ZIP code for customer address may be verified as part of the input process. To avoid duplication

3. Try to enter North Carolina in a drop-down that has full state names. How many keystrokes does it take?

of functionality that would require duplication of testing, the user interface should use the same module as the middle tier. The means for doing so depend on the technology involved and are beyond the scope of this book.[4]

Reuse extends beyond a single application. If a function, such as ZIP Code Lookup, is used by multiple applications, Debbie would put the component into an infrastructure or core system library. That would eliminate needing to have tests applied to each application.

Summary

- Developer acceptance tests should be created for every service.
- A common API should be created for services that have multiple implementations.
- Create performance tests for service implementations.
- Create completeness and accuracy criteria for service implementation, when appropriate.
- Create comparative tests for checking old versus new implementations.
- Keep tests for services separate from tests for user interfaces.
- Consider whether services are application services or core services.

4. For example, you might use Ajax [Riordan01].

Chapter 18

Entities and Relationships

"The pure and simple truth is rarely pure and never simple."

Oscar Wilde

This chapter presents a more complex system and introduces a model diagram and its representation in tables.

Relationships

Sam's system started off with a simple setup—a Customer table and a CD table. The CD table had an entry for each physical CD. This corresponded to Sam's paper system, in which each CD had a separate index card that recorded its being rented. The table looked like this.

CD Data					
ID	Title	CD Category	Rented	Customer ID	Rental Due
CD3	Janet Jackson Number Ones	Regular	Yes	007	1/23/2011
CD7	Janet Jackson Number Ones	Regular	No		

Entities and Relationships

A system is often more complex than Sam's example. There are more entities than just a CD, and there are relationships between these entities. The business is the source of the information. Any diagrams, models, and tables are based on the business's understanding of the entities, not an underlying implementation.

For Sam's application, there are CDs that are physical copies of an album. If Cathy describes the system with these two concepts, the triad should use these terms. The relationship between CDs and albums can be shown in a diagram. A common diagramming method is Unified Modeling Language [UML].[1] The entities are shown in boxes in Figure 18.1. A simple way to represent the relationship that a CD "is a copy of" an album is to have an arrow with a label drawn between the two boxes.

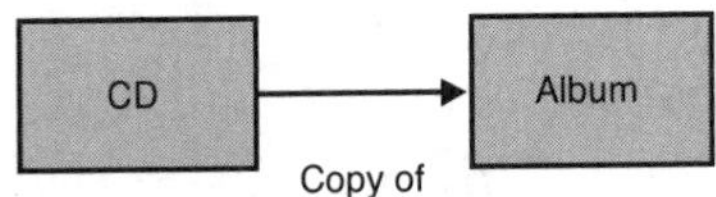

Figure 18.1 *Diagram of CD/Album Relationship*

In addition, the ends of the arrow can be labeled with an indication of how many entities are on each side of the relationship, as in Figure 18.2. The * states that there can be many CD copies of an album, and the 1 says that each CD is a copy of only one album. If there is a value, such as the UPC code, that relates the CD to the album, you can add that to the diagram.

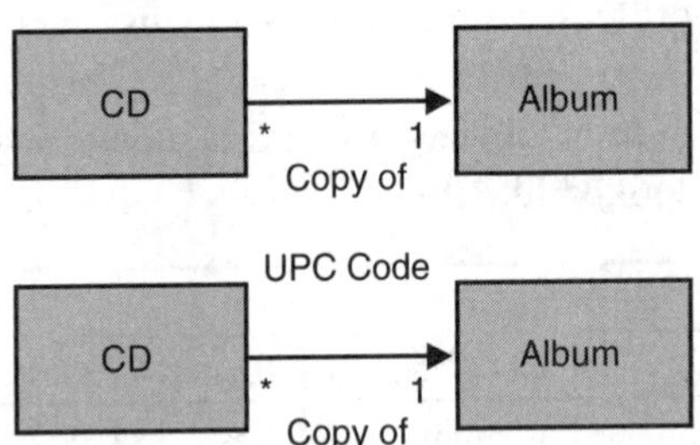

Figure 18.2 *Diagram of CD/Album Relationship with Specific Relationship*

Because the UPC code is what relates this CD to an album, the data for both CD and album would include that value. The CD table now refers to the Album table, as follows.

Album Data		
UPC Code	Title	CD Category
UPC123456	Janet Jackson Number Ones	Regular

1. See [Wiki06] and [Ambler01] for details.

and

CD Data				
ID	UPC Code	Rented	Customer ID	Rental Due
CD3	UPC123456	Yes	007	1/23/2011
CD7	UPC123456	No		

Multiple Relationships

There could be another entity that Cathy talks about. Instead of a CD containing the state of being rented, there could be a separate concept of a rental. The rental is related to and to the CD by the CD ID and to the customer by the customer ID. Figure 18.3 shows this relationship.

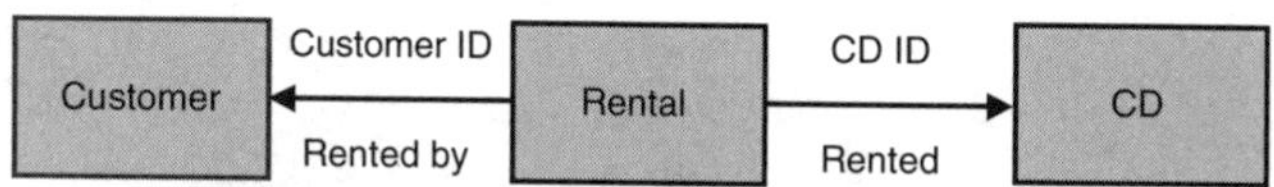

Figure 18.3 *Diagram of CD Customer Rental*

With this new organization, the CD does not contain the concept of whether it is rented or not. That information is now kept in another entity: Rental. This separation of concerns makes a better design and easier testing. Here's what the tables look like.

CD Data	
ID	UPC Code
CD3	UPC123456
CD7	UPC123456

Rental Data			
CD ID	Rented	Customer ID	Rental Due
CD3	Yes	007	1/23/2011
CD7	No		

Customer Data	
Name	ID
James	007

You can further simplify these tables if the triad approves. For example, the Customer ID and Rental Due fields are blank if the CD is not rented. There could be a convention that if the CD is not rented, an entry does not appear in the Rental Data table. So if only CD3 was rented and not CD7, the table would look like this.

Rental Data		
CD ID	Customer ID	Rental Due
CD3	007	1/23/2011

With the additional entities, redundant information is eliminated. The number of columns in each table is reduced, so there is less information to process. Using these additional tables, the test for check-in[2] can be as follows. The setup part could be in common with a number of other tests.

Check-In CD

Setup:

Album Data		
UPC Code	Title	CD Category
UPC123456	Janet Jackson Number Ones	Regular

CD Data	
ID	UPC Code
CD3	UPC123456
CD7	UPC123456

Customer Data	
Name	ID
James	007

2. The first three tables might be part of a common setup, as shown in Chapter 31, "Test Setup."

Given a customer with a rental:

Rental Data	Customer ID = 007
CD ID	Rental Due
CD3	1/23/2011

When the clerk checks in the CD:

Test Date
Date
1/23/2011

Check-In CD		
Enter	CD ID	CD3
Press	Submit	

Then the CD is recorded as not rented and the rental fee is computed. (The fee includes one late day.)

Rental Data	Customer ID = 007
CD ID	Rental Due

Rental Fee				
Customer ID	Name	Title	Returned	Rental Fee?
007	James	Janet Jackson Number Ones	1/23/2011	$2

You could discover this more complex relationship after creating the initial tests (in Chapter 10, "User Story Breakup") that used a single table, such as the first table in this chapter. You may not need to alter the original tests. You could use them with what is called a *view*. The data in these three tables is combined to appear as a single table.[3] The view decouples the way data is represented in the database from the way the business deals with the data.

---

3. An exercise for the technical reader is to determine how the three tables can be viewed as the original single table.

Alternative Representations

The Rental data could be kept after the CD is checked in as a history of rentals. This history could be represented as a separate table for use in tests (such as in Chapter 13, "Simplification by Separation"). For example, as shown here:

Rental History Data			
CD ID	Customer ID	Rental Due	Returned
CD3	88	12/21/2009	12/23/2009
CD3	007	1/23/2011	1/23/2011

If the business requirements stated that the rental history was only needed in relationship to a CD, the history could be shown as a table embedded in another table.[4] This cuts down on the number of tables, but it also increases the table's size. For example, as shown here:

CD Data				
ID	UPC Code	Rental History		
CD3	UPC123456	Customer ID	Rental Due	Returned
		88	12/21/2009	12/23/2009
		007	1/23/2011	1/24/2011

Summary

- Relationships between entities can be diagramed for ease of understanding.
- Entity relationships can be shown in multiple ways in tables.
- The customer unit determines the preferred form of showing relationships.
- Tests should reflect the entities and relationships.

---

4. In domain-driven design (DDD) terminology, CD is the root of an aggregate.

Chapter 19

Triads for Large Systems

"It always takes longer than you expect, even if you take Hofstadter's Law into account."

Douglas Hofstadter

This chapter shows how larger systems can have more and different triads. Some projects do not require new customer acceptance tests. This chapter also examines a lack of acceptance tests.

Large Systems

Sam's system had just two people, Debbie and Tom, as developer and tester. Debbie was an omnipotent developer. She did everything from creating the overall architecture to designing the user interface to administering the database. Tom did all sorts of testing, from helping with acceptance test development to running performance testing tools to checking usability and performing exploratory testing. Teams for larger projects are sometimes composed of such ambidextrous individuals. But often the range of technology involved and the scope of the project do not allow individuals to cover the entire gamut of development and testing. Nor does a single customer, such as Cathy, know every detail about what needs to go into the system. Subject matter experts specify the requirements in their own particular area of expertise.

The triad still exists, just with different people. It becomes the subject matter expert, the developer (or developers if you are doing pair programming), and the functional tester (or people whose focus is one of these roles). They develop acceptance tests for the particular stories or requirements with which the expert is familiar.

For projects with larger implementations, teams often have an architect or technical lead focus on the overall structure of a system to keep it consistent with other systems. The system may encompass a single application or multiple applications.

For teams like this, you have another triad: the architect, developer, and tester (see Figure 19.1). The architect, Al, helps the developer unit make design decisions that are consistent with the larger picture. The three work together to determine a system's modules and their interrelationships. The responsibilities of each module are specified with acceptance tests, like the ones Debbie created in Chapter 16, "Developer Acceptance Tests." The triad develops these tests collaboratively. Because all involved people are of a technical bent, the tests may incorporate many non-customer-related terms. But everyone in the triad needs to understand the terms and their implications.

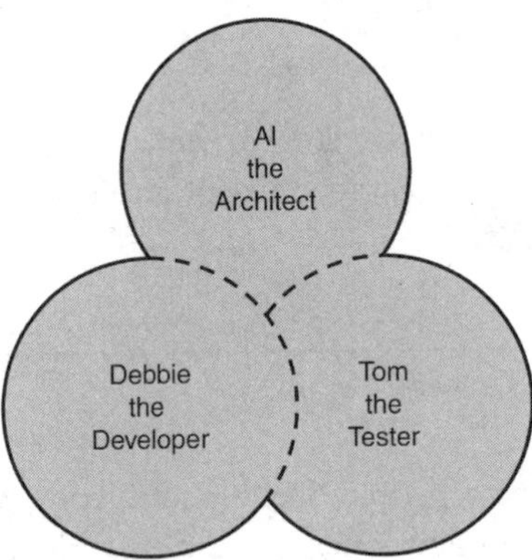

Figure 19.1 *The Technical Triad*

Some tests for the modules are derived from the customer acceptance tests, just as unit tests are derived from them. The process of deciding how many modules are required and which modules are responsible for fulfilling which parts of the acceptance tests is a major facet of the architectural design process. This process is covered in other books, such as [Fowler01].

One key that the team should focus on is getting an end-to-end system working soon after the start of the project. One customer acceptance test should be demonstrated on the entire system. The feedback from the ease or non-ease of developing for that test can yield helpful information to the triad as to whether a particular architecture is suitable for the project. It also gives a baseline against which to measure additions. When a new story is implemented, a customer acceptance test may fail because an implementation changed its behavior. If the behavior represented by the test is still required, the triad can review and possibly revise the architecture. This is before much work has been spent writing code dependent on the architecture.

With larger systems, you may have a database architect, Dana. Dana creates the persistent storage that multiple applications require. She ensures that there is no redundancy of information, such as storing a customer's address in two different places. A different triad—the developer, the tester, and Dana (see Figure 19.2)—works to ensure that the developer has a way to make persistent all the information needed to solve the story that the developer is working on. This collaboration operates the same way as the customer-developer-tester triad. Debbie states what she needs and creates an acceptance test. Dana delivers the persistence methods required. Tom may suggest additional tests. Again, the three people in the triad may not have these titles; they are just the roles they play.

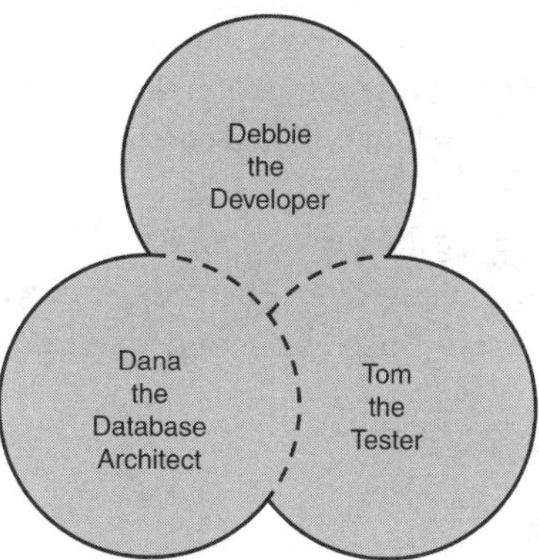

Figure 19.2 *Another Technical Triad*

As we have seen, the triad concept can work all the way up and down the chain, from an overall software application down to the individual modules. The triad consists of the requester, the implementer, and the tester who ensures that all bases are covered. The triad is meant as a minimum for the number of people in collaboration. You may have a quad, a penta, or a larger group as required. However, it is often the case that the larger the group, the less members interact and the less effective they are. So limit the number to those actually required rather than those who just have a possible "want to know what's happening."

When a Customer Test May Not Be Required

Sam's business is booming. He now rents not just CDs, but electronic books, videos, and games. He has bought up a number of competitors. So now Al, the architect, has the work of keeping a large set of diverse programs working together. Al needs to combine systems so that the counter clerks use the same system if they switch stores. The combination involves taking the data, such as customers, from one system, and converting it to another. There are projects like these that may not necessarily involve new customer acceptance tests.

Data Conversion

Al and Dana work together on the data conversion project. This conversion is a mostly technical project, not a customer project. Al will be the one to write the acceptance tests for the conversion. He will specify the measures of the cleanliness of the conversion. For example, he may create the rules to determine that a customer who resides on two systems is a duplicate. Al knows that Sam does not want a customer showing up twice on the converted system.

There may be some business issues, such as differences in customer status from one system to another. For example, Sam's business rule for allowing someone to reserve may be different from the business rule for an acquired competitor. You can keep track of where a customer came from and incorporate both rules. But that is Sam's call.

There should be no new customer acceptance tests, because they have already been created for the working system. The only exceptions would be tests that check that the business issues, such as customer status, have been appropriately handled.

Database Conversions

Dana has been informed that there is not going to be support for the current database version that Sam's systems use. Dana needs to convert to the next version, or perhaps to a different system. This is not a customer need, but a technical issue. There are no new customer acceptance tests because the behavior of the system should not change. All acceptance tests can work as a regression suite. When the conversion is complete, the tests should still run as before.

If a project involves lots of stories for which there are no customer acceptance tests, it may well be a technical project. Often, large technical issues such as database conversion are incorporated into customer-focused projects. The customer often does not have knowledge of the underlying issues and therefore has no ability to provide acceptance tests. If this is the case, the technical parts should be broken into a technical project with a technical lead playing the part of the customer. Projects such as an upgrade to a new database, a new version of a language, or a new operating system are technical infrastructure issues.

What If There Are No Tests?

You have a system that has been acquired and for which there are no acceptance tests: no manual ones, and no automated ones. You need to make some changes, but what can you do? Let's look at a couple of conditions. In one, you may acquire the system from a vendor; in the other, you may inherit it from an acquisition.

When you buy a vendor application, it may be configurable or customizable. *Configurable* means that you set up values to make the application run in your environment or with your set of data. The logic in the application uses this configuration information to alter its operation in predetermined ways. You may be able to add some additional features, such as a Microsoft Word macro, but these macros use existing operations. Because the vendor should have tested all operations, having acceptance tests is less critical.

Customizable means that you are provided with some source code for the system that you alter to make a system work for your particular purpose. The code provides some existing behavior that you are changing. In this case, you should ask the vendor for acceptance tests—either manual or automatic. The vendor response might be as follows:[1]

- Don't have any
- Have some, but all manual
- Have full set, but all manual
- Have full set: some manual, some automated
- Have full set, completely automated

If a vendor doesn't have a full set, ask him how he knows the system works. It could be that he has a full set, but contractually he is not required to provide them to you. If you can't find another vendor that will provide acceptance tests, you are in the same situation as from an acquisition.

You have to change an acquired system that has few or no acceptance tests in the area that you want to change. Chances are that the system has not been designed to be tested [Feathers01].

First, create acceptance tests for the functionality you are going to change. Inject the tests beneath the user interface if you can. Otherwise, run the tests through the user interface, and automate the tests if possible. Every test should pass as it documents the current working of the system. These tests will now run as a regression test. Create an acceptance test for the change you are going to make. Determine which of the current tests, if any, should fail once the change is made. Then implement the change and test.

---

1. There are some gray areas that might be considered either configurable or customizable.

Legacy Systems

One common issue with legacy systems is the lack of tests: both external acceptance tests and internal unit tests.[2] And often when there are external acceptance tests, they are not automated. Making changes in the system and ensuring that the changes do not have unintended effects is difficult.

Just as for an acquired system without tests, before making a change, create acceptance tests around the portion of the system that is involved with the change. The acceptance tests document how the system currently works. You sometimes have more control over legacy systems, then those acquired from a vendor. So the acceptance tests you write may be able to be run beneath the user interface.

Then write acceptance tests for how the system should work once the change is implemented. Initially, they should fail. Otherwise, the system is already doing what the change request asks for. The feature was just not documented.

In many instances, you may have to write the tests as user interface tests. If it's possible, automate these tests. If the system design allows it, write the tests to the middle-tier layer and automate them. Then proceed with the change. When your new tests pass and any identified as "should break" fail, the system has been changed correctly.

Suppose you don't have tests around every functional piece of the system. With the tests around the part of the system you are changing, you ensure there are no side effects in that part. But you cannot be sure that the change has not affected anything else.

Lack of Acceptance Tests Is a Debt

An acquaintance of mine asked me to estimate the cost of converting a web application from a commercial application server to an open-source one to save licensing fees. The application had been coded by a third party. I examined the code and determined that there were only a very few vendor-specific methods that would need to be changed. I gave him the estimate, and he said it seemed reasonable.

I said that the estimate did not include fixing bugs that currently existed in the system. He agreed to that. I suggested that my responsibility would be over when the converted system passed all the automated acceptance tests. He hesitated and replied that there were no automated acceptance tests. I said then my responsibility would end when the system passed all the

---

2. Michael's Feather's definition of a legacy code is anything without tests [Feathers01].

manual acceptance tests. He again paused and acknowledged that there were no acceptance tests for the system.

I looked at him and stated that I could then have a converted system that passed all the acceptance tests that afternoon for half the price. He smiled. I then proposed that I would help develop acceptance tests for the current system, because his staff did not have time to do so. That was agreed to. In the end, the total cost of creating the tests and doing the conversion far exceeded the license fees, so the project never got off the ground.

Projects such as conversions cost more due to the technical debt represented by the lack of acceptance tests.

Manual Testing

In one instance, a legacy system had acceptance tests, but they were severely out of date. They were mostly manual tests, so they were executed infrequently (if at all). In addition, the developers could not be sure whether the results were correct. A situation like this could become a nightmare, because it appeared that the tests were available, but they really were not. Sometimes with manual tests, the entire team participates in manual regression testing. The testers provide scripts, and everyone devotes a day or two every iteration to testing. This motivates the team to automate the regression testing. With automation, the tests are run frequently.

Summary

- Larger teams have more triads consisting of the requester, the implementer, and the tester.
- Focus on getting an end-to-end system passing the simplest tests.
- Some projects are developer related and should have developer-created acceptance tests.
- If there are no acceptance tests for the portion of a system that needs to change, create acceptance tests before making the change.

PART III

General Issues

This part contains general issues regarding acceptance testing.

Chapter 20

Business Capabilities, Rules, and Value

"Price is what you pay. Value is what you get."

Warren Buffett

The triad discusses delivering value to the business in other ways.

Business Capabilities

Cathy would like to provide customers with discounts for repeat business to keep them loyal to Sam's store. She's heard rumors about a competitive CD rental store that Salvatore Bonpensiero is opening in town the end of the week. Cathy has a vague idea for new things she can do for her customers, such as giving discounts for renting a lot of CDs.

Debbie notes that the system currently does not keep track of the number of rentals for each customer. She roughly estimates that it would take at least an iteration to start keeping track of this information and then applying it to the invoices that are sent out.

After hearing Debbie's estimate, Tom asked Cathy if she'd really like it by the end of the week. Cathy replies with a definite yes. Debbie then suggests that Cathy should print up some discount cards, as some other retail stores use. The counter clerk can mark off the number of rentals on the card. When the card is filled in, the customer gets a free rental.

Cathy loves the idea. It could be in place by the afternoon without software changes. She and Tom start discussing ways to avoid a customer misusing the system, such as faking the marks. Debbie suggests putting the customer ID on the card. Cathy can record in a spreadsheet each day the customer IDs of the discount cards that have been turned in for a free rental. If a customer has used an abnormal number of cards, Cathy can investigate whether an issue needs to be dealt with. Also, Cathy can get a good idea of how many CDs each customer rents to see whether it makes business sense to spend the money on automating the discounts.

Morale of the story: Not all capabilities need to be met by software. The triad should consider any means that implements the requested capability.

Scenario Handling

Sam is reviewing the demo that Debbie and Tom are presenting. Sam asks a question, "So what happens if something goes wrong with the hardware? Or we have a hurricane that knocks out the power. Or..."

Debbie interjects, "Then we go back to a manual system. You won't have index cards anymore, but we'll have blank contracts that Cary can fill out. He'll record the CD ID, the customer ID, the date rented, the date due, and the amount. We'll keep a printout of all CDs, with their categories, the number of days in the base rental period, and the amount. We'll see how long it takes Cary to find information on a CD. If it's really long, you might have a power outage special in which all CDs can be rented for the lowest amount and the longest time."

"When the hardware comes back up, Cary, Mary, or Harry can enter the information into the system. We'll create a special screen for input of all the information, rather than have the system calculate the return date and the amount. In fact, because of the way we've designed the system for testing, we already have a way to do this in the code. We just have to add a user interface to the program."

Morale of the story: Don't try to deal with every possible scenario in software.

> *Every Exception Need Not Be Handled*
>
> My wife and I travel frequently. When we're on the road, we like to pick up a quick breakfast at a fast food place. We're vegetarians, so that makes it a little more difficult. Usually we stop at McDonald's and order Egg McMuffins, hold the meat. That item usually stops the order taker in her tracks. She looks down at the keyboard and then back up. There's no key for Egg McMuffin without meat. Many times, the cashier has to call the manager over to help her. There is a combination of keys that allows her to enter such a weird order, but sometimes it takes three or four minutes to enter our food order.

One time, we stopped at a Burger King. We ordered two Breakfast Croissants, hold the meat. The order taker responded almost instantly with the total. I couldn't figure out whether the employee was better trained, more experienced, or had a better keyboard layout. I looked at the receipt. It said "2 Breakfast Croissants—Ask Cashier." In the event of any off-menu requests, the procedure was to ask the order taker for the details. It sped up taking the order, which was a great benefit to the customer.

Not handling every exception in software not only saved development time, but increased customer satisfaction. It was a win-win.
P.S. Someone finally fixed the issue of off-menu requests at McDonald's. Ordering goes a lot faster now.

Business Rules Exposed

A business rule is something that is true regardless of the technology that is employed. Whether rentals are kept on paper or in the computer, Sam wants to limit the number of simultaneous rentals by a customer.

Sam has the business rule that a customer cannot rent more than three CDs at any one time. He created this rule because he had a limited stock of CDs, and he wanted to ensure there was sufficient choice in CDs for other customers. As Sam's inventory grows, the reason for the business rule may change. He may want to increase the limit so that good customers who rent numerous CDs are not disappointed. He might add a rule so that a customer is informed that they had already rented a particular CD. In this case, the business rule could help a long term customer save money on rentals by avoiding duplicates.

One of the primary purposes of a system is to make transactions comply with the business rules. Business rules should be exposed so that they are easy to test and easy to change.

A Different Business Value

The check-out workflow was modeled from what Sam had noticed in a regular video store. The flow looked like this.

As-Is Workflow

- The customer looks at CD cases that contain the title sheet.
- The customer picks the CD he wants.
- The customer brings the CD to the counter.
- The clerk retrieves the corresponding CD in its case from shelves behind the counter and puts the title sheet case in its place.
- The clerk returns to the counter with the CD.
- The clerk scans the CD ID and customer ID.
- The contract is printed, and the customer signs it.
- The customer heads out the door with the CD he picked out.

The triad created a value-stream map from the renter's point of view. The renter wants to rent a particular CD, so that is the starting point. The end point is the renter heading out the door with the CD. The renter wants to get in and out as quickly as possible. So the triad figured that instead of the customer walking around looking at CD cases, he could just look on a computer screen and select the CD. No more looking for the physical case. So the workflow would be as follows:

Possible To-Be Workflow

- The customer selects the CD on the system.
- The customer enters his customer ID.
- The system notifies the clerk that a CD had been requested by the customer and prints a contract.
- The clerk gets the CD and places it in a check-out box with the contract.
- The customer walks up with his customer card.
- The clerk retrieves the CD and contract and gives it to the customer.
- The customer signs the contract.
- The customer heads out the door with the CD.

This workflow is quicker and faster for both the clerk and the customer. Sam also figured he could save a large chunk of store rental by eliminating the display shelves with all the CDs. The clerks wouldn't have to replace the CD cases when the CD was returned. However, customers may prefer to browse titles being displayed on the shelves to find something new. Before implementing the change, Sam needs to investigate how his customers would react to this change. That's in accordance with the principles of the charter (see Chapter 5, "The Example Project").

By looking at a larger value stream, the triad found a possible win-win situation for everyone. Software teams that consider the larger context may find non-software improvements.

Summary

- Not all capabilities need to be met by software solutions.
- Software does not need to be able to handle every scenario.
- Software teams should examine workflows in which their software participates for bigger-picture improvements.

Chapter 21

Test Presentation

"Ring the bells that still can ring
Forget your perfect offering.
There is a crack in everything,
That's how the light gets in."

Leonard Cohen

There is no perfect way of writing a test or a table. Alternative ways are presented here.

Customer Understood Tables

The key in selecting the form of a table is to pick the one that the customer unit most easily understands. For example, here is the business rule table for rental fees.

CD Rental Fees			
Category	Standard Rental Days	Standard Rental Fee	Extra Day Rental Fee
Regular	2	$2	$1
Golden Oldie	3	$1	$.50
Hot Stuff	1	$4	$2

There are various ways you can document the tests for this table. You can have a standard calculation-style table, such as this.

Rental Charges		
Category	**Days**	**Cost?**
Regular	3	$3
Golden Oldie	3	$1
Hot Stuff	3	$8

Alternatively, you could have an individual table for each computation, as here.

Rental Charges	
Category	Regular
Days	3
Cost?	$3

Rental Charges	
Category	Golden Oldie
Days	3
Cost?	$1

Rental Charges	
Category	Hot Stuff
Days	3
Cost?	$8

There are forms of tables with labels that make the test read almost like a sentence.[1]

---

1. This is a DoFixture table from the Fit Library by Rick Mugridge [Cunningham01]. Slim also has a version like this [Martin03].

Rental Charges						
When renting a CD	with category	Regular	for	3 days	the charge should be	$3
When renting a CD	with category	Golden Oldie	for	3 days	the charge should be	$1
When renting a CD	with category	Hot Stuff	for	3 days	the charge should be	$8

You do not need to use the same style table in all tests. The triad should select the one most appropriate to the behavior being tested. In case of a disagreement, the decision should be deferred to the customer unit.

Table Versus Text

The tests in this book have used tables to indicate the setups, actions, and expected results. If the customer prefers, the tests can be expressed in pure text. For example, the previous actions could be written as follows.

Rental Charges

Given a CD that is a Regular, when it is rented for 3 days, then the charge should be $3.

Given a CD that is a Golden Oldie, when it is rented for 3 days, then the charge should be $1.

Given a CD that is a Hot Stuff, when it is rented for 3 days, then the charge should be $8.

Specifying Multiple Actions

Sam's application has the business rule that a customer should not be allowed to rent another CD after that customer exceeds the rental limit. You could show this test as a sequence of action tables, such as this.

CD Rental Limit Reached

Given these rentals:

First rental:

Start	Check-Out	
Enter	CD ID	CD1
Enter	Customer ID	007
Press	Check-Out	OK

Second rental:

Start	Check-Out	
Enter	CD ID	CD3
Enter	Customer ID	007
Press	Check-Out	OK

Third rental:

Start	Check-Out	
Enter	CD ID	CD5
Enter	Customer ID	007
Press	Check-Out	OK

Then the next rental should fail:

Fourth rental:

Start	Check-Out	
Enter	CD ID	CD2
Enter	Customer ID	007
Press	Check-Out	Rental_Limit_Exceeded

Alternatively, you can specify all the actions in a calculation-style table. This reduces the size of the test and can make it more understandable to all members of the triad.

CD Rental Limit Reached			
CD ID	Customer ID	Check-Out Status?	Notes
CD1	007	OK	1st rental
CD3	007	OK	2nd rental
CD5	007	OK	3rd rental
CD2	007	Rental_Limit_Exceeded	4th rental

In the first version, the notes appear before each table. In this version, those notes are included in the table to explain each step in the test.

Complex Data

An embedded table can show the individual parts of particular columns. For example, a customer with a name and an address that have individual parts could be shown with embedded tables, as here.

Customer Data							
Name			Address				Date Joined
First	Last	Prefix	Street	City	State	ZIP	03/04/2003
John	Doe	Mr.	1 Doe Lane	Somewhere	NC	99999	

Another way of representing parts such as the address is to use a different organization of the table. Each column represents a different level. As shown below, the leftmost column is the topmost level. The next column breaks the level into its parts. The rightmost column contains the values for each element.

Customer Data		
Name		
	First	John
	Last	Doe
	Prefix	Mr.
Address		
	Street	1 Doe Lane
	City	Somewhere
	State	NC
	ZIP	99999
Date Joined		03/04/2003

Custom Table Forms

The tables in the test can represent whatever is most appropriate for the application. If you were creating an acceptance test for an application that solves Sudoku puzzles, you might have an input table that looked like this.

Sudoku Puzzle								
1			4			7		
	2			5			8	
		3			6			9
4			7			1		
	5			8			2	
		6			9			3
7			1			4		
	8			2			5	
		9			3			6

The output table would look like the following.

Sudoku Solution								
1	6	5	4	9	8	7	3	2
9	2	4	3	5	7	6	8	1
8	7	3	2	1	6	5	4	9
4	9	8	7	3	2	1	6	5
3	5	7	6	8	1	9	2	4
2	1	6	5	4	9	8	7	3
7	3	2	1	6	5	4	9	8
6	8	1	9	2	4	3	5	7
5	4	9	8	7	3	2	1	6

You might also have a test in which the puzzle has no solution or has multiple possible solutions to see if the results match your expectation. A tester like Tom might create a puzzle that has thousands of possible results or one that has only a single digit in it to see how long it takes to get all the possible solutions.

In any event, the form of the test should be as compatible as possible with the way the customer unit deals with the functionality.

Summary

- Use the form of the table that is easiest for the customer unit to understand.
- If a standard table form is unsuitable, create a table form that is more appropriate for the test.

Chapter 22

Test Evaluation

"Program testing can be a very effective way to show the presence of bugs, but it is hopelessly inadequate for showing their absence."

Edsger Dijkstra

This chapter describes the characteristics of good tests. These characteristics include being understandable to customers, not fragile, and test a single concept.

Test Facets

The following discussion of things to look for in tests came partly from Gerard Meszaros [Meszaros01], Ward Cunningham, and Rick Mugridge [Cunningham01]. Overall, remember that the tests represent a shared understanding between the triad.

Understandable to Customers

The test should be written in customer terms (ubiquitous language) (Chapter 24, "Context and Domain Language"). The tables should represent the application domain. If the standard tables shown in the examples are not sufficient, create tables that the user can understand (Chapter 21, "Test Presentation"). Use whatever way of expressing the test most closely matches the customer's way of looking at things. Try multiple ways to see which way is most suitable to the customer.

The bottom line is to use what is easiest for the customer. If a basic action table is not as understandable, add graphics to make it look like a dialog box. If the customer needs something that looks like a printed form to understand the material, rather than just the data, use that as expected output. You can also have a simple test for the data to more easily debug what might be wrong with the printed form (Chapter 12, "Development Review").

Unless the customer wants values, use names. For example, use Good and Excellent as customer types, not customer types 1 and 2.

As presented in this book, acceptance tests are customer-defined tests that are created prior to implementation (see the book's Introduction). You can execute them as unit tests, integration tests, or user interface tests. Make the acceptance tests written in unit testing frameworks readable, as shown in the example in Chapter 4, "An Introductory Acceptance Test," so that you can match them with the customer's expectations.

Spell Checked

Spell-check your tests. Tests are meant for communication, and misspelled words hinder communication. The spell-check dictionary can contain triad-agreed-upon acronyms and abbreviations. Define these acronyms and abbreviations in a glossary.

Idempotent

Tests should be idempotent. They should work the same way all the time. Either they consistently pass or they consistently fail. A non-idempotent test is erratic; it does not work the same way all the time. Causes of erratic tests are interacting tests that share data and tests for which first and following executions are different because something in the state has changed. Paying attention to setup (Chapter 31, "Test Setup") can usually resolve erratic tests.

Not Fragile

Fragile tests are sensitive to changes in the state of the system and with the interfaces they interact with. The state of the system includes all code in the system and any internal data repositories.

Handle sensitivity to external interfaces by using test doubles as necessary (Chapter 11, "System Boundary"). In particular, functionality that depends on the date or time will most likely need a clock that can be controlled through a test double. For example, testing an end-of-the-month report may require the date to be set to the end of the month. Random events should be simulated so that they occur in the same sequence for testing.

Changes to a common setup can cause a test to fail. If there is something particular that is required for the test, the test could check for the assumptions it makes about the condition of the system. If the condition is not satisfied, the test fails in setup, rather than in the confirmation of expected outcome. This makes it easier to diagnose why the failure occurred.

Tests should only check for the minimum amount of expected results. This makes them less sensitive to side effects from other tests.

Confirm the Environment

Many programs require that the platform they are installed upon meet a particular requirement, such as a particular version of an operating system. When the program is installed, the installation process verifies that these requirements are met. If they are not, the installation terminates.

This approach is more user friendly than letting a program be installed and then having the program fail because the environment is wrong. However, the program assumes that the environment does not change after it is installed. Sometimes the installation of another program changes the environment and causes the first program to fail.

To be less fragile, the program should confirm the required environment every time it starts up. If the environment is not as expected, the program should notify the user with an error message. That makes it much easier for a user to determine what the problem is than a "This program had a problem" message.

Test Sequence

Ideally, tests should be independent so they can run in any sequence without dependencies on other tests. To ensure that tests are as independent as possible, use a common setup (Chapter 31) only when necessary. As noted in that chapter, the setup part of a test ("Given") should ensure that the state of the system is examined to see that it matches what the test requires. Internally, this can be done by either checking that the condition is as described or making the condition be that which is described.

Workflow Tests

Often, there are workflows: sequences of operations that are performed to reach a goal. You should test each operation separately. Then you might have a *workflow test.* A workflow tests includes multiple operations that need to be run in a particular order to demonstrate that the system processes the sequence correctly.

Use case tests should have a single action table in them. Workflows that have multiple use cases within them may have multiple action tables in their tests. Try not to have too many complicated workflow tests. They can be fragile or hard to maintain. See Chapter 28, "Case Study: A Library Print Server," for an example of a workflow test.

Test Conditions

A set of tests should abide by these three conditions:[1]

1. A test should fail for a well-defined reason. (That is what the test is checking.) The reason should be specific and easy to diagnose. Each test case has a scope and a purpose. The failure reason relates to the purpose.
2. No other test should fail for the same reason. Otherwise, you may have a redundant test. You may have a test fail at each level—an internal business rule test and a workflow test that uses one case of the business rule. If the business rule changes and the result for that business rule changes, you will have two failing tests. You want to minimize overlapping tests. But if the customer wants to have more tests because they are familiar or meaningful to him, do it. Remember: The customer is in charge of the tests.
3. A test should not fail for any other reason. This is the ideal, but it is often hard to achieve. Each test has a three part sequence: setup, action/trigger, and expected result. The purpose of the test is to ensure that the actual result is equal to the expected result. A test may fail because the setup did not work or the action/trigger did not function properly.

Separation of Concerns

The more that you can separate concerns, the easier it can be to maintain the tests. With separation, changes in the behavior of one aspect of the application do not affect other aspects. Here are some parts that can be separated, as shown earlier in this book:

- Separate business rules from the way the results of business rules are displayed (Chapter 14, "Separate View from Model").

1. These came from Amir Kolsky.

- Separate the calculation of a business rule, such as a rating, from the use of that business rule (Chapter 13, "Simplification by Separation").
- Separate each use case or step in a workflow (Chapter 8, "Test Anatomy").
- Separate validation of an entity from use of that entity (Chapter 16, "Developer Acceptance Tests").

You can have separate tests for the simplest things. For example, the customer ID formatting functionality needs to be tested. The test can show the kinds of issues that the formatting deals with. If the same module is used anywhere a customer ID is used, other tests do not have to perform checks for invalid customer IDs. And if the same module is not used, you have a design issue. A test of ID might be as follows.

Customer ID Format		
ID	Valid?	Notes
007	Y	
1	N	Too few characters
0071	N	Too many characters

Test Failure

As noted before in Chapter 3, "Testing Strategy," a passing test is a specification of how the system works. A failing test indicates that a requirement has not been met. Initially, before an implementation is created, every acceptance test should fail. If a test passes, you need to determine why it passed.

- Is the desired behavior that the test checks already covered by another test? If so, the new test is redundant.
- Does the implementation already cover the new requirement?
- Is the test really not testing anything? For example, the expected result may be the default output of the implementation.[2]

2. Any new test that passes the first time without a change in the implementation should be made to fail by briefly changing the implementation. This ensures that the test is actually testing something.

Test Redundancy

You want to avoid test redundancy. Redundancy often occurs when you have data-dependent calculations. For example, here are the rental fees for different category CDs that were shown in Chapter 10, "User Story Breakup."

CD Rental Fees			
Category	Standard Rental Days	Standard Rental Charge	Extra Day Rental Charge
Regular	2	$2	$1
Golden Oldie	3	$1	$.50
Hot Stuff	1	$4	$2

Here were the tests that were created.

Rental Charges		
Type	Days	Cost?
Regular	3	$3
Golden Oldie	3	$1
Hot Stuff	3	$8

Do you need all these tests? Are they equivalent? They all use the same underlying formula (Cost = Standard Rental Charge + (Number Rental Days – Standard Rental Days) * Extra Day Rental Charge).[3] When the first test passes, the other tests also pass.

What if there are lots of categories? Say there are 100 different ones that all use this same formula. That would be a lot of redundant tests. If there was an identified risk in not running them, then they may be necessary.[4] A collaborative triad should be able to cut down these tests to the essential ones.

Test variations of business rules or calculations separately, unless they affect the flow through a use case or user story.

In an effort to avoid redundancy, don't shortcut tests. Have at least one positive and one negative test. For example, there should be a test with a customer

3. Depending on how the code is written, a single test might provide 100% code coverage. If you have that coverage, do you need more tests?

4. These tests may not be performed during the standard build-test cycle if they take excessive time.

ID that is valid and one that is not valid. Be sure to test each exception. For example, with the CD rental limit of three, have a test for renting three CDs (the happy path) and four CDs (the exception path).

No Implementation Issues

Tests should be minimally maintainable. Make them depend on the behavior being tested, not the implementation underneath. This way they require little maintenance work. Unless the desired behavior has changed, the test should not have to change, regardless of any implementation changes underneath. To achieve this, design tests as if they had to work with multiple implementations.

Tests should not imply that you need a database underneath. You can have a slew of file clerks who took down the data, filed it away in folders, and retrieved it when requested. Of course, the system would take a little bit longer. The tables in the tests such as CD Data represent the business view of the objects, not the persistence layer view. They will be used to create the database tables, so there will be similarities.

Points to Remember

When creating and implementing tests, consider the following:

- Develop tests and automation separately. Understand the test first, and then explore how to automate it.
- Automate the tests so that they can be part of a continuous build. See Appendix C, "Test Framework Examples," for examples of automation.
- Don't put test logic in the production code. Tests should be completely separate from the production code.[5]
- As much as practical, cover 100% of the functional requirements in the acceptance tests.

5. In some cases, such as hardware chip design, it is acceptable for production code to have a built-in self-test to confirm that assumptions about the system's environment still hold and all elements of the system are functioning correctly.

In structuring tests, remember the following:

- Tests should follow the Given-When-Then or the Arrange-Act-Assert form [AAA01].
- Keep tests simple.
    - Only have the essential detail in a test.
    - Avoid lots of input and output columns. Break large tables into smaller ones, or show common values in the headers (Chapter 18, "Entities and Relationships").
    - Avoid logic in tests.
- Describe the intent of the test, not just a series of steps.

A test has several costs involved in writing and testing it, executing it, and maintaining it. The tests deliver the benefits of communicating requirements and identifying defects. The incremental cost of a new test should be less than the incremental benefit that that test delivers.

Summary

- Make acceptance tests readable to customers.
- Separate concerns—test one concept with each test.
- Avoid test redundancy.

Chapter 23

Using Tests for Other Things

"By fighting, you never get enough, but by yielding, you get more than you expected."

Lawrence G. Lovasik

Acceptance tests define the functionality of a program. But you can use them for more than just that—measuring doneness, estimating, and breaking down a story.

Uses of Acceptance Tests

Acceptance tests are a communication mechanism between the members of the triad. They clarify the customer requirements and are a specification of how the system works. But you can also employ them for other purposes. They are a measure of how complete an implementation is; a means of estimating the effort to implement a story, and a method for story breakdown.

Degree of Doneness

If there are multiple acceptance tests for a business rule or a story, the ratio of successful tests to the total number of tests can provide a rough guide to how much of the story has been implemented. For example, if you have ten acceptance tests and three are passing, the story is "about" 30% complete.

It is possible that the "worst" test case was saved for last. So the effort to implement that story represents more than its fair share of the total effort. That is why this is only a guide to doneness, rather than an exact measurement.

Make all the tests pass for a story before moving to another story. Otherwise, you may wind up with lots of stories that are not done.

Estimation Aid

An estimate may be required for implementing a story in many environments. The number and complexity of the acceptance tests can be a rough guide to the effort required to implement a story. The tests for a new story can be compared to the tests run against completed stories. You can develop your own heuristics as to how the number and complexity influence the effort. Large custom setups (givens) and numerous state changes (thens) usually imply a much larger effort than tests with small setups and few state changes.

Breaking Down Stories

You may need to break down a story into smaller stories for the purposes of fitting stories into iterations. Mike Cohn [Cohn01] offers some ways to break down a story. For example, you can start with a basic user interface and then add more bells and whistles, such as images. You can implement something manually, such as calling users about overdue rentals, and later automate it with robot calling. You can do something simple, such as a single check-out per CD, and then have a story for checking out multiple CDs at once.

In addition, you can use acceptance tests as a breakdown mechanism. The test for each scenario of a use case can become a separate story. A complex business rule can become a separate story. The test for a complicated business rule calculation may be expressed in a table with lots of rows. You can break the calculation into separate stories by assigning a set of rows to each story.

With the address example in Chapter 17, "Decouple with Interfaces," the tests themselves suggest a way to break down the story. The tests for a U.S. address are separate from the tests for a Canadian address. Therefore, U.S. address verification can be a different story than Canadian address verification.

Developer Stories

Another reason for breaking down a story is so that multiple teams can help implement it. Chapter 16, "Developer Acceptance Tests," showed how Debbie made up acceptance tests for user interface components and functional modules that are to be created by other developers. If a story has to be broken down, you should create acceptance tests for each of the substories. The acceptance tests help decouple the stories by clarifying the responsibilities of each of the stories. They provide doneness criteria for each story. It is far more effective for distributed teams to work on decoupled stories than to work on tasks for the same story [Eckstein01].

Tests as a Bug Report

For nontrivial bugs, you can write a test as documentation of the bug. The definition of a nontrivial bug is something more than a misspelled word, a bad color, or an unaligned dialog box. For each bug, the discoverer should create an acceptance test that shows that the desired behavior has not been achieved. With the bug, the acceptance test fails. When it passes, the bug has been fixed.[1]

For example, suppose that you were coding the discount example in Chapter 4, "An Introductory Acceptance Test," and you did not have an acceptance test. If a bug was reported for a Good customer, you would create an acceptance test. To ensure that the bug fix does not affect other behavior, include related test cases that are currently passing. For example, here are tests around other values for a Good customer. You might also have tests for the Excellent customer as well, depending on the situation - the cost involved if the bug fix might alter that Customer Rating as well.

Discount Acceptance Test		
Item Total	Customer Rating	Discount Percentage?
$10.00	Good	0%
$10.01	Good	1%
$50.01	Good	1%

Root Cause Analysis

If a bug like the preceding appears, you have an opportunity to do root-cause analysis.[2] What you are looking for is why the bug appeared. Is it something in the process itself, or was it a random event? Was the case in production not covered by a test case, and if so, why not? Were the data values not expected? For example, suppose a data value was supposed to be between 1 and 100, but the value in production was found to be 101. In that case, you create an acceptance test that demonstrates the correct behavior—limiting the value to 100. Because an acceptance test represents a requirement, the need for this acceptance test being created after implementation may represent a missed requirement An acceptance test that has the wrong values is a misinterpreted requirement.

1. In some complex situations, you can write an "unacceptance" test that passes with the bug. The "unacceptance" test should fail when the bug is fixed. If it does not, the changes did not totally fix the problem.

2. Other resources give detailed explanations of how to do this [Systems01] [Wiki07] [Wiki09].

The missed or misinterpreted requirement may be traced to a random event, such as, "We had to get this done in four hours before release." Alternatively, it may be traced to a common cause, such as, "The customer never collaborates with us before we start implementing."[3]

If you find yourself getting buried in analysis, try something you think might prevent the problem from reoccurring and see what happens. If it doesn't work, try something else.

Production Bugs

One of the most important measures for a team process is the number of bugs that have escaped to production. You should examine the root cause or causes of each escaped bug so you can discover how to prevent more of them from escaping in the future.

Regression Testing

The primary purpose of acceptance tests is to translate the customer requirements into code. If you have acceptance tests for all requirements, you can use the set of acceptance tests as a regression test suite. Unless the requirement associated with an acceptance test changes, all acceptance tests should pass. If a change is made to the implementation to accommodate a new requirement, all previous acceptance tests should still pass. If previous tests break when a new requirement is introduced, you may have issues in the design of your code.

If the acceptance tests are automated, run them as often as possible. This provides immediate feedback that a change in the application has caused some previously implemented functionality to break.

Summary

- You can use acceptance tests as any of the following:
  - A rough guide to story completeness
  - A rough way to estimate relative story effort
  - A way to break up stories

---

3. If the "We had to get this done in four hours before release" occurs more than once, it is a common cause rather than a random event.

- Distributed teams that break up a story should have acceptance tests for their part of the story.
- Examine the root cause of why an acceptance test was missed or incorrect. If possible, change the process to eliminate the cause.

Chapter 24

Context and Domain Language

> *"England and America are two countries separated by a common language."*
>
> George Bernard Shaw

Communication requires a common language. During the collaboration in the creation of acceptance tests, a common language emerges.

Ubiquitous Language

Domain-driven design (DDD) [Evans01], refers to the *ubiquitous language*. The ubiquitous language involves the terms in which the customer and developers talk about a system. The language arises from explanations given by a customer or subject matter expert about the entities and processes in a system. The ubiquitous language transforms itself and becomes more refined as developers and customers discover ambiguities and unclearness.

The language evolves during the collaboration on the requirements and the tests, as shown in Chapter 6, "The User Story Technique." Contributions to the language come from the column names in tables, the names of use cases and their exceptions, and the business rules. Each term in the language should be documented with a one-sentence description that the customer unit provides and the developer and tester units understand. The customer unit leads the terminology effort, but the developer unit can suggest that terms are unclear, ambiguous, or redundant.

For example, the triad referred to entities as customer, CD, rental, and album. They could be defined with single sentences as:

- A customer is someone to whom we rent CDs.
- An album is an artist's release.
- A CD is a physical copy of an album that is rented.
- A rental contains the information on a CD that is rented.

You can use tables in defining the terms. For example, the discount example in Chapter 4, "An Introductory Acceptance Test," referred to the terms Customer Type and Item Total. The Customer Type can be defined by a table, such as this.

Customer Type	
Name	**Meaning**
Regular	A common customer
Good	One we want to keep
Excellent	One we will cater to his every whim

Order Total might be part of a larger picture table. You might show relationships to other entities if that clarifies the picture.

Order Fields		
Name	**Meaning**	**Formula**
Item Price	What we charge for the item	
Order Item	Item on an order	
Item Quantity	Count of how many of an item is ordered	
Item Total	Total price for a single item	Item Price * Item Quantity
Order Total	Total price for all items on an order	Sum of all Item Totals

The triad should agree not only on the meanings of the entities, but their *identity* and *continuity*. *Identity* is whether two entities are the same. For example, if a rental contract is reprinted, it represents the same entity as the first printout. However, a credit charge that is resubmitted may be construed as a new charge, and the customer will get double-billed. If a customer checked in two CDs within a short period, two legitimate charges could look the same. The credit processor might interpret that as a duplicate billing and reject the second.

Continuity is how long an entity should persist. If a store customer wants rental history to be completely private, a rental entity should persist only until it is complete (that is, until the customer has checked-in the CD). On the other hand, if Sam wants the rental history to determine favorite CDs for a customer so he can offer him new releases in that same genre, the rental should be persistent.

Two Domains

The applicability of a ubiquitous language could be the entire enterprise. But often, that is too big a context, so it's just for the portion of the enterprise. (DDD refers to this as the *bounded context*.) So each portion of the enterprise has its own domain. Two domains may overlap if they use common resources.

Figure 24.1 is an example of overlapping domains. Both Check-Out/In System and the Accounting System use a common domain—Rental Fees and Charges. This requires that for the two domains, the customers agree on a shared language for the interface to the common one.[1]

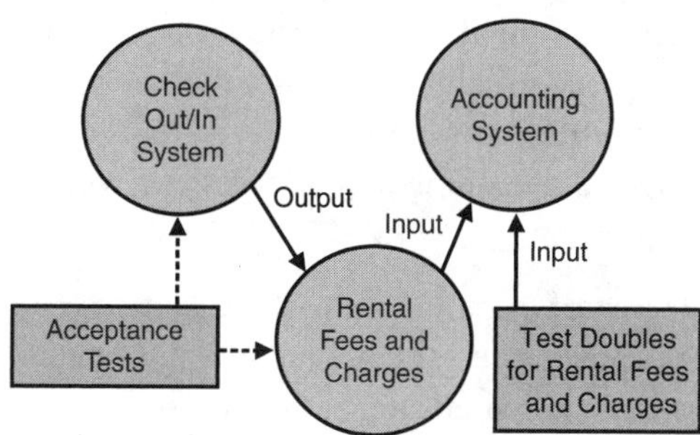

Figure 24.1 *A Common Domain—One-Way Interface*

The existence of a common domain impacts the acceptance tests. In Figure 24.1, the interface between Check-Out/In and Rental Fees and Charges is one-way (output only). The acceptance tests ensure that the proper data is being created. The interface between Rental Fees and Charges and the Accounting System is one way (input only). The test doubles allow the Accounting System to be tested separate from the Check-Out/In system.

1. It would be ideal if the terminology of both domains matched so that developers and testers did not have to switch meanings when working on the other domain. But the coordination effort required may not be worth it.

What Is a Flight?

An airline system is really large. There are reservation systems, ground operations systems, and flight operations, to name a few. The term *flight* is pretty common. Consider how you, the customer, think of a flight. You are going to catch a flight. Do you use the same reference whether your journey is going to be on a single plane or whether you have to transfer between planes?

The airplane you board is for a particular flight, identified by the flight number. A particular flight number can represent the same airplane traveling to many cities, only one of which you are interested in going to. For example, Flight 1000 may go to Boston, then Philadelphia, then Raleigh-Durham, then Atlanta. However, you may only be interested in the Boston to Philadelphia portion.

As an example of continuity, the association between the airplane entity and the flight entity is not persistent. You may fly on the same flight number multiple times and get a different airplane.

Each part of an airline system may use the term *flight* in its own domain context. For some parts, a flight represents the entire travel of a physical airplane through its entire day. For others, it represents the route of an entity identified by a flight number, regardless of what physical airplane is flying it.

To keep some degree of commonality, there is an agreed-upon term for the portion between a single takeoff and the subsequent landing: a *leg*. When airline systems communicate with each other, they can communicate about this common entity. For example, a leg is Flight 100 from Boston to Philadelphia.

Summary

- From collaboration on acceptance tests, a ubiquitous language emerges.
- Tests should be written using the ubiquitous language.
- Multiple systems using a common system need to agree on a ubiquitous language for that common system.

Chapter 25

Retrospective and Perspective

> *"There are those who look at things the way they are, and ask why... I dream of things that never were, and ask why not?"*
>
> Robert Kennedy

We've looked at acceptance tests from many different viewpoints. Here is a look back at of some of the salient points and a look-forward to see how you can apply it.

Recap

Now that the details of acceptance testing have been explored, it's time for a recap of how acceptance testing fits into the overall development process, as well as a few overall facets. The tale in this book of Debbie the developer, Tom the tester, and Cathy the customer has been a narrative one, with the goals and benefits of acceptance test-driven development (ATDD) woven in. ATDD is a communication tool between the customer, developer, and tester. It is about writing the right code (fulfilling the requirements), rather than writing the code right (design of the implementation). To summarize, the primary goals are as follows:

- Discover ambiguous requirements and gaps in requirements early on.
- Create a record of business/development understanding.
- Give feedback on quality.

The secondary goals are these:

- Use acceptance tests as an executable regression test.
- Measure your progress toward completeness.
- Measure the complexity of requirements.
- Use the tests as a basis for user documentation.

Passing the functional acceptance tests is necessary, but it's insufficient for verifying a system. The system must pass other tests, such as those for quality attributes (performance and reliability) and usability.

The Process

The project started with a charter that included objectives—acceptance tests for the whole project. Features with acceptance criteria were developed. The features gave an overall picture of what the system was going to do. Then the features were broken into stories, each with its own acceptance criteria. The stories were detailed in use cases or alternatively in event/response tables. Specific acceptance tests were written for the scenarios in the use cases, for individual events, or for individual state transitions. Workflow tests could be created that exercised more than a single use case.

Testing Layers

Acceptance tests, as used in this book, are customer-defined tests created prior to implementation. You can use many of these acceptance tests at multiple levels both as implementation validation tests and design verification tests. For example, you can run the check-out and check-in tests as follows:

- Run manually as full integration tests through the user interface. The rental contract values are checked on the printer output, and the credit charge output is checked on the bank statement.
- Used as the basis for usability tests. As a user runs the test, he may see how usable the system is.
- Run beneath the user interface with real databases in an almost-full integration test.
- Run with an in-memory database to run faster in a partial integration test.
- Run automatically as regression tests.

As another example, an almost-complete integration test might use a mock mail server to which it sends mail. A complete integration test involves using a real mail server (and appropriate e-mail addresses so that the tests aren't a source of spam).

The information in the acceptance tests provides information to all the developers in a project. For example, the flow associated with the tests and the actions performed give a framework that the user interface developers can employ in designing the user experience. The database developers can design the database structure based on the relationships between data, as shown in rows and columns of the tests.

The Tests

Acceptance tests are customer-understood tests. They come from user stories, business rules, or event/response tables. They exercise different scenarios in use cases—the happy path and every exception path. A *passing acceptance test* is a specification of how the system works. A *failing acceptance test* is a requirement that the system has not yet implemented. Initially, all acceptance tests for a new system should fail. Otherwise, the system is already doing what has been requested. An acceptance test failure may not help diagnose what caused the problem. It simply indicates that there is a problem.

Unit tests are employed by the developers to help maintain and design the implementation. A developer can use the acceptance tests as a basis for developing unit tests. If there is a test at the outer layer, some module inside must help to pass that test. The unit tests can diagnose where the problem exists that causes a failing acceptance test.

Architects or developers create component or module tests. These tests work as internal acceptance tests to ensure that the individual pieces of a system correctly perform their responsibilities.

Acceptance tests suggest ways that a system might be controlled or observed at levels lower than the user interface. For example, a business rule test may connect directly with a module that implements it. A data lookup test may go to a data access layer to retrieve information to ensure that the data has been properly stored. Many tests are round-trip on the same layer. For example, they perform actions on the middle tier and check the results at the middle-tier level. Other acceptance tests may cross layers, such as input through the user interface layer and output checking from the data access layer. Having an implementation required to meet the needs of acceptance tests for inputs and outputs makes the system more testable. The proof of testability is that a system can be tested. If the system provides a way to run the acceptance tests, the system is testable.

Implementing an acceptance test may require additional output that is not part of the set of requirements. For example, a CD status report might show the status of every CD (rented or not rented). Such a report could be used to view the results of a check-out or check-in test. Bret Pettichord calls the additional control points and reporting points *touch-points* in the code [Pettichord01].

Communication

There are two points to remember about communication:

- Acceptance tests are not a substitute for interactive communication.
- Acceptance tests can provide focus for that communication.

What's the Block?

Each member of the triad has read this book on ATDD. Okay, one hasn't. That's a block. You need to be on the same page to collaborate. Just one party such as the developer raving about how wonderful ATDD is may not help with the change. All members of the triad have to realize the benefits of ATDD and be in a position to implement it.

Often, customers feel they do not have the knowledge to give the specifics necessary for the tests. They do not have to have all the information. The people who have it need to be identified and brought into the collaboration process. Customers may not have the time, or they may not be used to working at the level of precision that acceptance tests require. Once again, they need to identify someone—such as a business analyst or subject matter expert—who has the time and can work at that level of precision. Just because the triad includes the customer doesn't mean that she has to be present; her designated representative with the authority to make decisions can fill the chair.

Monad

Are you a monad? You get requirements without tests. You have no communication with the customer. You have no tester to help you. If you have no acceptance tests, you have no requirements. Why are you writing code if there are no requirements? If the situation is such that it is absolutely necessary to start developing, write the acceptance tests from what you understand the requirements to be, and code to them.

Unavailable Customer

The customer says, "Go away and work. I've given you all the information." Now if it's an internal customer, you can appeal to shareholder fiduciary responsibility. You waste shareholder resources if you create a program that does not provide business value or one that does not meet the real needs of the customer. Don't work on that project until the customer provides specific acceptance tests. If you are assigned to two projects, work on the other project or spend some time learning a new skill. Alternatively, you can investigate who else has the subject matter expertise to create the tests and request that person be assigned to the project.

If it's an external customer, be sure you are on a time-and-materials basis, not fixed price. You may make money in reworking the implementation of unclear requirements, but you may get an unsatisfied customer who never comes back.

Change

Virginia Satir [Satir01] developed a change model that describes how people adapt to change. When a foreign element, such as ATDD, is introduced into an organization, it upsets the status quo, which may cause chaos. Chaos comes from the change in peoples' roles. The customer unit is more involved with providing examples. Testers create tests for an application that has not yet been written instead of seeing a user interface. Developers test more.

Exiting the chaos comes from a transforming idea—"a sudden awareness of and understanding of new possibilities." In this book, you've seen examples of the possibilities for ATDD. When you integrate the practice of ATDD into your process, you will be in a new status quo—a more effective software development organization. How to exit the chaos involves many aspects that are covered in [Rising01].[1]

> ***What Will It Take?***
>
> I was teaching a course a few years ago on being lean and agile. I always ask why the students are in the course and what their backgrounds are. One student said that he had completed an agile project. The customer was more satisfied than with previous waterfall projects. The project was completed under budget and in less time. He wanted more ammunition he could present to management as to why the company should do another agile project. I said that the points he raised were the best shot. I could give confirming information, but if someone isn't satisfied with those results, I'm not sure I could convince him otherwise.

---

1. See [Koskela02] and [Adzic01] for other change issues.

Risks

There are risks associated with acceptance tests—particularly automated acceptance testing. Tests require maintenance, and changing requirements cause tests to break. If the number of broken tests is large, there may not be time to fix all of them before a release. If the broken tests are not fixed, their failure may start to be ignored or signal that it's okay to have a broken test. (See Broken Window Syndrome [Wiki10].)

ATDD verifies that a system delivers what the requirements and tests specify. It does not validate that the system is actually what the user needs. Having the user, such as Cary, the clerk, is involved in the development process can reduce the issues in delivering a useful system.

Benefits

A common complaint against acceptance testing is that it's too expensive. If you are going to test something and document these tests, it costs no more to document the tests up front than it does to document them at the end. Adding automation to the tests up front does add a little bit of work, but it can pay off in reduced time for changes and the courage to refactor code to make it more maintainable.

What have been the results of ATDD? The Epilogue contains success stories from teams that have adopted ATDD. These stories give concrete examples of how ATDD improves quality, maintainability, and the development process in general.

ATDD produces improved quality as the triad gains a better awareness of the system. Creating the tests forces the conversation of what the system should do. The translation errors between requirements and implementation are reduced because the tests form the common understanding between them. Thinking through scenarios for tests identifies unclear requirements and can identify where cases might have been missed. There is a reduced risk of delivering a system that does not meet the requirements, because it is not delivered until it passes all the tests.

ATDD can create a more maintainable system. The terms used in the test form a common language between customers and developers/testers. If the same terms are followed in the implementation, it can be easier to understand the relationship of the code to the requirement. Writing the tests acts as a domain modeling process. The relationships between the entities are captured in the tests.

Having the tests prior to implementation requires the code to pass those tests. In the process, the code becomes more testable. The tests document how the system works. Developer acceptance tests specify how a module works. Because passing the tests shows how the system or module works, the tests are executable specifications that, if run, will not become outdated.

In development, the tests provide a focus on what the developers should implement. They write the code that needs to be written to pass a test. If the code is not executed by a test, why is the code present?

Summary

- ATDD makes a system testable, which drives it to be of higher quality.
- The bottom line is that ATDD provides benefits to an organization.

PART IV

Case Studies

This part contains cases studies from real-life projects.

Chapter 26

Case Study: Retirement Contributions

"First thing that I ask a new client is, 'Have you been saving up for a rainy day? Guess what? It's raining.'"

Marty, *Primal Fear*

This case study presents testing a batch process with lots of exceptions and states.

Context

You probably have a company retirement account administered by a financial institution that receives money from your company each month and purchases the mutual funds or other investments that you specified for your account. The financial institution receives a contribution file from your company that has a list of retirement plan participants and the amount that should be added to each participant's account. When the institution receives a statement from its bank that your company has sent a deposit that matches the total in the contribution file, it purchases the funds for each participant.

Figure 26.1 presents the overall flow of the process. The matching process checks the participant identifiers in the contribution file against the corresponding retirement plan. If each identifier matches and the bank deposit is correct, the funding data is produced.

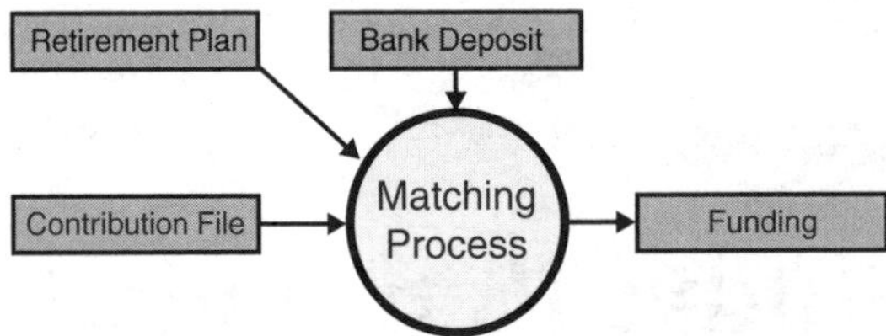

Figure 26.1 *Matching Process*

Many retirement administrators have dedicated staffs (such as Customer Service Representatives) that match each contribution file with the bank deposits. When a match is found, the customer service representative initiates the fund purchases. Several administrators have initiated projects to automatically perform the matching operation. The business case for these projects is to cut down on the time spent by the customer service representatives.

Many issues can occur with the matching process. The amount of the deposit may not exactly match the total in the contribution file. Or perhaps the deposit notification will not arrive for several days after the contribution file is received. Or multiple contribution files may be matched by a single deposit. Following are some of the acceptance tests for an application which performs the matching process.

The Main Course Test

The main course test assumes that the deposit amount exactly matches the total on the amounts in the contribution file and that all identifiers listed in the contribution file correspond to participants in the plan.

Setup

Each retirement plan has a set of participants who have decided how to invest their contributions. Each plan is associated with a bank account from which transfers are made to pay for purchasing of the funds.

Retirement Plan	Plan ID = XYZ	
Name	Participant ID	Fund
George	111111111	Wild Eyed Stocks
Sam	222222222	Government Bonds
Bill	333333333	Under the Mattress

Banking Relationship		
Plan ID	**Bank Routing Number**	**Account Number**
XYZ	555555555	12345678

Event

The event consists of two parts, which can occur in either order. One is the arrival of the contribution file, and the other is the arrival of the deposit notification. The Date Time Set makes the example repeatable.

Date Time Set
January 30, 2011 08:18 a.m.

Here is the contribution file where all participant IDs match those in the plan.

Contribution File	Plan ID = XYZ, File ID = 7777
Participant ID	**Amount**
111111111	$5,000
222222222	$1,000
333333333	$500

Here is the bank deposit whose amount matches the total of the amounts in the contribution file.

Bank Deposit			
Routing Number	**Account Number**	**Amount**	**Deposit ID**
555555555	12345678	$6,500	8888

Expected

Because the conditions for matching have been met, the expected output is funding instructions.

Funding	Plan ID = XYZ, File ID = 9999	
Participant ID	Fund	Amount
111111111	Wild Eyed Stocks	$5,000
222222222	Government Bonds	$1,000
333333333	Under the Mattress	$500

Matches			
Deposit ID	Contribution File ID	Funding File ID	Matched on Date Time
8888	7777	9999	January 30, 2011 08:18 a.m.

Implementation Issues

The way the setup works depends on your particular testing environment. The setup tables, Retirement Plan and Banking Relationship, can either check that the corresponding entries exist in the appropriate databases or insert them into the databases if they do not exist. If they do not exist and they cannot be inserted, the test fails at setup.

The contribution table and the bank deposit table can be converted by the fixture into data files that match the format of the data the system receives from the companies and the bank. The matching program can then process these data files as if they were actual files.

The matching program produces a funding file that another system processes. This funding file can be parsed and matched against the expected funding output.

Separation of Concerns

Many other problems can occur during the operation of the system. The received contribution file may not be in a readable format. This may occur the first time the file is received from a company due to setup issues, or it may occur repeatedly because of ongoing issues at the sending company. The files may be in different formats because of each company's human resource system. Those problems can be dealt with by using another set of tests that read samples of actual input files and check that either the file can be translated into a common format or a conversion error must be dealt with manually.

Business Value Tracking

Manual matching of deposits and contribution files takes an extensive amount of time for a customer service representative. In a majority of the instances, the match could be processed automatically. If the conditions did not hold (exact match of amounts and all participants already enrolled in the plan), the matching process could be performed with the current manual process. So there is high business value in creating a program that handles the main course as quickly as possible. The user story that encompasses doing the main course is given a large business value.

There can be a number of exceptions during the process. The deposit and contribution total may be off by a small amount (a few cents) or a large amount. A participant who is not entered as a participant on the plan may be listed in the contribution file. In that case, the matching program does not know what fund should be purchased for that participant.

The exceptions can be dealt with by ranking them by business value. The value represents some combination of the frequency of the exception and the cost for a customer service representative to process it. For example, one exception is for a match that is off by a few cents. This event might occur frequently, but the cost of the time involved to fix it exceeds the benefit.

One Exception

Each exception should have its own test to show that the exception is handled properly. The tests might use a common setup. The only difference may be in the event.

Here is an exception: The deposit is off by one cent. The customer unit decided that any discrepancy less than a dollar should be handled using the equivalent of "take a penny, give a penny." The discrepancies will be kept on some form of persistent storage, such as a database table or a log file. At some point, they can be analyzed to determine if there is a systemic issue such as one company always being two cents short. For the time being, the total of the discrepancies will be reportable to the appropriate financial officer so that the books can be balanced.

Event

The setup is as for the main course. The event is different.

Date Time Set
January 30, 2011 08:18 a.m.

Contribution File	Plan ID = XYZ, File ID = 7778
Participant ID	**Amount**
111111111	$5,000
222222222	$1,000
333333333	$500

Bank Deposit			
Routing Number	**Account Number**	**Amount**	**Deposit ID**
555555555	12345678	$6499.99	8889

Expected

Because the conditions for matching have been met, the expected output is funding instructions.

Funding	Plan ID = XYZ, File ID = 10000	
Participant ID	**Fund**	**Amount**
111111111	Wild Eyed Stocks	$5,000
222222222	Government Bonds	$1,000
333333333	Under the Mattress	$500

Matches			
Deposit ID	**Contribution File ID**	**Funding File ID**	**Matched on Date Time**
8889	7779	10000	January 30, 2011 08:18 a.m.

Now the issue is whether to show this as a separate table or as part of the Matches table. Because the purpose is for balancing nonmatching funding, it is shown as a separate table.

Discrepancy			
Deposit ID	Contribution File ID	Matched on Date Time	Discrepancy Amount
88889	7779	January 30, 2011 08:18 a.m.	$-.01

Another Exception

In this exception, a participant ID that is listed in the contribution file does not have a corresponding entry in the retirement plan.

Event

Once again, you could use a common setup. The difference in the event is that the contribution file contains an additional contributor who does not appear in the funding data. The total matches the deposit.

Date Time Set
January 30, 2011 08:18 a.m.

Contribution File	Plan ID = XYZ, File ID = 7779
Participant ID	Amount
111111111	$5,000
444444444	$100

Bank Deposit			
Routing Number	Account Number	Amount	Deposit ID
555555555	12345678	$5,100	8892

Expected

Because the conditions for matching have been met, the expected output is funding instructions.

Funding	Plan ID = XYZ, File ID = 10001	
Participant ID	Fund	Amount
111111111	Wild Eyed Stocks	$5,000

Matches			
Deposit ID	Contribution File ID	Funding File ID	Matched on Date Time
8892	7779	10001	January 30, 2011 08:18 a.m.

The missing participant needs to be reported somehow. A separate table shows the information that is attributed to the participant. A separate user story and set of tests will show how to handle this output.

Missing Participant			
Plan ID	Participant ID	Matched on Date Time	Participant Amount
XYZ	444444444	January 30, 2011 08:18 a.m.	$100

Two Simultaneous Exceptions

So what if two exceptions occur in the same processing? Should there be a test for that? Often it is difficult to form an automatic response to the occurrence of two exceptions for the same transaction, so the transaction is handled manually. However, it would be useful to know that there are two exceptions so that input doesn't have to be manually processed twice—once for each exception. The test then shows that two exceptions occurred. If the two exceptions are decoupled (the response to one does not depend on the response to the other), the tests for the individual exceptions may be sufficient, depending on the risk tolerance of the project.

Event

Once again, the setup matches what it was for the main course. But both a missing participant and a nonmatching deposit are involved.

Date Time Set
January 30, 2011 08:18 a.m.

Contribution File	Plan ID = XYZ, File ID = 7780
Participant ID	Amount
111111111	$5,000
444444444	$100

Bank Deposit			
Routing Number	Account Number	Amount	Deposit ID
555555555	12345678	$5,099	8893

Expected

No funding is produced. The output describes the exceptions that occurred during the matching process. These exceptions can be tracked to determine which combinations of multiple exceptions occur frequently. At some point, the frequent combinations could be handled in code, rather than left for manual processing.

Exception		
Contribution File ID	Deposit ID	Exceptions
7780	8893	Deposit_does_not_match_contribution_total Participant_in_contribution_file_not_in_plan

The Big Picture

These tests have been focused on the context of the system. In the big picture, not only do you have to create a funding file, you must actually purchase the funds and record the transactions in each participant's account. You need to develop a larger test for this entire workflow. It may not necessarily be run as an automated test. It may still require some test double. You would not want to keep purchasing mutual funds and adding them to a participant's account every time you run this large test. So a test double for the actual purchasing interface is required.

The big picture test may be beyond the developer unit's scope. Their job is to ensure that the funding instructions are correct based on the input. But the project is not complete until the full test is run by the testing unit.

Event Table

The matching process is a batch process. It is not driven by user input, but by events that occur. Therefore, an event table is appropriate for this case. Here's an example of some of these events.

Matching Events		
Event	**Response**	**Notes**
Contribution file received	Check for matching deposit If so, perform match Else store file	
Bank deposit received	Check for matching contribution file If so, perform match Else store deposit	
One week after contribution file received	If no bank deposit received, notify client	
One week after bank deposit received	If no contribution file received, notify client	
One minute prior to market close	Disallow matching until after market close	Prevents funding issues

State Transition Table

The contribution file goes through several states that track its progress through the matching process. These are some of the states that a file cvan be in.

Contribution File	
State	**Meaning**
Received	Contribution file received
Data Checked	File has been examined for format errors
Awaiting Match	Waiting for bank deposit
Edit Processing	Contribution file has bad format

External events and internal events cause the state of the contribution file to change or some processing to occur. This table describes some of the state transitions for the contribution file.

Contribution File State/Event Transitions				
State	**Event**	**Response**	**New State**	**Notes**
Initial	Received contribution file	Record contribution file	Received	
Received		Perform data check	Data checked	Examine file for format errors
Data checked	Data check is bad		Edit processing	Need to correct errors
Data checked	Data check is good		Awaiting match	

A test can be associated with each state transition that is not already being checked by another test. For example, for the first transition, you might have the following.

Transition to State Received

Given a retirement plan:

Retirement Plan	Plan ID = XYZ	
Name	**Participant ID**	**Fund**
George	111111111	Wild Eyed Stocks
Sam	222222222	Government Bonds
Bill	333333333	Under the Mattress

When a contribution file is received:

Date Time Set
January 30, 2011 08:18 a.m.

Contribution File	Plan ID = XYZ, File ID = 7777
Participant ID	**Amount**
111111111	$5,000
222222222	$1,000
333333333	$500

Then record it as received.

Contribution File States		
Plan ID	**File ID**	**Status**
XYZ	7777	Received

Summary

- Separate concerns to make testing easier.
- Give each exception its own test.
- Test every state transition.

Chapter 27

Case Study: Signal Processing

Lisa Simpson: Would you guys turn that down!
Homer Simpson: Sweetie, if we didn't turn it down for the cops, what chance do you have?

The Simpsons "Little Big Mom" (2000)

Acceptance tests for a real-time signal processing system are presented in this chapter.

It's Too Loud

I have produced software with Richard Cann of Grozier Technical Systems for a number of years. Grozier produces sound level measurement systems. Numerous concert sites, particularly outdoor ones, use these systems to monitor sound levels for regulatory reasons and to act as good neighbors.

The systems are composed of embedded systems that run multiple programs. Richard produces some of the programs, particularly the display and control components. I produce the real-time signal analysis portion [Wiki08].

Sound Levels

The programs input the sound through the microphone input. Each second, 22,500 samples are recorded. The signal analysis programs perform calculations on each of these sets of samples. The output is a measure of loudness, (technically the equivalent continuous sound level [Leq]). An overview of the process is shown in Figure 27.1.

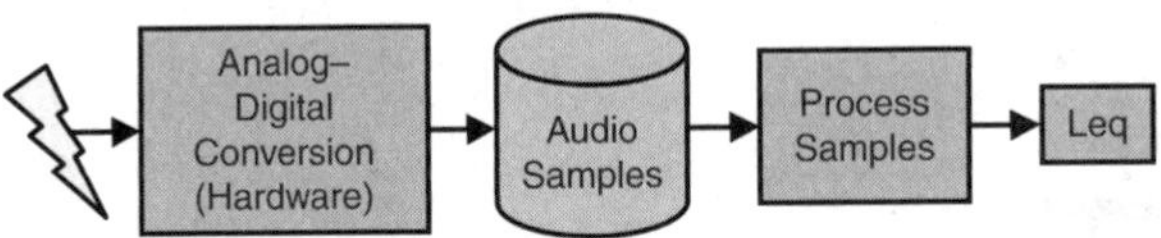

Figure 27.1 *Sound Level Process*

The sound is input through a microphone. The *gain* (how much the signal is amplified) varies based on both the microphone and the volume setting on the input. To correctly compute the Leq, you must adjust the gain so that a standard sound source (a calibration source) produces a specific Leq result.

It is difficult to replicate the entire system (microphone, calibration source, and so forth) for testing. However, you can capture the sounds by using regular recording methods and then replay them as input (a test double) for the tests. Suppose the sounds produced by the calibration source are captured in a calibration file and sounds of known Leq are captured in separate files. These files contain a second's worth of data (22,500 samples). Then the test of the overall system can be as follows.

Compute Leq

Given that the volume is adjusted so that calibration file (containing a 1KHz signal) yields the standard Leq:

Calibration	
File	Leq (db)
calibration.wav	94

The test files should produce values of the expected Leq.

Leq Tests	
Input File	Leq (db)?
test1.wav	88
test2.wav	95

To ensure that these Leqs are correct, the same test is repeated with calibrated specialized hardware. The results of the hardware test become the *oracle*—the agreed-upon expected result. This is similar to using the outputs of an existing system to be the expected results for a new system.

Developer Tests

The details of the process are shown in Figure 27.2. It shows that there are two intermediate results in the computation: the windowed samples and the A-weighted samples.

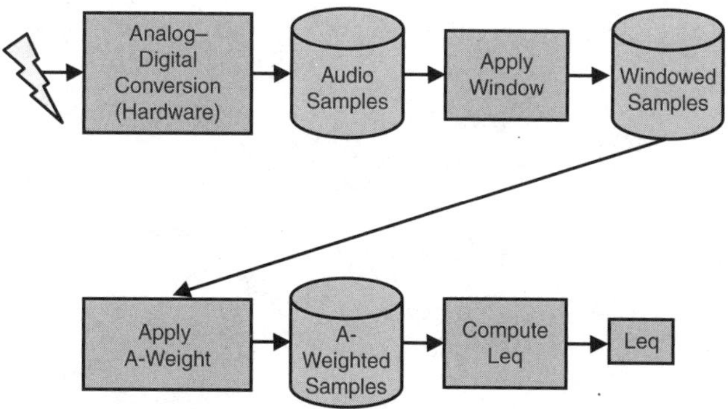

Figure 27.2 *Details of Sound-Level Process*

Richard is particularly interested in the final results. Is the Leq computed correctly for a particular file? As a developer, it helps if I can apply tests to intermediate results. These intermediate tests are usually termed *unit tests* because they apply to lower-level modules. However, because Richard is highly experienced in signal processing, he creates input and output files that can be used in acceptance tests for the intermediate processing works. For example, for the Compute Leq part, he creates an A-Weighted sample file.

Compute Leq	
A-Weighted Sample File	**Leq?**
Aweight1.data	77
Aweight2.data	44

The input and output files contain digital samples for 1 second. Equivalent files are available for each of the other steps in the process.

Summary

- Acceptance tests do not have to involve just simple values. They can be entire sets of values (often represented in files).
- A subject matter expert can often create lower-level tests that can be used as developer tests.

Chapter 28

Case Study: A Library Print Server

"There's no such thing as a free lunch."

Anonymous

Here is a library print server system. Libraries use such a system to charge for printouts of documents. The example shows how acceptance tests can cover a workflow and not just a use case.

The Context

I have consulted for Rob Walsh, the cofounder of EnvisionWare, in exploring a new object design for the print server system the company provides to libraries. In my book *Prefactoring,* I showed the unit test strategy and underlying object design for the system.[1] I described the work flow with a concentration on how it was implemented using the internal messaging system. The following workflow concentrates on the acceptance tests.

A library patron, Joe, wants to print a document created on one of the library's computers. He submits the document for printing and then goes over to a release station to print the job. There are two separate use cases that form the work flow—submitting the document for printing and actually printing the document—. Internally, the personal computer and the release station communicate with a central server (see Figure 28.1).

1. See Chapter 15 in [Pugh01].

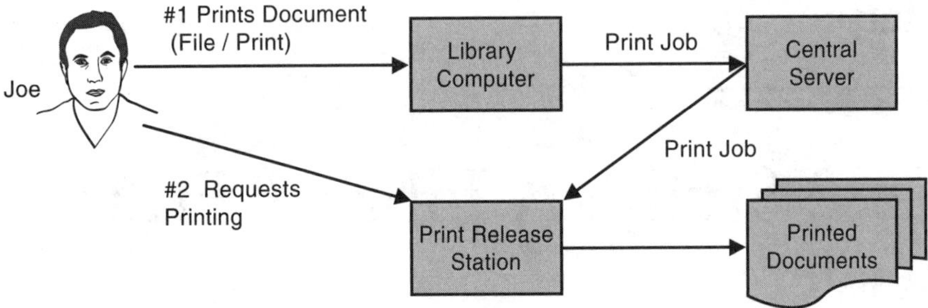

Figure 28.1 *Workflow*

There are a number of tests that ensure the individual steps work. For example, some tests ensure that the print cost is correctly computed for various users and different modes of printing—black-and-white and color. Other tests check that users can deposit money into their prepaid accounts. The following is the test for the entire workflow.

A Workflow Test

In this workflow, Joe submits two documents for printing and then goes to the release station. When Joe signs onto the release station, he sees a list of the two print jobs. Joe selects each one to print. Each job is printed, and Joe's account is charged. Here's the detailed test.

Workflow of Printing Two Documents to Print Queue

Given a user with an account on the system:

User		
Name	Balance	User ID
Joe	$1.00	123

And these print rates:

Print Rates	
B&W Per-Page Rate	Color Per-Page Rate
$.03	$.10

And two documents to be printed:

Document		
Name	Number of Pages	Contains
Joestuff.doc	1	The quick brown fox jumped over the lazy dogs

Document		
Name	Number of Pages	Contains
Morestuff.doc	7	--Lots of stuff--

And no print jobs currently on the print queue for that user:

Print Jobs	User ID = 123		
User ID	Filename	Print Mode	Job Number

And the next job number is set:

Next Job Number
Job Number
99991

When the user requests the first document to be printed:

Request Printing		
Enter	User ID	123
Enter	Filename	Joestuff.doc
Enter	Printing Mode	Black & White
Press	Submit	

Then the system responds with:

Approve Print Charge		
Display	Print Charge	$.03
Press	Accept	

If the user accepts, a print job is created.

Print Jobs			
User ID	Filename	Print Mode	Job Number
123	Joestuff.doc	Black & White	99991

When the user requests a second document to be printed:

Request Printing		
Enter	User ID	123
Enter	Filename	Morestuff.doc
Enter	Print mode	Color
Press	Submit	

Then the system responds with:

Approve Print Charge		
Display	Print Charge	$.70
Press	Accept	

If the user accepts, a print job is created.

Print Jobs			
User ID	Filename	Print Mode	Job Number
123	Joestuff.doc	Black & White	99991
123	Morestuff.doc	Color	99992

Now two print jobs have been created. The next step in the flow is for Joe to go over to the release station and request each job to be printed.

Workflow for Printing Jobs from Print Queue

Given that print jobs have been created for a user:

Print Jobs			
User ID	Filename	Print Mode	Job Number
123	Joestuff.doc	Black & White	99991
123	Morestuff.doc	Color	99992

When the user enters his user ID:

User ID Entry		
Enter	User ID	123
Press	Submit	

Then the list of print jobs is displayed.

Print Job List	
Filename	Job Number
Joestuff.doc	99991
Morestuff.doc	99992

When the user selects one file:

Select File to Print	
Filename	Joestuff.doc
Press	Submit

Then it is printed on the appropriate printer.

Printed Output	Selected File = Joestuff.doc
Output?	
The quick brown fox jumped over the lazy dogs	

And the file is eliminated from the display list and the print queue.

Print Job List	
Filename	Job Number
Morestuff.doc	99992

Print Jobs			
User ID	Filename	Print Mode	Job Number
123	Morestuff.doc	Color	99992

And the user's account is charged the print cost.

User		
Name	Balance	User ID
Joe	$.97	123

When the user selects another file:

Select File to Print	
Filename	Morestuff.doc
Press	Submit

Then it is printed.

Print Output	Selected File = Morestuff.doc
Output?	
--Lots of stuff--	

Then it is eliminated from the display list and the print queue.

Print Job List	
Filename	Job Number

Print Jobs	User ID = 123		
User IDh	Filename	Print Mode	Job Number

And the user's account is charged the print cost.

User		
Name	Balance	User ID
Joe	$.27	123

Additional tests could show the flow if the user does not have sufficient money to print a document or the user decides to cancel the printing of a document.

Summary

- A workflow test consists of more than one use case.

Chapter 29

Case Study: Highly Available Platform

"You just call out my name,
And you know wherever I am
I'll come running, oh yeah baby
To see you again."

Carole King, "You've Got a Friend"

Many corporate software systems depend on a highly available platform. This chapter shows increasingly detailed acceptance tests for such a platform.

Context for Switching Servers

A highly available platform has at least two independent computers. If one goes down, the other available computers take over the load. If the servers are running close to capacity, not all the applications may be able to run. A predetermined priority mechanism determines which applications get to run. In addition to switching applications when a server goes down, in the case study, the system administrator is notified either via email or a text message.

The capacity of a server to run applications depends on the demands of the applications, such as memory, processor usage, and input-output operations. Instead of being overwhelmed by all the details at once, this study shows how to introduce the details gradually. This is another manifestation of the separation of concerns guideline.

Test for Switching Servers

The first test uses a simplified capacity that considers just the number of applications that can be run on each server. This test demonstrates that the servers switch applications properly when one of them goes down. There will be a lot of technical work to perform to make that happen. Starting with this simple acceptance test keeps the developer unit working while the customer unit examines more detailed capacity issues.

Server Goes Down

Given these servers:

Servers	
Name	Capacity (Applications)
Freddy	5
Fannie	3

And these applications with their priority:

Applications	
Name	Priority
CEO's Pet	100
MP3 Download	99
Lost Episode Watching	98
External Web	50
Internal Web	25
Payroll	10

And the servers running these applications:

Server Load	
Name	Applications
Freddy	CEO's Pet External Web Internal Web Payroll
Fannie	Lost Episode Watching MP3 Download

When a server goes down, switch any applications running on it to the alternate server. If the alternate server does not have the capacity for all the applications, run the applications based on priority order.

Server Events			
Event	Servers Remaining?	Applications Running?	Action?
Freddy Goes Down	Fannie	CEO's Pet Lost Episode Watching MP3 Download	Send event alert "Freddy down"
Fannie Goes Down	Freddy	CEO's Pet Lost Episode Watching MP3 Download External Web Internal Web	Send event alert "Fannie down"

A second test ensures that the next part of the flow is proper. Now that an event has occurred, the administrator should be notified in the appropriate way.

Send Alert to Administrator

Given these preferences for an event alert:

Administrator Notification			
Notification Preference	Text ID	E-Mail	Action?
E-mail	123	AB@somewhere.com	Send mail to AB@ somewhere.com

When an event occurs, send the event alert to the system administrator based on the notification preference that the event occurred.

Event Response	
Event	Response?
Any event occurs	Send Mail to AB@somewhere.com

If the notification fails, send the event alert via the other method.

Notification	Previous Action = Send Mail to AB@somewhere.com
Event	**Response?**
Mail not deliverable	Send text to 123
No response to mail	Send text to 123

You can create a similar test for three servers if one of them is going down. That test would show how to distribute the applications among the remaining two servers.

Test for Technical Rule

Now that application switching works, more complex rules can be applied to the capacity of each server. The selection of what applications to run is a separable concern. The results can be tested independently of testing the switching functionality.

For example, if a single server is running, the applications that can be run depend on selecting the highest priority applications that can run within the capacity. It's possible that an application that has a higher priority cannot be run because there is insufficient capacity. Then a lower priority application that does not require as much capacity might be run.

In the following table, CPU usage is measured in millions of instructions per second (MIPS). Memory usage is calculated in megabytes (MB). Input-output usage is measured in total of reads and writes per second (RWS).

Determine Applications to Run on Server

Given applications with these characteristics:

Application Characteristics				
Name	**Priority**	**CPU Usage (MIPS)**	**Memory Usage (MB)**	**Input-Output Usage (RWS)**
CEO's Pet	100	1	1000	1000
MP3 Download	99	10	500	2000
Lost Episode Watching	98	5	200	3000

continues

Application Characteristics, Continued				
Name	Priority	CPU Usage (MIPS)	Memory Usage (MB)	Input-Output Usage (RWS)
External Web	50	3	400	500
Internal Web	25	1	100	500
Payroll	10	8	10	1000

And a single server with the following capacity:

Server Characteristics			
Name	CPU Usage (MIPS)	Memory Usage (MB)	Input-Output Usage (RWS)
Fanny	15	2000	5000

Then it should run the following applications.

Application Running			
Name	CPU Usage (MIPS)	Memory Usage (MB)	Input-Output Usage (RWS)
CEO's Pet	1	1000	1000
MP3 Download	10	500	2000
External Web	3	400	500

In this test, "Lost Episode Watching" requires 5MIPS. The two higher priority applications—"CEO's Pet" and "MP3 Download"—use 11MIPS of the 15MIPS available. So "Lost Episode Watching" cannot be run, but a lower priority application "External Web" requires only 3MIPS, so it can be run.

You can create similar tests for two or more servers. The creation of these tests brings up issues of how to balance applications between two servers. Given this test, it's clear that if there were a second server, at least "Lost Episode Watching" should be running, as long as the server's capacity was greater than that application's needs. Or perhaps "CEO's Pet" will run on the second server, allowing "Lost Episode Watching" to run on the first one.

The tests for what applications should be run on what servers can become fairly complicated. There are usually more issues, such as applications that need specific devices that are only available on some of the servers, so they cannot be run on the other servers.

At some point, an additional test that combines the switching and the selection is created. From the acceptance point of view, this test need only demonstrate that the switching takes into account selection based on the more complex selection rule. Lots of other combinations of applications and servers may be tested to ensure that the code and design do not have more esoteric defects. There would also be acceptance tests for the switching time performance.

Summary

- Separate tests so that each checks a different part of the flow.
- Separation of concerns makes for simpler testing.

PART V

Technical Topics

This part contains some topics of interest to testers and developers.

Chapter 30

How Does What You Do Fit with ATDD?

"Then the part comes to me and it fits like a glove because it's actually written about me... All I had to do was show up and learn the lines."

David Carradine

This chapter presents topics that are aimed at developers and testers, rather than customers. It examines testing and designing.

Test Platforms

Depending on how long it takes to run the tests, you can run them at different times. Tests on a developer's machine should run pretty quickly. When the code is transferred to the integration platform, you can run a series of longer tests. There is a limit, however, to the number of tests that can be run in a short time, say 15 minutes. So a smoke test[1] is used that consists of the most risky or the most relevant.

You can run longer-running tests on a separate platform (see Figure 30.1). There can be a set that is run at least a few times during the day, a set run at night, another set over the weekend, or still another for a week at a time. If the tests are successful on one platform, you start running the longer set on the next

1. The term derives from electrical engineers who used to design and build a circuit. If the circuit smoked when they turned it on, they knew immediately that something was wrong [Wiki04].

platform. You probably can't imagine tests that last a week, but a number of complex systems require that long (and even longer).[2]

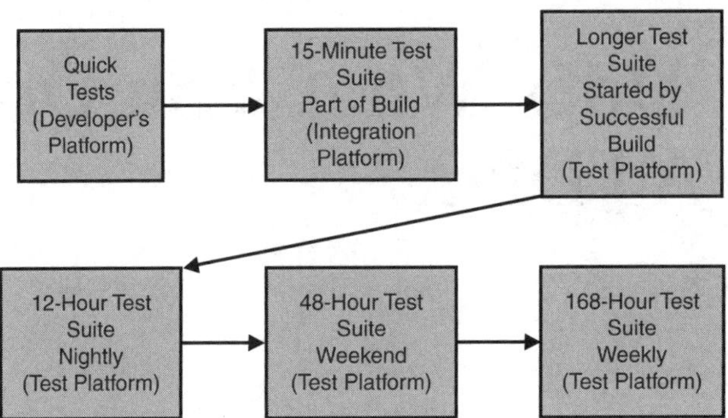

Figure 30.1 *Test Timing*

> ***A Little More Testing***
>
> In March 2007, a large airline migrated seven million reservations from the Sabre reservation system to SHARES, another reservation system. About one and a half million reservations did not transfer correctly. Passengers could not check-in for their flights. Kiosks in many cities stopped working. The conversion took place over a weekend. On Sunday, many passengers were stranded outside the security line because they could not obtain a boarding pass. Many millions of dollars in revenue were lost, not to mention customer dissatisfaction.
>
> A little more testing might have gone a long way toward preventing the problem [Fast01].

Internal Design from Tests

There has been little discussion on the internal design of an application. The one suggestion was to make the module implementing a business rule easily available to testing, such as shown in Figure 30.2.

The Model-View-Controller pattern states that the model should be separated from the view and controller. In this case, the model is the business rule for determining whether a customer can reserve a CD. The view is how the user

2. Tests of compilers can take a long time.

sees the result of this business rule—button or dialog box. The controller is how the user can make a reservation—the reservation dialog box. The view and the controller should be coded separated from the model.

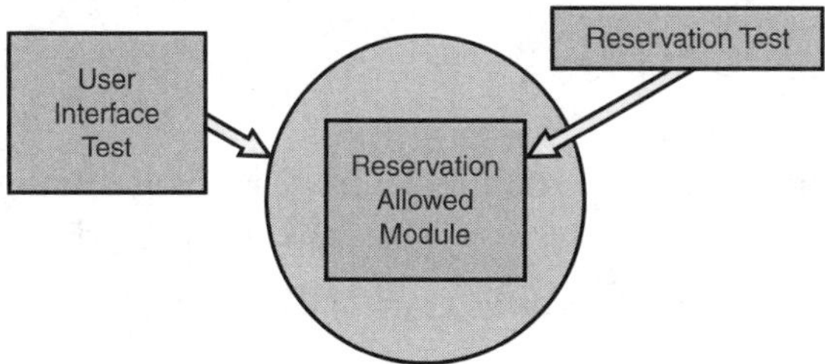

Figure 30.2 *User Interface and Logic Tests*

The tests in Chapter 14, "Separate View from Model," showed how the separation of the model from the view made the tests simpler. The simpler tests show up as simpler code. For example, suppose that the method used to determine whether a customer is allowed to reserve is called:

```
Boolean Customer.allowedToReserve()
```

What this method does is obvious from its name. It returns whether a customer is allowed to reserve by calculating the result according to Sam's business rule. The tests in Chapter 13, "Simplification by Separation," apply to this method.

The tests in Chapter 14 apply to the display. Because the calculation has already been tested, the display need only be tested to see if it displays appropriately. Simple tests usually correspond to simple underlying code. For example, the way the display code would look if the button was to be enabled or disabled might be this:

```
if (customer.allowedToReserve())
    enableReserveButton()
 else
    disableReserveButton()
```

If the button were to be shown or hidden, it might look like this:

```
if (customer.allowedToReserve()
   showReserveButton()
else
   hideReserveButton()
```

If there were different dialog boxes, it could be this:

```
OnReserveButtonClick() {
    if (customer.allowedToReserve())
       displayReservationDialog();
    else
       displayNotAllowedToReserveDialog();
    }
```

In any case, the two tests to run for a customer who is allowed to reserve and one who is not allowed to reserve will execute all the paths in this code. You don't have to run all the tests as shown in Chapter 13.

Device Testing

Every external device should have its own set of tests. For example, Debbie is investigating use a bar code scanner to read the CD ID and the customer ID. She needs to create developer tests for the bar code scanner to ensure that the scanner can properly read the bar code. These are going to be manual tests unless Debbie can get a robot that will move the scanner. Here are some tests she might come up with:

- Check that scanning a vendor-supplied bar code produces the correct output.
- Create a bar code image with the printer, scan it, and check that the output matches.
- Try scanning at different speeds, and check the output.
- Scan in both directions, and check the output.

Tom might come up with these ideas:

- Try a dirty bar code to see if it is readable.
- Try a ripped bar code to see if it is readable or produces an error.
- Try scanning a bar code in an off-axis direction.

You need to do all these tests with the device itself. These are developer acceptance tests. The change in input devices from the keyboard does not require new acceptance tests from the customer. Debbie will have at least one acceptance test that goes through the user interface to ensure that the connection to the scanner is properly made. But she does not have to test all the previous conditions through the user interface unless she identifies some risk in the integration of the scanner with the system.

Starting with User Interfaces

Some customers want to see user interface prototypes as part of the requirement process. You can use these prototypes as the basis for acceptance tests through the user interface or through the middle tier.

Once the user interface prototype is approved, you can employ it as the basis for tests. For each display screen, assign every entry field a label. For each screen, make up an action table with those labels. The tests can execute the action table either through the user interface or through the middle tier. Add "given" and "then" parts to the tests that give the conditions—the data required—and the expected results. Then create tables that show the business rules that apply to combinations of inputs, such as the ones presented in this book. The tables will clarify the cases that you may have missed by just looking at the user interface.

Black Box Testing

Acceptance test-driven development (ATDD) is closely related to black box testing. Both are independent of the implementation underneath, so common black box techniques apply. These include[3] the following:

- Equivalence partitioning, which divides inputs into groups that should exhibit similar behavior. (See the tests in Chapter 10, "User Story Breakup," section "Business Rule Tests.")
- Boundary value analysis, which tests values at the edge of each equivalence partition. (See the example discount percentage tests in Chapter 4, "An Introductory Acceptance Test," section "An Example Business Rule.")
- State transition testing checks the response from a system that depends on its state. (See Chapter 15, "Events, Responses, and States," section "States and State Transitions.")
- Use case testing to check all paths through a use case. (See the Check-Out Use Case in Chapter 7, "Collaborating on Scenarios.")

3. See [Myers01] or [Kaner01] for details on these techniques.

- Decision table testing for complex business rules. (See "The Simplified Rule" in Chapter 13.) Often, the decision table is presented in the opposite format, where rows and columns are interchanged from the format used in this book. This book's format follows that of many of the automated testing tools.

Unit Testing

Unit tests help with the design and quality of the implementation. You get more immediate feedback with unit tests, because only a small chunk of code is being tested. It may take a while to implement enough code to pass an acceptance test.

You don't want to duplicate testing between unit tests and acceptance tests. In many cases, business rule tests can be written in a unit test framework, as shown in Chapter 4. The purpose of acceptance tests is communication. Keeping customer-provided tests in a form that customers can understand helps in this communication.

If the terminology in an acceptance test changes, you may want to propagate the changes to the classes and methods in an implementation to keep things in sync.[4]

Summary

- Run acceptance tests as often as possible.
- Test devices separately from their connection to the system.
- Use black box testing techniques to develop acceptance tests.

4. See [Adjic01] for more tester and developer issues.

Chapter 31

Test Setup

"It's not what I do, but the way I do it. It's not what I say, but the way I say it."

Mae West

This chapter discusses the trade-offs between using an individual setup for tests and using a common setup. It also explores concerns about test order and persistent storage.

A Common Setup

You may have noticed that the setup for several of the triad's tests started to be repetitious. All the tests need customers and CDs to rent or return. It is tempting to place the repetitive setup into a common setup. There is a classic trade-off between decreasing duplication by the common setup and increasing the possibility that altering the common setup causes failing tests.[1] A common setup for all tests might be as follows.

Customer Data		
Name	ID	Credit-Card Number
James	007	4005550000000019
Maxwell	88	372700997251009

1. This is an example in the test world of the "Splitters versus Lumpers" prefactoring guideline for design [Pugh02].

Album Data		
UPC Code	Title	CD Category
UPC123456	Janet Jackson Number Ones	Regular
UPC000001	Beatles Greatest Hits	Golden Oldie

CD Data	
ID	UPC Code
CD2	UPC000001
CD3	UPC123456
CD7	UPC123456

This data forms a "test bed" for the other tests. If you make any changes to this setup, such as to James's ID or credit-card number, tests that depend on those values will fail. They will fail not because the behavior of the system changed, but because the test may now be specifying an invalid behavior. For example, the Card Charge test would have James's original credit-card number on it, but James's number has changed. A shared setup should remain constant.

On the other hand, the Rental table has more potential transactions than the CD Data and the Album Data tables. Many tests require different values in this table. For example, the data in this table are used for the tests of Check-In story and the Customer Limit on Simultaneous Rentals business rule.

Rentals		
CD ID	Customer ID	Due Date
CD12	007	1/21/2011
CD6	88	1/22/2011
CD20	88	1/23/2011
CD 21	88	1/24/2011

Customer ID 007 could be used for a regular check-in test. Customer ID 88 could not be used for a regular test, because ID 88 already has three CDs rented. Keeping track of which customers are suitable for which tests requires discipline. Without this discipline, using a separate setup in each test for the appropriate data is far easier to maintain.

The common setup could be run for each test to get a clean start—"a Fresh Fixture" as Gerard Meszaros terms it [Meszaros01]—or it could be run just once before a series of tests that do not affect the setup [Koskela02]. In this particular case, if the tests that are run add more rentals to ID 007 and this setup is not rerun, ID 007 may reach the rental limit. Subsequent tests that assume he is not at the limit will fail.[2]

Some Amelioration

You can do some things to ameliorate potential problems. First, never change existing data in the setup. Add to the setup if you need a different entity. For example, if you need a customer with different characteristics, add another customer. Some teams give names to the entities; customers who represent the kind of entity they are dealing with might be Big Spender, Prompt Returner, and so forth. For example, instead of Customer ID 88 being named Maxwell, he might be named Customer Who Reached Limit if the previous Rental table was used.

Another way of handling the issue is not to have a common setup that is used for every test, but ones that are common to a group of tests. The number of tests that a change in the setup can affect is limited.

Still another way is to create variables in the common setup. For example, you might define a variable (as shown in Chapter 17, "Decouple with Interfaces") to contain James's credit card, such as

4005550000000019 → JAMES_CREDIT_CARD

In each of the tests, you would reference JAMES_CREDIT_CARD rather than the number.[3] For example, in the setup for the credit-card charges (Chapter 11, "System Boundary"), you might use the following.

Credit-Card Charges from Rental System			**Day = 1/21/2011**
Card Number	**Customer Name**	**Amount**	**Time**
←JAMES_CREDIT_CARD	James	$2	10:53 a.m.

2. The approach taken starts to define a test architecture [Rup01], which should be designed with the same care as the application.
3. This is an example of the DRY—Don't Repeat Yourself—Principle from the Pragmatic Programmers [Hunt01]. It is also known as the Once and Only Once Principle. A corollary of this principle is Shalloway's Law. If there are N places where a change has to be made, Shalloway will find N–1 of them.

Still another way of making tests less dependent on the setup is to use relative results. For example, you might be testing the ability to add a customer, say Napolean Solo. Using this setup and an absolute result, the test would first check that there is one customer in the customer data, perform the add, and check the result to see that there are two customers. Using a relative result, the test would first determine the current number of customers and then check to see that the number of customers after the addition of Napolean Solo was the previous number plus one.[4] In both cases, the test would also check that Napolean Solo was a customer.

Test Order

In many acceptance test frameworks, you have control over the sequence in which tests are run.[5] If a test has no side effects, the order in which it is run relative to other tests is unimportant. A side effect is a change to the state of the system or an output to an external repository, as shown in Chapter 8, "Test Anatomy." If a test does have a side effect on the shared setup, such as deleting a customer, you may need to run the tests in an order such that the deletion comes last.

You may be able to take advantage of complementary side effects. Suppose one test adds a customer and another test deletes a customer. If you run these tests one right after the other, the side effects should cancel out.[6]

Running tests in a particular order, just like dependence on a common setup, requires discipline. It can decrease the amount of testing code, because a test assumes that the previous test has successfully executed. But maintenance of the tests may accidentally change the order and cause tests to break, or it could change the results of tests that later tests in the order depend upon. If tests are tied together to run in a particular order, reproducing a test that fails requires running all the preceding tests.

Persistent Storage Issues

Often, tests include altering entries in persistence storage, such as a database. Even if the tests do not use the same entities, such as customers, they may leave

4. A relative result is also referred to as a *delta*. A test that uses a relative result is called a *delta test*.
5. This is not the case for unit test frameworks.
6. A log of operations can include entries on both of these operations. So the side effect of logging is not cancelled out.

the database in a state in which it is not ready for the tests to be run again. In that case, you need to restore the database to its original state.

Depending on your test environment, you may have a couple of technical solutions to this problem. One solution is to simply restore the database from a backup copy. Although this takes some time, it may be small relative to the amount of time for all the tests. Alternatively, you could execute the tests within a virtual machine. The virtual machine is closed upon test completion, and a new clone of the virtual machine is used for the next test [Devx01].

A database on a test platform may consist of many records, so it may take considerable time to restore the entire database. You could create a procedure that backs up and then restores just the entities that have been affected by the test. Alternatively, you could have a process that eliminates all traces of an entity such as a customer. Then the tests could create that entity and use it for further tests.[7] Another approach to restoring persistent data to its original state, particularly for tests that add to the data, rather than modify it, is to time-stamp every record. When the test is over, you would delete all records whose timestamps are equal to or after the time at the beginning of the test. You could also create a log of records that have been modified during the tests and restore the original record once the tests have completed.

If you don't have control of the database, what you can do is document what the state of the system should be in the "Given" part of the tests. Then if the state is not as expected, the test will fail not in the "When" part, but in the "Given" part. That clarifies it is not the action that caused the failure. For example, suppose you are testing adding a customer and the customer you want to add is ID 99. You need to ensure that the customer does not already exist. So you place this in the "Given" section. If you have a lot of these conditions, you might separate them from the "Given" into an "Assume" section.

Customer Data		
Name	ID	Exists?
Agent	99	No

Summary

- There is a trade-off in eliminating redundancy and causing dependencies between a common test setup and individual test setups.

7. This is like what happened to George Bailey in *It's a Wonderful Life*.

- Use a common setup to create a test bed for further tests.
- Be cautious of tests that have side effects that alter conditions for other tests.
- If using shared resources, document assumptions as to their condition.

Chapter 32

Case Study: E-Mail Addresses

"Beware of bugs in the above code; I have only proved it correct, not tried it."

Donald Knuth

This study involves breaking down a complex test, which represents a complex business rule, into simpler tests. The simpler tests can decrease time in understanding and implementing the rule.

Context

Almost every application that involves communication requires an e-mail address. When you enter an e-mail address, you should parse it to ensure that it is in a valid format. The process of verifying that an e-mail address is actually valid requires an exterior action, such as sending an e-mail to the address and checking that it was not rejected.

The testers for one company had a set of e-mail address examples they uses to test every application that had an e-mail address entry. The examples included both correct and incorrect formatted addresses. The company also had a business rule that e-mail addresses from some domains were not acceptable. These domains included mail servers that allowed completely anonymous e-mail. A portion of the tests is shown here.

E-Mail Tests		
E-Mail	**Valid?**	**Reason**
George@sam.com	Yes	
George@george@same.com	No	Two @s
.George@sam.com	No	Invalid name

E-Mail Tests		
E-Mail	**Valid?**	**Reason**
George@samcom	No	Invalid domain
George+Bill@sam.com	Yes	+ is allowed in name
George@hotmail.com	No	Banned domain
George@iamoutogetyou.com	No	Banned domain
...and many more		

Every time an e-mail address was entered on an input screen, this entire set of tests was run.

An E-Mail Trick

You may notice that George+Bill@sam.com is a valid e-mail address. The + is allowed in the part prior to the @ sign. It has a special meaning in most e-mail systems. The e-mail is delivered to the part before the + (George in this case). The full address (George+Bill) is used in the To part of the e-mail. Your e-mail client (Eudora, Thunderbird, Outlook, and so on.) can filter based on the part after the + (Bill) to put the message in a particular folder or perform another action. Some e-mail systems or internal servers may discard the + so that the mail instead goes to a user named GeorgeBill. That represents a different user than George. If you try this trick, test this on your system to ensure that it works before using the trick.

Breaking Down Tests

This acceptance test is pretty clear. When I ask developers how much time they think it will take to program an e-mail validation routine that will pass this test, they suggest a couple of days. I then suggest breaking down this test into smaller ones may decrease the time.

We saw in Chapter 13, "Simplification by Separation," that breaking down a business rule into simpler business rules makes things easier to understand and test. Each smaller table represents either a requirement or a test. Sometimes it's hard to distinguish between the two. The tables presented here represent either details of an e-mail address from the business point of view or unit tests for a module that implements e-mail format verification.

In the e-mail situation, we can use the rules that the Internet standards provide in RFC 2822 [IEFF01]. The first rule for a valid e-mail address is that it contain one and only one @ symbol. The @ separates the name part of the address from the domain part. For example, with ken.pugh@netobjectives.com, ken.pugh is the name part and netobjectives.com is the domain. The official term for the name part is local-part. So we will use that in our tables.

E-Mail Split into Local-Part and Domain			
E-Mail	Valid?	Local-Part?	Domain?
X@Y	Yes	X	Y
XY	No	DNC	DNC
XY@XY@XY	No	DNC	DNC

DNC means "Do Not Care" because the e-mail is invalid. Usually, a developer says that it will take less than 15 minutes to implement code that performs this check. It all depends on how familiar the developer is with the regular expression library.

Local-Part Validation

According to the rules, the local-part must only contain the following characters:

- Uppercase and lowercase English letters (a through z, A through Z)
- Digits 0 through 9
- Period (.), provided that it is not the first or the last character and it doesn't appear two or more times consecutively
- ! # $ % & ' * + – / = ? ^ _ ` { | } ~

The maximum size of the local-part is 64 characters.[1] We can put this free text business rule into a table.

Local-Part Allowable Characters		
Characters	Allowed?	Notes
a through z	Yes	
A through Z	Yes	
0 through 9	Yes	
! # $ % & ' * + – / = ? ^ _ ` { | } ~	Yes	
.	Yes	If not first, last, or two consecutive
Anything else	No	

1. If you are actually following this case study to perform your own validation, you may also want to eliminate characters that can inject SQL [Security01]. You would not allow a single quote or a forward slash.

We could have a test of the allowed characters for the local-part. Of course, we need some test cases to see that the character rules are applied properly.

Local-Part Character Combination Tests		
Local-Part	**Valid?**	**Notes**
George	Yes	
George\	No	Character not allowed
George..a	No	Period appears twice in a row
.George	No	Period first
George.	No	Period last

And, of course, we should have some rules for length.

Local-Part Length Tests		
Local-Part	**Valid?**	**Notes**
	No	Zero length
a	Yes	Minimum length
1234567890123456789012345678901234567890123456789012345678901234	Yes	Maximum length
12345678901234567890123456789012345678901234567890123456789012345	No	Exceeds maximum length

Now when I ask a developer how long it will take to implement just the local-part rules, he usually says no more than an hour.

Domain Tests

The rules for domains are different than for the local part. The allowed characters are as follows.

Domain-Allowable Characters		
Character	**Allowed?**	**Notes**
a through z	Yes	
.	Yes	Must have at least one Cannot be first or last character
–	Yes	
0 through 9	Yes	
Anything else	No	

A domain has a maximum of 255 characters, and periods separate the parts. The top level is the rightmost part of the domain, the second level is the next-most right part, and so forth. So for a domain with two periods, the levels are as follows:

third-level.second-level.top-level

For example, the domain "www.netobjectives.com" has three levels. The third level is "www"; the second level is "netobjectives"; and the top level is "com". Most e-mail addresses use a two level domain, such as "netobjectives.com".

There must be at least a top-level domain and a second-level domain. Most e-mail addresses use just two levels, but there is no limit to the levels within the confines of the maximum of 255 characters. Top-level domains are standard, such as "com", "org", "net", "us", "ca", "mx", "tv", and so on.

We have a few alternatives for the top-level domain part. We could have a table that lists all valid top levels, such as this:

Top-Level Domain List	
Top Level	**Valid?**
com	Yes
net	Yes
us	Yes
...and so forth for all possibilities	Yes
Anything not listed	No

But it might be work to keep this table up to date. As an alternative, we could accept top-level parts that are at least two characters and at most four characters. However, some top-level domains that might not be valid would be accepted since they passed the simple rule. For example:

Top-Level Domain Parts		
Top Level	**Valid?**	**Notes**
c	No	Too short
co	Yes	Minimum length
come	Yes	Maximum length
comet	No	Too long

The issue with having something that lists all domains is that when a new top-level domain is created, the domain list table has to be updated. However, you can ensure that there is validation for all the ones that are currently in the table. There is a generic aspect to this trade-off. The more specific you are, the less possibility there is that something invalid will sneak through. However, the less specific you are, the less often you'll have to update anything if something new that fits into the model passes through. It's your choice, based on customer input.

Here are the tests for the domain structure.

Domain Breakdown Tests					
Domain	**Top-Level Domain?**	**Second-Level Domain?**	**Third-Level Domain?**	**Valid?**	**Notes**
A.B.COM	COM	B	A	Yes	
COM				No	Must have at least one period
B.COM	COM	B		Yes	Could require two
A.B.C.COM	COM	C	B	Yes	Fourth level is A
A.B.COM.				No	Cannot end in period
.A.B.COM				No	Cannot begin with period

And, of course, we can have a test for the maximum length of the domain. That is left to an exercise for the readers.

Developers, when asked, usually suggest that it would take an hour or so to code the method that this table could be tested against.

Disallowed Domain Tests

Finally, there is a list of disallowed domains, or domains that customers cannot use. These domains permit people to send anonymous e-mails. Whether a particular application wants to disallow these domains is up to it. The following list is static. If we wanted to be able to update the list, we would create tests to verify that the list is updated correctly. This table represents the list. We could use it as an input to the program or as a test to see that every domain on it is recognized to be a disallowed domain.

Disallowed Domains	
Domain	**Reason**
Hotmail.com	Anonymous mail
Imouttogetyou.com	Spam source
Anymore ???	

When developers are asked how long coding will take (without worrying about updating the list), they usually answer around an hour.

The total time estimates from the individual pieces is usually around four hours. The original time estimate from the combined test is often two days. By breaking down the tests into smaller parts, the estimated time decreases because each part appears simpler. In addition, the smaller parts are easier to program.

Test to Ensure Connection

You can run the same tests as presented at the beginning of this chapter against a module that passes all these tests. That would ensure that all the validation functions have been tied together properly. It's possible that the test cases in this table will fail because the results in these tables differ from the actual result. In that case, you get to decide whether you should alter the underlying implementation to agree with these tests or alter these tests, because they actually do not represent e-mail address validation correctly.

Verification Test

There are two parts to the validation process. The first is to make sure that the e-mail address is properly formatted. The second is to ensure that a properly formatted e-mail address actually represents a real e-mail address. Usually, you send an e-mail to the address. If it bounces, it is invalid. The e-mail often contains either a note to reply to the message or a link to a web page that can record that the message was received. The table might look like this.

Actual E-Mail Address Check			
Sent Message	**Bounced**	**Received Reply**	**Valid?**
Yes	No	Yes	Yes
Yes	Yes	Do not care	No
Yes	No	No	Unknown
No	Do not care	Do not care	Unknown

Summary

- Break up complicated conditions into smaller conditions.
- Smaller conditions are easier to test and code.
- Validation of correct format is only part of validation.
- Validate whether a correctly formatted value represents a real value (such as e-mail address, customer ID, or CD ID).

PART VI

Appendices

This part contains business value estimation, automation examples, and exercises.

Appendix A

Other Issues

"This sentence contradicts itself—or rather—well, no, actually it doesn't!"

Douglas Hofstadter

We're done with acceptance testing. No, not really. Here are a few more issues that didn't seem to fit in the other chapters.

Context

When developing Sam's system, the requirements and tests—check-out and check-in—were created first. The existence of CDs and customers were a given. Those tests form a context for other requirements and tests. Because entities such as CDs and customers are needed, there is an implicit requirement for a means to get them into the system.[1] The existence of those entities implies that we probably need Create-Read-Update-Delete (CRUD) functionality for each of them, as shown in Chapter 12, "Development Review." Because the form of acceptance tests for this functionality is fairly consistent, they may be created by just the developer or tester and reviewed by the others. However, a higher level of business rules may need to be applied to the operations. For example, the customer may want to limit access to the operations. The CRUD functionality gives the context for these limitations. A table can show the permissions for every user type, such as:

1. This is similar to Alexander's design by context [Alexander01].

Operation Security-CD				
User Type	Create	Read	Update	Delete
Counter clerk	No	Yes	Yes	No
Inventory maintainer	Yes	Yes	Yes	Yes
Customer	No	Yes	No	No

Another approach would be to create an entity, as a CD; determine its security requirements; and then do the CRUD functionality. Then repeat the sequence for the other entities.

Customer Examples

All examples that a customer creates can become tests [Marick01]. However, not all tests are created directly from examples. Some, like the previous entity tests, are indirectly developed. If the number of tests starts to cause confusion, you can separate test cases into those that come from customer-provided examples and those created by the tester or developer to check other states or calculations.

Fuzzy Acceptance Tests

Suppose Sam wants to suggest CDs that a user might rent. This could be both a user benefit and a sales tool. It's unclear exactly what CDs should be suggested. This is the case of a story that does not have absolute results. It's fuzzy.

You can come up with algorithms for determining CDs to suggest. You can test the implementation of these algorithms to see that they come up with the expected results. That is a definitive test.

However, it's difficult, if not impossible, to determine whether the resulting suggestions help meet Sam's expectations of more sales. Whether a suggestion grabs a customer enough to rent the CD cannot be measured with the types of acceptance tests we've been describing. It's too fuzzy to test.[2] Another means for measuring the results is needed.[3]

---

2. The sequel to the TV series *Lost* may address this.
3. It may be tested during system operations. A classic way is through A/B (Champion/Challenger) testing [Decision01].

Acceptance Test Detail

A customer such as Sam may know what he wants but not be able to specify all the detail. For example, he might want the check-out to be faster than his competitors, but he doesn't have the information on how fast that is. You can still specify acceptance tests without all the detail. You can fill it in later. Or you can use comparative results as shown in Chapter 17, "Decouple with Interfaces," as the expected outcome.

Requirements and Acceptance Tests

According to the Institute for Electrical and Electronic Engineers (IEEE), a requirement is a "condition or capability needed by a user to solve a problem or achieve an objective" or a "condition or capability met or possessed by a system component to satisfy a contract, standard, specification or regulation." A requirements document usually should not include ways to implement the requirements or a specific manifestation. Requirements should be testable/verifiable, modifiable, and prioritized. They should be clear, unambiguous, and complete (at the time of implementation). Creating acceptance tests aids in creating requirements that meet these characteristics.

The "manifestation" is how a system appears either externally or internally; it is a result of design and implementation. Requirements may include constraints on manifestation. Examples of external constraints are "The user interface shall follow the corporate web standard" or "The interface to the merchant bank shall follow its standards." Internal constraints may include specific implementation or design manifestations, such as "code in Java J2EE," "use JavaServer Faces," or "employ corporate architectural framework." Internal constraints are usually instituted to reduce the number of technologies that must be maintained. You may create acceptance tests for these constraints. However, tests are often more a subjective measure of how well a manifestation meets the constraints.

> ***An Anti-Missile Acceptance Test***
>
> The military likes to buy defensive weapons, such as anti-missile missiles. This has a pretty clear acceptance tests. The anti-missile missile needs to shoot down an incoming missile. If the system fails that test, it is useless. The acceptance tests need a little more detail, such as defining the characteristics of the incoming missiles—speed, size, ballistic or non-ballistic, maneuvering, and so forth.

The tests need not specify the characteristics of the anti-missile missile that is needed—speed, maneuverability, antonymous versus guided. Nor do they need to measure the accuracy for the radar that tracks the incoming missiles.

All the implementation needs to do is to meet the overall acceptance test—can it destroy an incoming missile with the stated characteristics?

Documenting Requirements and Tests

You can use traditional applications—such as Microsoft Word, Rational Requisite Pro, or Hewlett-Packard Quality Center—for keeping requirements and associated tests. Alternatively, you can keep the requirements and tests in an easily editable online format, such as a wiki.[4] All members of the triad can update the requirements and tests in a more collaborative environment. In either case, you should link the objectives to the features, the features to the stories, and the stories to the acceptance tests. As an application becomes larger, there becomes a greater need to keep the documentation well organized and cross-referenced.

Decoupling Requirements

Decoupling tests from each other helps to decouple requirements from each other. This decoupling follows along the same lines as Larry Constantine's [Constantine02] decoupling of program modules that makes for higher quality code. Decoupled requirements are easier to test. There is always a possibility that requirements are coupled to each other. Implementing one requirement may break the implementation of another requirement unless this dependency is recognized in advance. An example of coupled requirements was given in the highly available disk storage systems in Chapter 12.

Separation of Issues

Creating customer data that matches a particular business rule can be difficult. The initial discount example in Chapter 4, "An Introductory Acceptance Test," had discount levels based on whether a customer was good or excellent. There was no specification given for what determines a good or excellent customer. Suppose that a business rule using past order history determined the customer

---

4. For example, FitNesse is a wiki version of Fit created by Robert Martin and Micah Martin [Martin01].

rating. (This rule might be simpler than Sam's rules in Chapter 13, "Simplification by Separation," for determining whether a customer could reserve.)

Without worrying about how a good/excellent customer is determined, you can easily verify the discount business rule. You can then create good, excellent, and regular customers with the history required to match the customer rating rule and run the business rule against those customers. Then you should run one or more customers through the full test (the first test variation in Chapter 4).

Tom might come up with other tests for the customer rating rule. For example, he might run it against the entire production set of customers to see how many customers matched each rating. That test could suggest to the business representative in Chapter 4 that a report of that type might come in handy.

Testing Systems with Random Events

Many systems have random events to which they respond. For example, the sequence of check-outs and check-ins can vary dramatically. You can test the functionality of the response to each event. You can also test the correct functionality of a particular sequence of events. However, the testing of any random sequence is more difficult to test. In particular, testing an implementation in which timing of the events may expose a defect is a quality attribute issue. The types of tests to uncover defects caused by errors in technical areas such as threading or locking are beyond the scope of this book. See [IBM02] for more information.

The Power of Three

The triad represents one manifestation of the power of three. The number three occurs often in the world. Jerry Weinberg suggests that you should create at least three ways to implement a requirement so that you can make a design between them. You could explore at least three forms of tables to see which one is most suitable for the customer.

The number three appears in many solutions in the non-software world. For example, there are three ways to save on transport costs if you are shipping a product. You can ship the product in larger batches; you can send it by a slower method; or you can build it closer to your customers. With at least three alternatives, you have an opportunity to compare, contrast, and pick the best or merge the three options into a better one.

Summary

- Requirements and tests form a context for other requirements and tests.
- Separation of issues and decoupling requirement makes for easier testing.

Appendix B

Estimating Business Value

"What's it worth to you?"

Anonymous

Creating software is about delivering business value. Without some measure of business value, it's hard to determine whether the software has any.

Business Value

Every feature in a system such as Sam's should have business value. Business value can come from numerous areas, such as these:

- Increased revenue (sales, royalties, fees)
- Decreased expenses
- Using fewer resources
- More efficient use of resources
- Customer satisfaction
- Product promoters/satisfiers/detractors
- Staying in business
- Avoiding risk

Business value in some areas is easy to quantify because it is straight dollars. However, in other areas, quantification is more difficult. But without some way to compare these "apples and oranges," it is hard to determine which stories should have higher priority. For example, should a story that saves $10,000 be prioritized over a story that gives customers more satisfaction?

One way to compare is to assign a relative business value to every story. The customer unit has the responsibility to assign business value. The business value does not have to be an exact measure. It's just relative. If the $10,000 savings seems to be the same as giving customers more satisfaction, the stories have the same business value.

Relative determination may be made by putting the stories on the wall one at a time. If a story has more business value than another story, place it above that story. If it has less value, put the new story below, or if about the same, on one side. If a story fits between two stories, move the stories and make space for the new one in between. For example, in Figure B.1, Story Two has the highest value, Story One and Story Three are about the same, Story Four has less than those, and Story Five has a lot less.

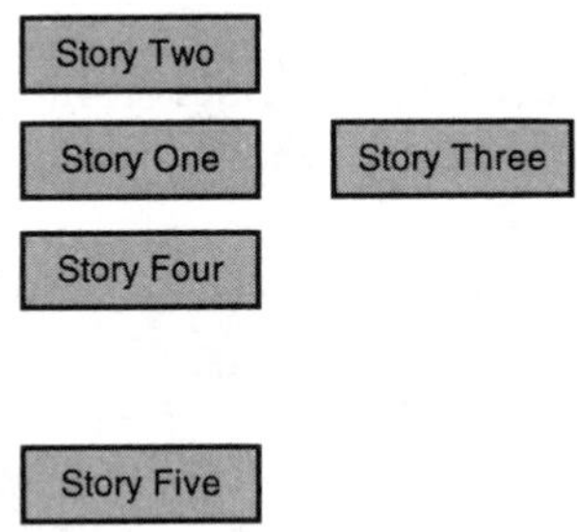

Figure B.1 *Relative Story Placement*

You can use a Fibonacci series (1, 2, 3, 5, 8, 13...) or a power-of-two (1, 2, 4, 8, 16, 32, ...) series to assign stories in each row a value (see Figure B.2). Where you start with the numbering is not important, as long as you assign the same numeric value to equivalent stories in the future.

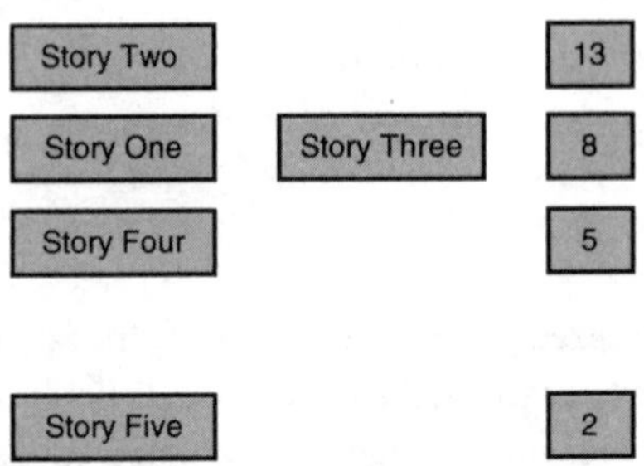

Figure B.2 *Relative Story Values*

Periodically, you can measure the cumulative business value of the delivered stories (see Figure B.3). Because the key in agility is to deliver business value quickly, such a chart provides feedback for everyone to see the project is progressing.

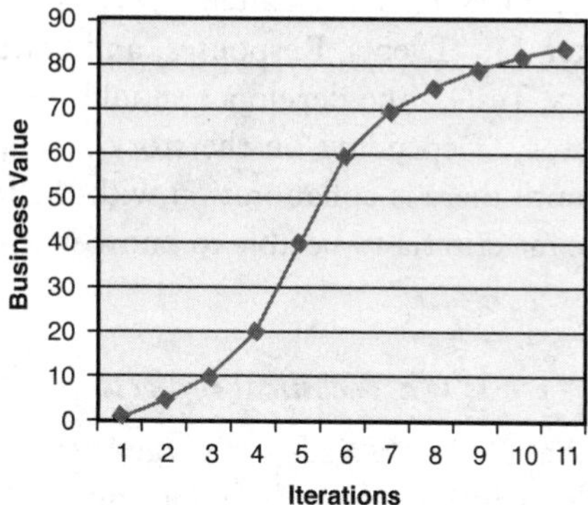

Figure B.3 *Business Value Chart*

The developer and tester unit can estimate story effort in story points using the same technique they used for business value.[1]

A story's business value estimate divided by the estimated story effort yields *rough return on investment.*[2] It is a rough guide to the relative return on investment. It can provide another value when the customer unit decides what stories to develop.

If the iterations involve approximately the same relative amount of effort, then the slope of the business value curve is roughly the return on investment. The rate of increase in business value may be lower in the initial phases of a project as either the business or technology domain is being learned. After an increase in the rate, it may slow down when stories that have a lower return on investment may be worked upon. At some point, the rate will be such that the project should be terminated. There certainly will be other potential projects that have higher return on investment.

Developer Stories

If a story is estimated to take a long time to implement, you can break it into smaller stories. However, the customer unit must be able to realize business value from one of the smaller stories. If he cannot, the smaller stories are

1. They could use story poker as described in [Shalloway01].
2. Also known as "Bang for the Buck."

developer stories; they exist to make it easier to track units of work. There may be technical value in completing a business story, such as having a new display component or a new service. When the technical value story is incorporated into a business story, the business value is credited.

As noted in Chapter 15, "Events, Responses, and States," and Chapter 16, "Developer Acceptance Tests," the developer should create an acceptance test for every developer story. Depending on the story, it may not be possible to create a specific test until there is collaboration with the implementer, but you should have at least some criteria to be able to know when the story is done.

Is It a Technical Project?

As referenced in Chapter 19, "Triads for Large Systems," some customer stories require a lot of framework development. This translates into a lot of developer stories. If you are in this situation, you have an embedded technical project. There should be a "technical product owner" who can break a customer story into "technical customer stories," each with acceptance criteria. And if the framework is vague enough, so these developer stories cannot be created, you should break this framework into its own technical project, with the customer project being a test bed for it, rather than vice versa.

Summary

- Estimate the business value for stories.
- Track the cumulative business value for delivered stories.
- If necessary, break stories into developer stories for tracking.
- The business value for a story is not achieved until all associated developer stories are completed.

Appendix C

Test Framework Examples

"There's more than one way to skin a cat."

Anonymous

There are many acceptance test frameworks. This appendix has a few examples for the application described in this book.

The Examples

These examples show how the tests in this book are expressed in different frameworks. The corresponding table-style tests are in Chapter 10, "User Story Breakup," and Chapter 11, "System Boundary." They all perform the following operations:

- Set up persistent storage with a customer and a CD.
- Check-out a CD.
- Check-in a CD with a simple rental fee computation.
- Verify the computation of the rental fee for an upcoming change in how rental fees are calculated, based on the CD category.

The Check-Out CD and Check-In CD tests are part of a workflow test. The Check-In test assumes that the CD has been checked-out. If the tests are run separately or not run in the required sequence, the setup would be performed for each test. Then the given part of the Check-In test has to ensure that the values for CD Data indicate that the CD is rented.

Fit Implementation

Here is the Fit version, which uses just the three original Fit table types. You can download the Fit version with the Java code from http://atdd.biz.

Setup

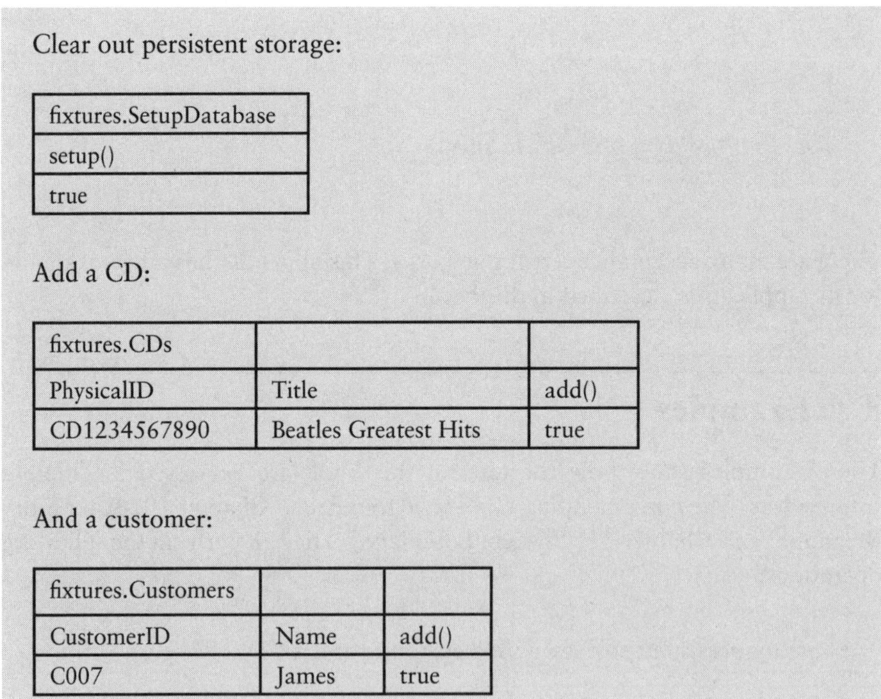

Clear out persistent storage:

fixtures.SetupDatabase
setup()
true

Add a CD:

fixtures.CDs		
PhysicalID	Title	add()
CD1234567890	Beatles Greatest Hits	true

And a customer:

fixtures.Customers		
CustomerID	Name	add()
C007	James	true

Check-Out CD

Given:

That a CD is not rented:

fixtures.CDData				
PhysicalID	Title	Rented	Customer ID	StartTime
CD1234567890	Beatles Greatest Hits	No		

And the date is:

fixtures.TestDate	
Date	set()
1/3/10 8:00 AM	true

When:

The CD is checked out:

fit.ActionFixture		
start	fixtures.CheckOut	
enter	CustomerID	C007
enter	CDID	CD1234567890
press	Rent	

Then:

The CD is recorded as rented at the checkout time.

fixtures.CDData				
PhysicalID	Title	Rented	Customer ID	StartTime
CD1234567890	Beatles Greatest Hits	Yes	C007	1/3/10 8:00 AM

And the following data is ready to be printed on the rental contract:

fixtures.RentalContractData					
CustomerID	Customer Name	PhysicalID	Title	RentalDue	check()
C007	James	CD1234567890	Beatles Greatest Hits	1/5/10 8:00 AM.	true

Check-In

Given:

At a later date:

fixtures.TestDate	
Date	set()
1/8/10 8:00 AM	true

And the CD is rented:

fixtures.CDData				
PhysicalID	Title	Rented	Customer ID	StartTime
CD1234567890	Beatles Greatest Hits	Yes	C007	1/3/10 8:00 AM

When:

The CD is checked in:

fit.ActionFixture		
start	fixtures.CheckIn	
enter	CDID	CD1234567890
press	Return	

Then:

The CD is recorded as not rented:

fixtures.CDData				
PhysicalID	Title	Rented	Customer ID	StartTime
CD1234567890	Beatles Greatest Hits	No		

And charge data is prepared for the charging system.

(This is computed at $2 per day.)

fixtures.RentalChargeData				
CustomerName	Title	Return-Date	Rental-Fee	check()
James	Beatles Greatest Hits	1/8/10 8:00 AM	$10.00	true

Category-Based Rental Fees

Given fees based on categories:

fixtures.CDCategoryValues				
Category	RentalDays	BaseRentalFee	ExtraDayRentalFee	add()
NewRelease	1	2.00	2.00	true
GoldenOldie	3	1.00	0.50	true
Regular	2	1.50	1.00	true
NotSet	2	1.00	1.00	true

When a rental is returned, the correct rental charge is computed.

fixtures.RentalFee		
Category	Rental Days	Rental Fee()
NewRelease	5	$10.00
GoldenOldie	3	$1.00
Regular	3	$2.50

Slim—Table Style

Here is the FitNesse version using Slim, created by Markus Gaertner. Some tables have been reformatted so they fit on the page. You can download this version with the Java code from http://atdd.biz.

Header

```
variable defined: TEST_SYSTEM=slim
classpath: lib/*.jar
classpath: *.jar
classpath: bin
```

import
fixtures.slim

Setup

Clear out persistent storage:

SetupDatabase
setup?
true

Add a CD:

CDs	
PhysicalID	Title
CD1234567890	Beatles Greatest Hits

And a customer:

Customers	
CustomerID	Name
C007	James

Check-Out CD

Given:

That a CD is not rented:

query:CDData				
PhysicalID	Title	Rented	Customer ID	StartTime
CD1234567890	Beatles Greatest Hits	No		

And the date is:

TestDate
Date
1/3/10 8:00 AM

When:

The CD is checked out:

script	CheckOut
CustomerID	C007
CDID	CD1234567890
Rent	

Then:

The CD is recorded as rented at the checkout time:

query:CDData				
PhysicalID	Title	Rented	Customer ID	StartTime
CD1234567890	Beatles Greatest Hits	Yes	C007	1/3/10 8:00 AM

And the following data is ready to be printed on the rental contract:

query:RentalContractData				
CustomerID	Customer Name	PhysicalID	Title	RentalDue
C007	James	CD1234567890	Beatles Greatest Hits	1/5/10 8:00 AM

Check-In

Given:

At a later date,

TestDate
Date
1/8/10 8:00 AM

And the CD is rented:

query:CDData				
PhysicalID	Title	Rented	Customer ID	StartTime
CD1234567890	Beatles Greatest Hits	Yes	C007	1/3/10 8:00 AM

When:

The CD is checked in:

script	CheckIn
CDID	CD1234567890
ensure	Return

Then:

The CD is recorded as not rented:

query:CDData				
PhysicalID	Title	Rented	Customer ID	StartTime
CD1234567890	Beatles Greatest Hits	No		

And charge data is prepared for the charging system.

(This is computed at $2 per day.)

query:RentalChargeData			
CustomerName	Title	ReturnDate	RentalFee
James	Beatles Greatest Hits	1/8/10 8:00 AM	$10.00

Category-Based Rental Fees

Given:

Fees based on categories:

CDCategoryValues			
Category	RentalDays	BaseRentalFee	ExtraDayRentalFee
NewRelease	1	2.00	2.00
GoldenOldie	3	1.00	0.50
Regular	2	1.50	1.00
NotSet	2	1.00	1.00

When :

A rental is returned, the correct rental charge is computed:

RentalFee		
Category	Rental Days	Rental Fee?
NewRelease	5	$10.00
GoldenOldie	3	$1.00
Regular	3	$2.50

Slim—Cucumber Style

Here is the Slim version created by Bob Martin. It gives an idea of what text-base tests look like. The text tests are connected to the scenario library. The scenario library in turn discusses methods written for a particular language.

Setup

```
-!|CDs|
```

CD ID	Title
CD1234567890	Beatles Greatest Hits

```
-!|Customers|
```

Customer ID	Name
C007	James

Check-Out CD

```
![ script
Given that CD1234567890 is not rented.
And it is 8:00 on 1/3/2010.
When that CD is rented by C007;
Then it should be marked as rented by C007 at 8:00 on
1/3/2010.
And the rental contract for C007 should have name: James,
CD id:CD1234567890, Title:Beatles Greatest Hits, Due
date:1/5/2010, and  time:8:00.
]!
```

Check-In CD

```
![ script
Given that CD1234567890 is recorded as rented at 8:00 on
1/8/2010 by C007
When that CD is returned at 8:00 on 1/8/2010.
Then it is recorded as not rented.
And the rental receipt for C007 should have Name: James,
Title: Beatles Greatest Hits, Return Date: 1/8/2010, Return
Time: 8:00, Fee: $10.00.
]!
]!
```

Scenario Library

scenario	Given that _ is not rented.	CD
$CD=	echo	@CD
clear rental status of	@CD	

scenario	And it is _ on _.	TIME, DATE
set time	@TIME	
set date	@DATE	

scenario	When that CD is rented by _;	CUSTOMER	
$CCUSTOMER=	echo	@CUSTOMER	
rent cd	$CD	to user	@CUSTOMER

scenario	Then it should be marked as rented by _ at _ on _.	USER, TIME, DATE				
ensure	cd	$CD	is rented to	@USER		
ensure	cd	$CD	was rented at	@TIME	on	@DATE

scenario	And the rental contract for _ should have name: _, CD id:_, Title:_, Due date:_, and time:_.	CUSTOMERID, CUSTOMERNAME, CDID, CDTITLE, DUEDATE, DUETIME									
rental contract for	@CUSTOMER ID	should have line with name	@CUSTOMER-NAME	cd id	@ CDID	title	@ CD TITLE	due date	@ DUE-DATE	due time	@ DUE TIME

scenario	Given that _ is recorded as rented at _ on _ by _.	CD, TIME, DATE, USER				
ensure	cd	@CD	is rented to	@USER		
ensure	cd	@CD	was rented at	@TIME	on	@DATE

scenario	When that CD is returned at _ on _.	RETURN_TIME, RETURN_DATE			
return cd	$CD	at	@RETURN_TIME	on	@RETURN_DATE

scenario	Then it is recorded as not rented.		
ensure	cd	$CD	is not rented.

scenario	And the rental receipt for _ should have Name: _, Title: _, Return Date: _, Return Time: _, Fee: _.	CUSTOMER, NAME, TITLE, RETURN_DATE, RETURN_TIME, FEE	
check	name on receipt for	@CUSTOMER	@NAME
check	title on receipt for	@CUSTOMER	@TITLE
check	return date on receipt for	@CUSTOMER	@RETURN_DATE
check	return time on receipt for	@CUSTOMER	@RETURN_TIME
check	fee on receipt for	@CUSTOMER	@FEE

Category-Based Rental Fees

CD Category Values			
Category	Rental Days	Base Rental Fee	Extra Day Rental Fee
NewRelease	1	2.00	2.00
GoldenOldie	3	1.00	0.50
Regular	2	1.5	1.00
NotSet	2	1.00	1.00

Rental Fee		
Category	Rental Days	Rental Fee?
NewRelease	5	10.00
GoldenOldie	3	1.00
Regular	3	2.5

Robot

Here is the Robot version created by Dale Emery. It is available at http://atdd.biz.

Setup

```
**Settings**
Resource _keywords/actions.txt
Resource _keywords/cd.txt
Resource _keywords/charge.txt
Resource _keywords/contract.txt
Resource _keywords/date.txt

**Test Cases**
Sams Add a CD
   Sams Adds CD "CD1234567890" with Title "Beatles Greatest
   Hits"

Sams Add a Customer
   Sams Adds Customer "C007" with Name "James"
```

Check-Out CD

```
Verify that the CD is Not Rented
   Verify that the Rental Status for CD "CD1234567890" is "No"

Set the Date for Rental
   Set Date "1/3/10 8:00 AM"

The Customer Rents the CD
   Customer "C007" Rents CD "CD1234567890"

Verify that Sams Recorded the Rental
   Verify that the Rental Status for CD "CD1234567890" is "Yes"
   Verify that the Rental Customer ID for CD "CD1234567890" is
   "C007"
   Verify that the Rental Start Time for CD "CD1234567890" is
   "1/3/10 8:00 AM"

Verify that the Rental Contract Describes the Rental
    Verify that the Rental Contract Customer ID Is "C007"
    Verify that the Rental Contract Customer Name is "James"
    Verify that the Rental Contract CD ID is "CD1234567890"
    Verify that the Rental Contract CD Title is "Beatles
    Greatest Hits"
    Verify that the Rental Contract Due Date is "1/5/10 8:00 AM"
```

Check-In CD

```
Set the Date for Return
   Set Date "1/8/10 8:00 AM"

The Customer Returns the CD
   Customer Returns CD "CD1234567890"

Verify that Sams Recorded the Return
   Verify that the Rental Status for CD "CD1234567890" is
      "No"

Verify that the Rental Charge Describes the Rental
    Verify that the Rental Charge Customer Name is "James"
    Verify that the Rental Charge CD Title is "Beatles
       Greatest Hits"
    Verify that the Rental Charge Return Date is "1/8/10
       8:00 AM"
    Verify that the Rental Charge Fee is "$10.00"
```

Category-Based Rental Fees

```
** Settings **
Resource _keywords/fee_structures.txt

** Test Cases **
Add Fee Structure Categories
#             Category     Rental         Base           Extra
                           Days           Rental Fee     Day Rental Fee
 Add Category NewRelease    1             2.00           2.00
 Add Category GoldenOldie  3             1.00           0.50
 Add Category Regular       2             1.50           1.00
 Add Category NotSet        2             1.00           1.00

Verify Rental Fees
#             Category     Rental Days  Total Rental Fee
 Verify Fee  NewRelease     5           $10.00
 Verify Fee  GoldenOldie    3           $1.00
 Verify Fee  Regular        3           $2.50
```

Cucumber

Here is the Cucumber version created by John Goodsen.

Check-Out CD

```
Scenario: Two-Dollar Rental for 5 Days

    Given I am "James"
    And the CD "Beatles Greatest Hits" with status "Not
       Rented"
    When I rent the CD "Beatles Greatest Hits"
    Then the rented CD status is "Rented"
    And the rented CD Checkout time is NOW
    And the CD rental contract has customer data for "James"
    And the CD rental contract has rental data for "Beatles
       Greatest Hits"
```

Check-In CD

The previous scenario continues here:

```
    When I come back "5 days" later
    And I return the CD "Beatles Greatest Hits"
    Then the rented CD status is "Not Rented"
    And the rental charge is $10
```

Category-Based Rental Fees

```
Scenario Outline: Category Based Rentals

  Given the following Category fee schedule:
    | Category       | Rental Days | Base Fee | Extra Day Fee |
    | NewRelease     | 1           | $2.00    | $2.00         |
    | GoldenOldie    | 1           | $1.00    | $0.50         |
    | Regular        | 1           | $1.50    | $1.00         |
    | Not Set        | 1           | $1.00    | $2.00         |

  When I rent a CD from the <category> for <n-days>
  Then the bill will reflect the correct rental <fee>

  Examples:
    | category       | n-days | fee    |
    | NewRelease     | 5      | $10.00 |
    | GoldenOldie    | 3      | $1.00  |
    | Regular        | 3      | $2.50  |
```

Test Frameworks

To get more information about these and other common test frameworks, Table C.1 provides links. You can find other frameworks and tools at www.opensourcetesting.org/functional.php.

Table C.1 *Some Acceptance Test Frameworks and Associated Links*

Framework	Website
JBehave	http://jbehave.org/
Fit	http://fit.c2.com/
FitNesse	http://fitnesse.org/
Easyb	http://www.easyb.org/
Cucumber	http://cukes.info
Robot	http://code.google.com/p/robotframework/
Arbiter	http://arbiter.sourceforge.net/
Concordian	http://www.concordion.org/
Selenium	http://seleniumhq.org
Watir	http://watir.com/

Summary

- Tests can be implemented in a number of frameworks.

Appendix D

Tables Everywhere

"It is tempting, if the only tool you have is a hammer, to treat everything as if it were a nail."

Abraham Maslow

"Everywhere around the world
There'll be dancing
They're dancing in the streets"

Marvin Gaye, William Stevenson, and Ivy Hunter

Tables can be used to drive manual acceptance tests and to clarify not just functional requirements, but quality attribute requirements.

User Interface Tests with Tables

In Chapter 4, "An Introductory Acceptance Test," Debbie and Tom presented the test cases used for a discount business rule. The cases were as follows.

Discount Calculation		
Item Total	Customer Rating	Discount Percentage?
$10.00	Good	0%
$10.01	Good	1%
$50.01	Good	1%
$.01	Excellent	1%
$50.00	Excellent	1%
$50.01	Excellent	5%

That chapter presented several ways to execute the test. One way was to use a test script for the user interface. No test script was presented in that chapter. You could express the test script with tables that give the information needed to run the test. For example, the following tables have the setup necessary for all the test cases and an example of the table flow for the first test case.

Compute Discount Amount

Given these items:

Items for Sale	
Item Number	Cost
I1	$10.00
I2	$10.01
I3	$50.01
I4	$.01
I5	$50.00
I6	$50.01

And these customers:

Customers		
Name	Rating	Password
George	Good	12345678
Edward	Excellent	11111111

When a customer logs on:

Logon		
Enter	Name	George
Enter	Password	12345678
Press	Submit	

And adds an item to the shopping cart:

Add Item		
Enter	Item Number	I1
Press	Add	

And checks out:

Check-Out	
Press	Check-Out

Then the discount on the order should match the percentage in the Discount table.

Order		
Item Total	Discount?	Discount Percentage? (Discount/Item Total)
$10.00	$0.0	0%

The setup for this test could be part of a standard setup for all the tests for the system. It would usually not go through the user interface but be a programmatic setup, as shown in Chapter 31, "Test Setup."

You could execute this test manually or automatically. When driven manually, the tester should be able to determine from the screens how to enter the information in this table. If not, the user interface probably has issues.

As an automatic test, each table could be associated with a script that drives the corresponding user interface screen. These scripts could then be reused in other tests that employ the same tables with the same or different data.

Requirement Tables

The original requirement for the discount was expressed in textual form. The requirement itself could be put into a table for clarification [Parnas01]. Here was the original discount business rule:

> If Customer Type is Good and Item Total is less than or equal to $10.00,
>
> Then do not give a discount,
>
> Otherwise, give a 1% discount.
>
> If Customer Type is Excellent,
>
> Then give a discount of 1% for any order.
>
> If Item Total is greater than $50.00,
>
> Then give a discount of 5%.

In table format, this rule could look like one of the following tables. The form of the table should be whatever is appropriate to the problem, as discussed in Chapter 21, "Test Presentation."

Discount Rule		
Type	**Item Total**	**Discount Percentage**
Good	<= $10.00	0%
Good	Otherwise	1%
Excellent	Any	1%
Excellent	> $50.00	5%

Or it might be like this.

Discount Rule		
Type	**Item Total**	**Discount Percentage**
Good	<= $10.00	0%
	Otherwise	1%
Excellent	Any	1%
	> $50.00	5%

The table format clarifies what was potentially unclear or ambiguous in the text. For example, the "any" of the original text statement appears more unclear when it is placed in this table. In addition, filling out the tables may bring to light suppressed premises, unstated requirements, or assumptions. In this example, having a column for Type may suggest that there are other types for which the discount rule may be applicable. For example, is there a regular customer who is neither good nor excellent? If so, there needs to be another entry, such as this one.

Type	Item Total	Discount Percentage
Regular	< $1,000	0%
	Otherwise	1%

Another Table

To be complete, the discount percentage example assumes that a customer has a rating of Good or Excellent without specifying how that rating was arrived at. The separation of concerns of what discount to apply from the determination of the customer type makes the tests for both more robust.

Similar to what was done in Chapter 13, "Simplification by Separation," here is a business rule for determining the customer rating.

Customer Rating Rule	
Total of Orders	Customer Rating
<= $1,000	Regular
>$1,000	Good
> $5,000	Excellent

When rules are expressed as tables, making up the tests often is straightforward. In this example, you simply create tests at each of the transition points between each rating.

Customer	
Total of Orders	Customer Rating?
$1,000	Regular
$1,000.01	Good
$5,000	Good
$5,000.01	Excellent

Now you need a test that shows that the Total of Orders for a particular customer is correct. Creating tables showing a set of orders for customers that total up to the amounts in this table is left as an exercise for the reader.

Quality Attribute Requirements

You can use tables to indicate the required quality attribute measures that an application must meet. For example, in Chapter 12, "Development Review," Tom showed a table for performance of check-outs.

Check-Out Performance	
Number of Simultaneous Check-Outs	Response Time Maximum (Seconds)
1	.1
10	.2
100	.3

If platform capacity was a constraint, the triad could create a resource table, such as this one.

Maximum Resources		
Number of Users	Memory in Megabytes	CPU Cycles in Million of Instructions Per Second
1	10	1
10	30	5
100	50	20

Data Tables

Can you use the customer tables as the data? Sure. You need to have a translation mechanism, but that's fairly simple. For example, Chapter 10, "User Story Breakup," had a table for rental rates.

Rental Rates			
CD Category	Rental Period Days	Rental Rate	Extra Day Rate
Regular	2	$2	$1
GoldenOldie	3	$1	$.50
HotStuff	1	$4	$6

This table could be the actual source for the rates. The program would read this table and use the values as the rates. If Sam wants to change the rates, he just changes this table and tells the program to reread it.

Summary

- You can use tables to drive user interface tests manually or automatically.
- Use tables for requirements for clarification and to expose unexpressed details.

Appendix E

Money with ATDD

"Money frees you from doing things you dislike. Since I dislike doing nearly everything, money is handy."

Groucho Marx

Developers who have been exposed to test-driven development (TDD) often come across the money problem. This problem was introduced in Kent Beck's book, *Test-Driven Development by Example* [Beck01]. An example with unit tests accompanies many of the xUnit frameworks.

The Context

An organization owns shares of stocks in different companies, and the shares are valued in different currencies. You want to add up the money in different currencies and convert it to a total in a given currency. An example of this follows, where CHF are Swiss francs.

Total Share Value			
Shares	Value Per Share	Total Value	
100	1 USD	100 USD	
50	2 CHF	100 CHF	
		150 USD	If 2 CHF = 1 USD

The Original Tests

Kent Beck's book showed how to develop the code using a test-driven approach. The tests he created using JUnit could be expressed in tables. The first table is for currency conversion and demonstrates how Swiss francs are converted in U.S. dollars.

Currency Conversion		
From Currency	To Currency	Rate
CHF	USD	2

This table is the setup for the remaining tests. Given this table, we need to be sure that we understand how to apply the rate. Do you multiply or divide Swiss francs by 2 to get U.S. dollars? Here's an example table for that.

Conversion	
From Amount	To Amount?
10 CHF	5 USD

You need to multiply an amount by the number of shares. The tests for this multiplication operation are expressed in the following table.

Currency Multiplication		
Amount	Multiplier	Product?
5 USD	2	10 USD
5 CHF	2	10 CHF

Finally, you need to add two values that may be in different currencies. There are four possibilities, and this table expresses two of them. Note that the sum is always expressed in USD.

Currency Addition		
Amount One	Amount Two	Sum?
5 USD	5 USD	10 USD
5 USD	10 CHF	10 USD

The preceding two tests demonstrate our understanding of how addition should work. The sums in the first two cases resulted in USD. Two more tests, which were not in Kent's book, may help in further understanding of the addition issue.

Currency Addition		
Amount One	**Amount Two**	**Sum?**
5 CHF	5 CHF	10 CHF ??
10 CHF	5 USD	10 USD ??

Should the sum of two amounts in Swiss francs result in Swiss francs or U.S. dollars? Should the sum always represent USD, or should it reflect the currency of the first amount? The sums in this table are shown with ?? to reflect that the answers are uncertain and need further definition.

Now we can express the desired calculation in a table. The Accumulated Value is the sum of the Total Values of the current and preceding rows.[1]

Total Share Value			
Shares	**Value Per Share**	**Total Value**	**Accumulated Value?**
100	1 USD	100 USD	100 USD
50	2 CHF	100 CHF	150 USD

These tables do not drive the details of the underlying implementation. That's what the steps in test-driven design do. These tables were derived from the JUnit tests to demonstrate to the customer how the conversion works. Let's next approach this from the opposite direction.

The Acceptance Test Approach

Acceptance tests do not indicate how to design a solution. Rather, they are a communication mechanism between the customer, developer, and tester. Let's start by stating the problem as a user story: "As an accountant, I need to convert amounts that are in different currencies to a total in a common currency." The role of the accountant is the customer with whom we can collaborate in developing acceptance tests.

Our initial collaboration reveals that currencies are converted into other currencies by applying exchange rates. These exchange rates are time dependent, so we need a context for the conversion. In the context of accounting, the user says that the exchange rates for this conversion will be fixed at an instance of

1. This table has a second row with values that do not appear in the original tests.

time. He wants all conversions in the reports he is preparing to use the same exchange rates. These rates will be those as of midnight on the day prior to the report being prepared.

Decoupling the issue of conversion from the issue of time-dependent exchange rates allows for easier testing. We can create a separate set of tests for the exchange rates.

We start by making up an exchange rate table. The values in the table are representative of the actual conversion rates. In real life, the conversions may use more digits after the decimal places. They are shown with two decimal digits to keep the example simple.

Conversion Rates			
Currency To/ Currency From	EUR	USD	CHF
EUR	1.0	1.51	.91
USD	.67	1.0	.73
CHF	1.1	1.35	1.0

Here are examples of how to convert from one currency to another.

Currency Conversion		
Input	Convert to Currency	Converted Amount
5 EUR	USD	7.55 USD
7.55 USD	EUR	5.06 EUR ??

The accountant came up with the first example to show what he meant by conversion. The developer created the second example. It shows that the reverse conversion produces a different value than the original conversion. This inconsistency causes a discussion, because the conversion is not symmetric. Is that what is desired? Should there be separate exchange rates for USD to EUR and EUR to USD? Or should one rate be just the inverse of the other rate? Will the non-symmetry cause problems? It's time for clarification. This is a fundamental issue in the conversion that can affect the rest of the situation. Let's assume that the accountant decided that the conversion should be symmetric, so we'll rewrite the setup and the tests.

Conversion Rates			
Currency To/Currency From	EUR	USD	CHF
EUR	1.0	1.51	.91
USD	X	1.0	.73
CHF	X	X	1.0

Here are the corresponding examples.

Currency Conversion		
Input	Convert to Currency	Converted Amount?
5 EUR	USD	7.55 USD
7.55 USD	EUR	5 EUR

The tester suggests a few more examples that come to mind, all dealing with precision. When converting from USD to EUR, the result turns out to have a large number of digits after the decimal point. The ... shows that the digits do not just stop at 2. What should be done with these digits?

Currency Conversion		
Input	Convert to Currency	Converted Amount?
5.01 EUR	USD	7.5651 USD ??
7.57 USD	EUR	5.0132... EUR??

These examples bring up a discussion of round-off. How should round-off be handled? Should it be tracked by putting the round-off into a separate account (such as the developer's 401K plan)? Should it be accounted for by some report output? Should the amounts be rounded up or rounded down? Or is the direction of rounding based on certain conditions? There are certain decisions that can be delayed, such as what to do with the round-off. The tests for now can at least ensure that round-off is calculated properly.

Currency Conversion Round-Off			
Input	Convert to Currency	Converted Amount?	Round-Off?
5.01 EUR	USD	7.57 USD	.0049 USD
7.57 USD	EUR	5.01 EUR	–.32... EUR

Next to be developed were a few examples of conversion for multiple currencies. The examples looked like this.

Currency Conversion with Round-Off			
Input	Convert to Currency	Converted Amount?	Round-Off?
5 EUR + 10 USD	USD	17.55 USD	.0 USD
5 EUR + 7.57 USD	EUR	10.01 EUR	–.32... EUR
5.01 EUR + 5.01 EUR	USD	15.14 USD ??	.0098 USD ??

The accountant gave the first two examples. The developer wrote the last one. It demonstrates an outstanding issue. Should the amounts be individually converted, or should amounts be totaled before conversion? If the former, the values in the table are correct. If the latter, the table should be corrected to be as follows.

Input	Convert to Currency	Converted Amount?	Round-Off?
5.01 EUR + 5.01 EUR	USD	15.13 USD	.0002 USD

The tester comes up with one more example. This one asks the question of how to handle the round-offs between two currencies. Should the converted values be added prior to round-off or afterward? This test needs a second example to show that the underlying implementation does things correctly.

Input	Convert to Currency	Converted Amount?	Round-Off?
5.01 EUR + 5.01 CHF	USD	14.42 USD	.0019... USD

Now the developer understands the overall picture of the problem. She can pick one of the acceptance tests and use that as the starting point for a test-driven design. Unit tests, some of which may be derived from these examples, can check that the classes and methods are giving the desired behavior, such as the round-off. Passing these acceptance tests demonstrates to the accountant that the conversion module as a whole performs as desired.

Summary

- You can use acceptance tests to derive unit tests.

Appendix F

Exercises

"Arithmetic is where the answer is right and everything is nice and you can look out of the window and see the blue sky—or the answer is wrong and you have to start over and try again and see how it comes out this time."

Carl Sandburg

"You can't become a snowboarder by just reading about it."

Anonymous

To round out the exercises that are suggested throughout this book, here are some additional exercises for you. The calculator test exercise gives you an opportunity to create acceptance tests for an existing system and then use these tests as the basis for creating a new implementation of that system. The other exercises are to create detailed requirements and acceptance tests.

Calculator

Almost everyone has used a calculator. In some elementary schools, students are required to demonstrate proficiency with one. The type of calculator for which the tests are being written is a simple one with a single memory for a number, such as the one available on the Windows operating system (see Figure F.1).

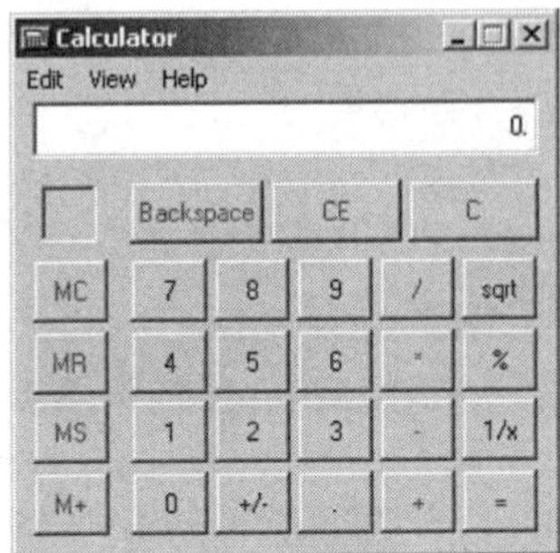

Figure F.1 *Calculator*

The table could specify a single input key, with the conditions of the previous step. Note that MS is "memory save" and MR is "memory recall."

Calculator				
Current			New	
Memory	Display	Input Key	Display?	Memory?
		2	2	
	2	+	2	
	2	3	3	
	3	1	31	
	31	=	33	
		MS	33	33

Alternatively, the table could state the sequence of steps.

Calculator		
Input	Display?	Memory?
2 + 31 =	33	
2 + 31 = MS	33	33

For the memory save and recall, you could create even more tests.

Calculator			
Memory	Input	Display?	Memory?
NA	2 + 3 =	5	
NA	2 + 3 = MS	5	5
5	2 + MR =	7	5

Now you apply a number of inputs to see what the results might be, such as the following.

Calculator			
Memory	Input	Display?	Memory?
NA	2 + + 3 =	5	
NA	2 + – 3 =	-1	
NA	2 – – 3 =	???	
NA	2 / – 3 =	???	

Create Some Tests

Because you have an existing application (a calculator), check the results of these inputs on that application. The 2 – – 3 test could produce –1 or 5, depending on how your existing calculator works. Change the results in the examples to match that calculator. Now give the examples to a developer, and have him create a program that passes these acceptance tests. Do you need a user interface? How much effort would it be to run the tests with a user interface than without one?

If the developer feels that the program is too large to complete easily, you can break up the acceptance tests. One way to do that is to separate tests involving the memory from the other tests. The memory is a separable feature. Another way is to have tests that specify only series of input that are "normal." That is, you would leave out sequences that had two symbols immediately following each other, such as "/–".

After the developer creates a program that passes the test as originally specified, change the result so that the other answer is expected. The acceptance test should fail. The developer now needs to alter the program to create the expected result. When the developer does so, do any other tests fail? Do you have redundant tests? Are all tests consistent?

More Exercises

Here are some other exercises. Create detailed requirements and the corresponding acceptance tests for each. Answers will be posted on atdd.biz.

Sam's CD Rental

As the inventory manager, I want to get a list of all rentals for a CD so I can see whether it is popular.

As the owner, I want to see a record of all activities, such as when CDs are checked-out and checked-in. This helps me determine whether I need to hire more staff.

As an auditor, I need to be able to keep track of all money transfers for Sam's CD Rental.

As a customer, I want to search for CDs by title, artist, or song.

As a customer, I also want to search for songs whose lengths fall between a minimum and maximum length expressed in seconds.

Triangle

A program inputs three values representing the lengths of the sides of a triangle. The program is to determine whether the triangle is scalene, isosceles, or equilateral [Myers01].

File Copying Exercise

A module is being written for an operating system to copy a file from one directory to another. The desired user interface follows.

For example:

```
copy some_directory another_directory a_file
```

The happy path includes the conditions where some_directory and another_directory exist and a_file exists in some_directory. There are many other conditions, such as another_directory does not exist.

List these conditions and create other cases.

References

"And now for the rest of the story."

Paul Harvey

Referenced

The following books and websites were referenced in this book.

[AAA01] http://www.arrangeactassert.com/why-and-what-is-arrange-act-assert/.

[ABA01] http://www.abajournal.com/news/article/judge_calls_for_end_to_lawyers_obfuscation_suits_madness/.

[Adzic01] Adzic, Gojko. *Bridging the Communication Gap: Specification by Example and Agile Acceptance Testing*. Neuri Limited, 2009.

[Adzic02] Adzic, Gojko. *Test Driven .NET Development with FitNesse*. Neuri Limited, 2008. Available at http://fitnesse.s3.amazonaws.com/tdd_net_with_fitnesse.pdf.

[Agile01] http://agilemanifesto.org/principles.html.

[Alexander01] Alexander, Christopher, Sara Ishikawa, and Murray Silverstein. *A Pattern Language: Towns, Buildings, Construction*. Oxford University Press, 1977.

[Ambler01] Ambler, Scott W. *Agile Modeling: Effective Practices for eXtreme Programming and the Unified Process*. Wiley, 2002.

[Anderson01] Anderson, David J. *Kanban*. Blue Hole Press, 2010.

[Answers01] http://www.answers.com/topic/acceptance-test.

[Answers02] http://www.answers.com/topic/system-test.

[Aston01] Meszaros, Gerard, and Janice Aston. "Adding Usability Testing to an Agile Project." Agile Conference, 2006.

[Bach01] Bach, James. "Exploratory Testing Explained". http://www.satisfice.com/articles/et-article.pdf.

[Beck01] Beck, Kent. *Test Driven Development: By Example*. Addison-Wesley Professional, 2002.

[Beust01] Beust, Cedric, and Hani Suleiman. *Next Generation Java Testing: TestNG and Advanced Concepts*. Addison-Wesley Professional, 2007.

[Chelimsky01] Chelimsky, David, Dave Astels, Zach Dennis, Aslak Hellesøy, Bryan Helmkamp, and Dan North. *The RSpec Book: Behaviour Driven Development with RSpec, Cucumber, and Friends*. The Pragmatic Bookshelf.

[Cimperman01] Cimperman, Rob. *UAT Defined: A Guide to Practical User Acceptance Testing*. Addison-Wesley Professional, 2006.

[Cockburn01] Cockburn, Alistair. *Agile Software Development: The Cooperative Game*. Addison-Wesley Professional, 2006.

[Cockburn02] Cockburn, Alistair. *Writing Effective Use Cases*. Addison-Wesley Professional, 2000.

[Cohn01] Cohn, Mike. *Agile Estimating and Planning*. Prentice Hall, 2005.

[Cohn02] Cohn, Mike. *User Stories Applied: For Agile Software Development*. Addison-Wesley Professional, 2004.

[Constantine01] Constantine, Larry, and Lucy Lockwood. A.D. *Software for Use: A Practical Guide to the Models and Methods of Usage-Centered Design*. Addison-Wesley Professional, 1999.

[Constantine02] Stevens, W., G. Myers, and L. Constantine. "Structured Design". IBM Systems Journal, 13 (2), 115–139, 1974.

[Cooper01] Cooper, Alan. *The Inmates Are Running the Asylum: Why High Tech Products Drive Us Crazy and How to Restore the Sanity*. Sams, 2004.

[Coplien01] Bjørnvig, Gertrud, James Coplien, and Neil Harrison. "A Story about User Stories and Test-Driven Development". Better Software 9(11), November 2007, ff. 34. http://www.rbcs-us.com/images/documents/User-Stories-and-Test-Driven-Development.pdf.

[Craig01] Mackinnon, Tim, Steve Freeman, and Philip Craig. "EndoTesting: Unit Testing with Mock Objects". http://www.mockobjects.com/files/endotesting.pdf.

[Crispin01] http://lisacrispin.com/wordpress/tag/power-of-three/.

[Crispin02] Crispin, Lisa, and Janet Gregory. *Agile Testing: A Practical Guide for Testers and Agile Teams*. Addison-Wesley Professional, 2009.

[Cunningham01] Mugridge, R., and W. Cunningham. *Fit for Developing Software: Framework for Integrated Tests*. Prentice Hall PTR, 2005.

[Cunningham02] http://fit.c2.com/wiki.cgi?FrameworkHistory.

[Cunningham03] http://c2.com/wikisym2007/pnsqc2007.pdf.

[Decision01] http://www.decisionanalyticsblog.experian.com/blog/collections/0/0/championchallenger-collections-strategy-testing.

[Devx01] http://www.devx.com/vmspecialreport/Article/30410.

[DrDobbs01] http://www.drdobbs.com/architecture-and-design/187900423;?pgno=3.

[EATDD01] http://ase.cpsc.ucalgary.ca/index.php/EATDD/Home.

[Eckstein01] Eckstein, Jutta. *Agile Software Development with Distributed Teams: Staying Agile in a Global World*. Dorset House Publishing Company, Incorporated, 2010.

[Evans01] Evans, Eric. *Domain-Driven Design: Tackling Complexity in the Heart of Software*. Addison-Wesley Professional, 2003.

[Fast01] http://www.fastcompany.com/blog/charles-fishman/usair-asks-fliers-%E2%80%98can-we-get-hallelujah%E2%80%99.

[Faught01] http://sadekdrobi.com/.

[Feathers01] Feathers, Michael. *Working Effectively with Legacy Code*. Prentice Hall, 2004.

[Fowler01] Fowler, Martin. *UML Distilled: A Brief Guide to the Standard Object Modeling Language*. Addison-Wesley Professional, 2003.

[Gottesdiener01] Gottesdiener, Ellen. *Requirements by Collaboration: Workshops for Defining Needs*. Addison-Wesley Professional, 2002.

[Gottesdiener02] http://ebgconsulting.com/articles.php#wkshp.

[Gottesdiener03] http://ebgconsulting.com/facassets.php.

[Hillside01] http://www.hillside.net/plop/plop2003/Papers/Brown-mock-objects.pdf.

[Hunt01] Hunt, Andrew, and Dave Thomas. *The Pragmatic Programmer: From Journeyman to Master*. Addison-Wesley Professional, 1999.

[Hussman01] Hussman, David. *Practical Agility*. The Pragmatic Bookshelf (in production 2010).

[IBM01] http://publib.boulder.ibm.com/infocenter/rbhelp/v6r3/index.jsp?topic=/com.ibm.redbrick.doc6.3/wag/wag29.htm.

[IBM02] http://publib.boulder.ibm.com/infocenter/iseries/v5r3/index.jsp?topic=/rzahw/rzahwdetco.htm.

[IEFF01] http://www.ietf.org/rfc/rfc2822.txt.

[III01] http://www.drdobbs.com/architecture-and-de-sign/184414956.

[Isolum01] http://lsolum.typepad.com/copyfutures/2004/10/a_lesson_from_j.html.

[Jefferies01] http://xprogramming.com/articles/expcardconversationconfirmation/.

[Kaner01] Kaner, Cem, Jack Falk, and Hung Q. Nguyen. *Testing Computer Software*. Wiley, 1999.

[Kerievsky01] http://industriallogic.com/papers/storytest.pdf.

[Koskela01] http://www.methodsandtools.com/archive/archive.php?id=72.

[Koskela02] Koskela, Lasse. *Test Driven: TDD and Acceptance TDD for Java Developers*. Manning Publications, 2007.

[Larman01] Larman, Craig, and Bas Vodde. *Scaling Lean & Agile Development: Thinking and Organizational Tools for Large-Scale Scrum*. Addison-Wesley Professional, 2008.

[Larman02] Larman, Craig, and Bas Vodde. *Practices for Scaling Lean & Agile Development: Large, Multisite, and Offshore Product Development with Large-Scale Scrum*. Addison-Wesley Professional, 2010.

[Marick01] http://www.exampler.com/.

[Martin01] http://fitnesse.org.

[Martin02] http://butunclebob.com/FitNesse.UserGuide.FitLibraryUserGuide.DoFixture.

[Martin03] http://fitnesse.org/FitNesse.UserGuide.SliM.

[Melnik01] Martin, Robert C., and Grigori Melnik. "Tests and Requirements, Requirements and Tests: A Möbius Strip". IEEE_Software Vol. 25, No. 1. January/February 2008, at http://www.gmelnik.com/papers/IEEE_Software_Moebius_GMelnik_RMartin.pdf.

[Melnik02] Melnik, G., F. Maurer, and M. Chiasson. "Executable Acceptance Tests for Communicating Business Requirements: Customer Perspective". Agile Conference, 2006.

[Melnik03] Melnik, Grigori, and Frank Maurer. "Multiple Perspectives on Executable Acceptance Test-Driven Development". http://www.springerlink.com/content/34w2q2561k471175/.

[Meszaros01] Meszaros, Gerard. *xUnit Test Patterns: Refactoring Test Code*. Addison-Wesley, 2007.

[Meszaros02] Melnik, Grigori, Jon Bach, and Gerard Meszaros. "Acceptance Test Engineering Guide, Vol. I". http://testingguidance.codeplex.com.

[Mindtools01] http://www.mindtools.com/CommSkll/ActiveListening.htm.

[Myers01] Myers, Glenford J. *The Art of Software Testing*. Wiley, 2004.

[Nielsen01] Nielsen, Jakob. *Usability Engineering*. Morgan Kaufmann, 1993.

[OSHA01] http://www.osha.gov/dts/osta/otm/noise/health_effects/physics.html.

[Parnas01] http://www.cs.iastate.edu/~colloq/new/David_Parnas_slides.pdf.

[Patton01] http://www.agileproductdesign.com/presentations/user_story_mapping/index.html.

[Pettichord01] Kaner, Clem, James Bach, and Bret Pettichord. *Lessons Learned in Software Testing*. Wiley, 2001.

[Pichler01] Pichler, Roman. *Agile Product Management with Scrum: Creating Products that Customers Love*. Addison-Wesley Professional, 2010.

[Poppendieck01] http://www.poppendieck.com/design.htm.

[Poppendieck02] Poppendieck, Mary, and Tom Poppendieck. *Implementing Lean Software Development: From Concept to Cash*. Addison-Wesley Professional, 2006.

[Poppendieck03] http://www.poppendieck.com/papers/LeanThinking.pdf.

[Poppendieck04] http://www.poppendieck.com/pdfs/Lean_Software_Development.pdf.

[Project01] http://www.projectsmart.co.uk/smart-goals.html.

[Pugh01] Pugh, Ken. *Interface-Oriented Design*. Pragmatic Bookshelf, 2006.

[Pugh02] Pugh, Ken. *Prefactoring—Extreme Abstraction, Extreme Separation, Extreme Readability*. O'Reilly Media, 2005.

[Reinertsen01] Reinertsen, Donald G. *The Principles of Product Development Flow: Second Generation Lean Product Development*. Celeritas Publishing, 2009.

[Riordan01] Riordan, Rebecca M. *Heads First Ajax*. O'Reilly Media, 2008

[Rising01] Manns, Mary Lynn, and Linda Rising. *Fearless Change: Patterns for Introducing New Ideas*. Addison-Wesley Professional, 2008.

[Rup01] http://rup.hops-fp6.org/process/artifact/ar_tstatmarc.htm.

[Satir01] http://www.satirworkshops.com/files/satirchangemodel.pdf.

[Security01] https://www.pcisecuritystandards.org/security_standards/pci_dss.shtml.

[Security02] http://www.securiteam.com/securityreviews/5DP0N1P76E.html.

[Shalloway01] Shalloway, Alan, James R. Trott, and Guy Beaver. *Lean-Agile Software Development: Achieving Enterprise Agility*. Addison-Wesley Professional, 2009.

[Sutherland01] http://jeffsutherland.com/JakobsenScrumCMMIGoingfromGoodtoGreatAgile2009.pdf.

[Systems01] http://www.systems-thinking.org/rca/rootca.htm.

[Tabaka01] Tabaka, Jean. *Collaboration Explained: Facilitation Skills for Software Project Leaders*. Addison-Wesley Professional, 2006.

[Tavares01] http://www.tavaresstudios.com.

[Usability01] http://www.usabilitynet.org/trump/documents/Suschapt.doc.

[Vinoleo01] http://vinoleoinc.com/Documents/How%20to%20create%20your%20Project%20Charter.pdf.

[Wake02] http://xp123.com/xplor/xp0308/.

[Weinberg01] Gause, Donald C., and Gerald M. Weinberg. *Exploring Requirements: Quality Before Design*. Dorset House Publishing Company, 1989.

[Whittaker01] Whittaker, James A. *Exploratory Software Testing: Tips, Tricks, Tours, and Techniques to Guide Test Design*. Addison-Wesley Professional.

[Wiegers03] Wiegers, Karl. Practical *Project Initiation: A Handbook with Tools*. Microsoft Press, 2007.

[Wiegers04] http://www.projectinitiation.com/process_assets/Project%20Charter%20Template.doc.

[Wiki01] http://en.wikipedia.org/wiki/N-body_problem.

[Wiki02] http://en.wikipedia.org/wiki/Four_color_theorem.

[Wiki03] http://en.wikipedia.org/wiki/Software_architect.

[Wiki04] http://en.wikipedia.org/wiki/Smoke_test.

[Wiki05] http://en.wikipedia.org/wiki/Myers-Briggs_Type_Indicator.

[Wiki06] http://en.wikipedia.org/wiki/Unified_Modeling_Language.

[Wiki07] http://en.wikipedia.org/wiki/Root_cause_analysis.
[Wiki08] http://en.wikipedia.org/wiki/Sound_level_meter.
[Wiki09] http://en.wikipedia.org/wiki/Five_whys.
[Wiki10] http://en.wikipedia.org/wiki/Broken_windows_theory.

References

Following are other books involved with aspects and topics related to acceptance test-driven development, including requirements, testing, and process.

[Astels01] Astels, David. *Test-Driven Development, A Practical Guide*. Prentice Hall, 2003.

[Bain01] Bain, Scott L. Emergent Design: *The Evolutionary Nature of Professional Software Development*. Addison-Wesley Professional, 2008.

[Copeland01] Copeland, Lee. *A Practitioner's Guide to Software Test Design*. Artech House Publishers, 2004.

[Coplien02] Bjørnvig, Gertrud, James Coplien, and Neil Harrison. "Chapter 2: A Story about User Stories and Test-Driven Development, into the Field." Better Software 9(12), December 2007, ff. 32.

[Coplien03] Coplien, James O., and Neil B. Harrison. *Organizational Patterns of Agile Software Development*. Prentice Hall, 2004.

[Craig02] Craig, Rick, and Stefan P. Jaskiel. *Systematic Software Testing*. Artech House, 2002.

[Demarco01] Demarco, Tom, Peter Hruschka, Tim Lister, and Suzanne Robertson. *Adrenaline Junkies and Template Zombies: Understanding Patterns of Project Behavior*. Dorset House, 2008.

[DeMarco02] DeMarco, Tom, and Timothy Lister. *Waltzing with Bears: Managing Risk on Software Projects*. Dorset House Publishing Company, Incorporated, 2003.

[Denne01] Denne, Mark, and Jane Cleland-Huang. *Software by Numbers: Low-Risk, High-Return Development*. Prentice Hall, 2003.

[Elssamadisy01] Elssamadisy, Amr. *Agile Adoption Patterns: A Roadmap to Organizational Success*. Addison-Wesley Professional, 2008.

[Elssamadisy02] Elssamadisy, Amr. "Test-Driven Requirements" Chapter 44 in *Agile Adoption Patterns: A Roadmap to Organizational Success*. Addison-Wesley Professional, 2008.

[Fowler02] Fowler, Martin. *Patterns of Enterprise Application Architecture*. Addison-Wesley Professional, 2002.

[Galen01] Galen, Robert. *Software Endgames: Eliminating Defects, Controlling Change, and the Countdown to On-Time Delivery*. Dorset House Publishing Company, Incorporated, 2004.

[Graham01] Fewster, Mark, and Dorothy Graham. *Software Test Automation.* Addison-Wesley, 1999.

[Graham02] Graham, Dorothy, Erik Van Veenendaal, Isabel Evans, and Rex Black. *Foundations of Software Testing.* Cengage Learning, 2008.

[Grenning01] Grenning, James W. *Test Driven Development for Embedded C.* Pragmatic Bookshelf, 2010.

[Highsmith01] Highsmith, Jim. *Agile Software Development Ecosystems.* Addison-Wesley Professional, 2002.

[Hiranabe01] Hiranabe, Kenji. Kanban. "Applied to Software Development: From Agile to Lean". http://www.infoq.com/articles/hiranabe-lean-agile-kanban.

[Janzen01] Janzen and Saledian. "Does Test-Driven Development Really Improve Software Design Quality?" IEEE Software 25(2), March/April 2008, pp.77–84.

[Jefferies02] Jeffries, Ron. *Extreme Programming Installed.* Addison-Wesley Professional, 2000.

[Kerievsky02] Kerievsky, Joshua. *Refactoring to Patterns.* Addison-Wesley Professional, 2004.

[Kerth01] Kerth, Norman L. Project Retrospectives: *A Handbook for Team Reviews*, Dorset House Publishing Company, 2001.

[Ladas01] Ladas, Corey. *Scrumban—Essays on Kanban Systems for Lean Software Development.* Modus Cooperandi Press, 2009.

[Marick02] Marick, Brian. *The Craft of Software Testing: Subsystems Testing Including Object-Based and Object-Oriented Testing*, Prentice Hall, 1994.

[Osherove01] Osherove, Roy. *The Art of Unit Testing: With Examples in .Net.* Manning Publications, 2009.

[Pardee01] Pardee, William. *To Satisfy & Delight Your Customer: How to Manage for Customer Value.* Dorset House Publishing Company, Incorporated, 1996.

[Poppendieck05] Poppendieck, Mary, and Tom Poppendieck. *Lean Software Development: An Agile Toolkit.* Addison-Wesley Professional, 2003.

[Poppendieck06] Poppendieck, Mary, and Tom Poppendieck. *Leading Lean Software Development: Results Are Not the Point.* Addison-Wesley Professional, 2009.

[Rainsberger01] Rainsberger, J. B. *JUnit Recipes: Practical Methods for Programmer Testing.* Manning Publications, 2004.

[Richardson01] Richardson, Jared, and William A. Gwaltney. *Ship It! A Practical Guide to Successful Software Projects.* Pragmatic Bookshelf, 2005.

[Rothman01] Rothman, Johanna. *Hiring the Best Knowledge Workers, Techies & Nerds: The Secrets & Science of Hiring Technical People.* Dorset House Publishing Company, Incorporated, 2004.

[Shore01] Shore, James, and Shane Warden. *The Art of Agile Development.* O'Reilly Media, 2007.

[Siniaalto01] Siniaalto, M., and P. Abrahamsson. *Comparative Case Study on the Effect of Test-Driven Development on Program Design and Test Coverage.* ESEM 2007.

[Siniaalto02] Siniaalto, M., and P. Abrahamsson. "Does Test-Driven Development Improve the Program Code? Alarming Results from a Comparative Case Study". Proceedings of Cee-Set 2007, 10–12 October, 2007, Poznan, Poland.

[Stott01] Stott, Will, and James W. Newkirk. *Using FIT Inside Visual Studio Team System: Better Software Development for Agile Teams.* Addison-Wesley Professional, 2007.

[Wake01] Wake, William C. *Extreme Programming Explored.* Addison-Wesley Professional, 2001.

[Weinberg02] Weinberg, Gerald M. *Perfect Software: And Other Illusions About Testing.* Dorset House, 2008.

[Whittaker02] Whittaker, James A. *How to Break Software: A Practical Guide to Testing.* Addison-Wesley Professional, 2002.

[Wiegers01] Wiegers, Karl. *Software Requirements, 2nd Edition.* Microsoft Press, 2003.

[Wiegers02] Wiegers, Karl. *More About Software Requirements: Thorny Issues and Practical Advice.* Microsoft Press, 2006.

[Williams01] George, Boby, and Laurie Williams. "An Initial Investigation of Test Driven Development in Industry." Proceedings of the 2003 ACM symposium on Applied computing table of contents, 2003.

[Williams02] Williams, Laurie, and Robert Kessler. *Pair Programming Illuminated.* Addison-Wesley Professional, 2002.

Epilogue

"All good things must come to an end."

English Proverb

Acceptance test-driven development (ATDD) has been presented through stories and examples. Here is the final word.

Who, What, When, Where, Why, and How

The Preface stated the context of this book and the questions to be answered. Here are the questions again, and if you skipped the entire book, here are the answers.

- **Who**—The triad—customer, developer, and tester communicating and collaborating
- **What**—Acceptance criteria for projects and features, acceptance tests for stories
- **When**—Prior to implementation—either in the iteration before or up to one second before, depending on your environment
- **Where**—Created in a joint meeting, run as part of the build process
- **Why**—To effectively build high-quality software and to cut down the amount of rework
- **How**—In face-to-face discussions, using Given/When/Then and examples

So What Else Is There?

Feel free to write to me at ken.pugh@netobjectives.com if you have comments or questions. Let me know what topics you would like covered in more depth. With the web world, it's easier to increase the amount of information, so check out atdd.biz. If your triad needs an in-person run-through of creating acceptance tests, Net Objectives offers courses and coaching. (www.netobjectives.com)

Legal Notice

Based on Sam's growing business, some readers may decide they want to open a CD rental store. For information regarding the legality of renting CDs in the United States, please see 17 USC 109 (b)(1)(A). In Japan, it is legal to have a licensed CD rental store that pays royalties to JASRAC (Japanese Society for Rights of Authors Composers and Publishers) [Isolum01].

Experiences of Others

I asked people to describe how ATDD was introduced to their teams and the benefits it produced. Here are their stories.

Rework Down from 60% to 20%

One team I have worked with was asked how much of their time they would estimate they spend on reworking features. Their estimate was about 60%. Having seen this situation a few times, I have found a method that seems to work with some pretty amazing results. Using FitNesse and Selenium, development items are written as executable specifications. The business analyst, tester, and developer define the feature in a FitNesse wiki and run automated tests on the feature from the same place. Using the Slim Scenario tables, features are written as English-readable sentences and then translated into commands below the covers. This makes the tests readable by the less technical members of the team so they can feel confident that they know what is being tested.

The business analyst types up what the feature should do. The developer and tester ask questions to define the scope, and the answers are added to the wiki. The tester translates the English sentences into Selenium scripts, and the developer starts to write unit tests. Once the Selenium scripts are complete, the developer runs them to check on the development process. The customer can run the tests at any time to see how much has been completed. After [the team members] started working through features this way, they estimated that their time spent on rework decreased to about 20%.

Dawn Cannan, agile tester
www.passionatetester.com/

Workflows Working First Time

I have experience with acceptance test-driven development on automated workflows. My team works on automated workflows for a European Mobile virtual network operator. When I started to coach/manage this team, the challenge was to keep (regain) the control on the software. With unit testing and then test-driven development, we took the control of the code base and we started to refactor and redesign workflow's actions.

After that appeared our most difficult challenge. Individually, each action worked fine, but each time the development team or the QA team tested workflows from the beginning to the end, we found a lot of defects.

To solve that problem, we wrote some acceptance tests with Junit. It was a difficult job because workflows generate many outputs (messages, database change, web services calls, etc.) and need many inputs. The first results were not convincing: We added a lot of mocks and fakes and so missed a lot of little defects. The tests were difficult to understand and hard to maintain.

Then we decided to use Concordion and reduce the use of mocks and fakes. We sold the idea to the QA team, the CIO, and the business people. On the following project, we built a proof of concept on some new workflows to convince people that the time required to build the tests was valuable. It was a technical success: All the workflows covered by acceptance testing worked the first time, and the defects that were found were just special cases not covered by the tests.

We generalized the use of acceptance test-driven development to other parts of the information system. For us, that was a success because we reduced the number of defects delivered to QA, and we could start to work on the subject of continuous delivery. Our only regret is that, for the moment, the tests are prepared and used only by QA and the development team, not the business people. Perhaps the root cause of this issue is that we use the acceptances tests to check a lot of details that are not directly useful to the business people or that the most useful client for our automated workflow is our QA team.

Gabriel Le Van
Paris, France

Little Room for Miscommunication

I helped develop the Visual Hospital Touchscreen Solution for energizedwork. (See http://lean-health.blogspot.com/2010/02/visual-hospital-system.html for details.) The approach we took was:

1. Quality assurance (QA) and product owner prepare the stories.
2. QA pair with the developers at the start of a story, breaking the acceptance criteria up into slices and agreeing the probable order in which the slices will be delivered. We keep our stories small—2 days or less. There may be around eight acceptance criteria per story and usually one or two acceptance criteria per slice.
3. QA and developers jointly write the automated acceptance tests for the first slice. We use Selenium IDE with a custom extension enabling Given-When-Then style tests, e.g.

   ```
   given a male, cardiovascular patient called Joe Bloggs in
   Bed05, Holborn
   when I tap Joe's discharge icon
   then the discharge dialog should appear
   ```

   We feel using Selenium IDE creates less of a barrier to entry for the QA and makes it easier to write the tests. Using the IDE, you can easily step forward and backward through a test or jump halfway through it. The drawback of the IDE is that it's harder to set up test data, and comparatively slow. (We've written more extensions that go a long way to mitigating both these problems.)
4. When the developers have the tests passing, we ask the QA to review, discuss any changes we had made to the tests, and assuming all is well, check in, then repeat from step 3 until all the slices are complete.

The benefits:
I think the biggest win is that because the automated acceptance tests are written jointly by the QA and developers, using near-plain English (as permitted by Given-When-Then), there is very little room for miscommunication. This means less rework and a happier QA/developer relationship. Other benefits include that the source code closely matches the business domain language and you can return to a test after 6 months and understand exactly what it was supposed to be doing.

Stephen Cresswell
Acuminous Ltd.

Saving Time

Acceptance test-driven development dovetails nicely with what I've called mock client testing. When creating automated tests for any body of code, write a test that pretends to be the client. Consume the code in the way you think the client will use the code. If you're writing an API, write a test that uses the API the way you expect it to be used, [and] then write the code behind the API call. The goal is to create a suite of tests that exercise the system the way you expect it to be used. This never completely exercises the code, but it's a great way to ensure all the basic functionality is in place.

A few years ago I was managing a small group of very talented developers at a startup. We had an existing product that was fairly complicated, and we were adding a network API. As the effort began, the team bogged down almost immediately. The work that one person finished would be broken by a teammate or by the same developer! The work was not going well, and it appeared that we had a great deal of frustrating work ahead of us.

I looked for a solution to this problem. This was a while before the current test automation movement, but that's essentially what we hit upon. I asked the team to create a series of tests, one for each API, and then implement the feature.

Every person on the team disagreed with me. They didn't like this new direction. One of the developers said, "We don't have the cycles to write tests, then write code as well! If you insist, I'll do it, but I want you to know how I feel. This is going to slow us down even more."

I insisted, and [the] team moved forward. It's worth noting that the team was already using a continuous integration system, but only for compiles, not testing.

Resistance was high during the first week, but I kept asking about the tests and checked to make sure they were being checked in. The second week, it was grudgingly conceded that the tests weren't a waste of time, but it was still just breaking even when you considered how much time it took to write them. But week three was the turning point.

By week three, the team had finally written enough tests that they could create them rapidly and generated enough tests that they started to see the benefit. They'd touch a piece of code, a test for a completely different API would break, and they'd fix it. The long hours in the debugger evaporated. When a problem occurred, the test found it within minutes instead of days later.

In my mind, the effort had truly succeeded when my skeptical co-worker came to me and said, "Jared, I was completely wrong. I had no idea how much time this would save us. It keeps us on track, catches problems when they occur, and now that we've had some practice, it doesn't take much time to add to the test suite."

Whether you call it acceptance test-driven development or mock client testing, create the tests that drive your product. Keep your team focused on building what you need, and catch the problems as quickly as they occur.

Jared Richardson
http://agileartisans.com/main

Getting Business Rules Right

Scenarios for testing:

Years ago, I delivered software for primary care to the National Health Service (NHS, the UK's public health provider). Every year we received new requirements that we had to meet to get our software accredited as providing the functionality someone in primary care needed. We received this in two packages. One was a conventional list of requirements; the other was a test pack. The test pack had a set of scenarios—some end to end, some covering a specific feature that needed to pass before you could get accreditation. Early we learned that the test pack was the best source of information on what we needed to build to be "done." Requirements are vague and open to interpretation. Scenarios are concrete, specific, and rarely have interpretation. Ever get that moment where you built something and then had an argument with the person who wrote the requirement because [he] just told you that your implementation is nothing like [his] requirements? Ever had [him] point to some sentence that you overlooked that changes the whole perception of how you deliver the story? Scenarios avoid that problem because they call attention to the correct behavior of the software.

So the ideal is to capture the scenarios that the software should support. Those give you the conditions for accepting the story as done. These are the acceptance tests. Now the composition of your team will dictate to some extent who is responsible for the parts of this process. In most cases, I have found it unlikely that the users of your software will be able to express the scenarios, though sometimes you might get acceptance criteria from them. In our case we have domain experts who act as proxies for real customers, so we ask them to define acceptance criteria—usually just a list—of things that a successful implementation will represent.

Interestingly, we occasionally fall down on getting scenarios written and end up developing off the acceptance criteria. The result is all too predictable. What gets developed is not quite right or what was quite intended, and we end up with rework. We certainly need to get better at this discipline. A root cause analysis tends to suggest that what fails for us here is the communication about what we should build. The storytest first approach is forcing the correct behavior of understanding the story before we build it.

Acceptance tests and unit tests:

There is definitely some pressure here with folks occasionally feeling that we are "testing twice:" once in the acceptance test and once in the unit test. Most developers would prefer just to write the unit test and not have to implement the acceptance test. I believe that acceptance testing comes into its own for ensuring we have developed the right work and during large-scale refactoring.

However, I think this feeling—that the acceptance tests are not adding value—occurs most often when you slide into post-implementation FitNesse testing because your scenarios were not ready. A lot of the value-add comes from defining and understanding the scenario up front. Much of the value in acceptance testing comes from agreeing what "done" means. That is often less clear than people think, and defining a test usually reveals a host of disagreements and tacit assumptions.

It is hard to write unit tests as part of the definition of the story. You don't necessarily know how you will build the story at planning or definition. The classes that implement the functionality probably don't exist, and you cannot exercise them from a test fixture at that point. Tools like Cucumber and FitNesse decouple authoring a test from implementing the test fixture for that test. This enables you to author the scenario in your test automation tool before you begin implementing the fixture that exercises the SUT. This is the key to enabling a test-first approach, where you need to communicate the scenario for confirmation prior to commencing work such as planning. Tools like FitNesse and Cucumber provide an easy mechanism to communicate your scenarios. We find that FitNesse allows customers and developers to communicate about the scenario before implementation. You can also see the results of executing it.

Because the conversation is more important than the tool, a tool like FitNesse or Cucumber may not be appropriate for the acceptance test. The most likely case is that you do not have any business rules to put under test. Don't feel constrained to use a particular tool. The most important thing is to define the acceptance test and then decide what tool is appropriate to automate the test. We even have some cases where the value of automation is too low. Where we are configuring the system, for example, it may be easier to test the rules that work with the configured system than test the act of configuring the system itself.

No user interface:

One obvious point here is that no user interface has been defined as yet. One obvious problem is that testing through the UI depends on the UI being completed to define tests. However, it can be worth thinking about mocking up the UI at the same time as you write the scenarios using a tool like Balsamiq.

We had a struggle at the beginning of the project over responsibility for defining how this should look before realizing that it needed to be cooperative. In the end, it all comes back to the agile emphasis on communication. The customer asks for features, but the developers need to negotiate how the features will be implemented.

Some folks still like to work from the UI down, whereas I want them to work from the acceptance tests on down, then hook up to the UI. It's probably all tilting at windmills at some point, but for me while both are essential to getting it right, I see more cost in the majority of cases to the rework for not getting the business rule right than to changing the UI.

Ian Cooper
Codebetter.com

Game Changing

I am an in-house software development consultant at Progressive Insurance and a proponent of ATDD. Here's my story....

In 2006, I started an assignment with a group that published service APIs to other parts of our company for the purpose of retrieving data from external vendors. At the time, they were testing most of their services manually, using the GUIs of the calling applications. Their testing was dependent upon the availability of both their own and their clients' test environments, and disruptions were common. Additionally, their service request and response schemata consisted of thousands of fields, but only dozens of those fields were exposed directly in the client GUIs. The rest were calculated, defaulted, or simply ignored. Not surprisingly, the test team felt squeezed by schedule pressure and quality problems.

Their management decided that they were simply out-gunned by the technical challenge before them, so they recruited some programmers with testing skills (and vice versa) to join the team. That's where I and a couple of other test engineers came onto the scene. One of the first things we did was raise awareness about the low level of coverage for these relatively complex interfaces. (This was somewhat disconcerting for veteran team members, and a tribute to the maturity of all involved that these conversations were rarely contentious.) We also began surveying other test teams within our company to see if there were any tools already in-house that we could use to circumvent the client GUIs and go directly at our service interfaces. We discovered a group that was using Fit for a similar purpose, and it was love at first sight.

We copied their implementation (Fit and OpenWiki with some customizations) to our environment, and within days we were creating and executing tests for some of our larger projects. Within a few weeks we had these tools well integrated into our infrastructure and processes. Tests were now being defined during or shortly after requirements definition, frequently serving to clarify requirements, but we didn't know then to call it ATDD. Soon, developers were asking for our tests to run before check-in and were helping with fixture design and development.

The number of tests for our systems typically increased five-fold as we introduced our implementation of automated ATDD, and we moved from executing a handful of test passes per project to a handful of passes per day. Defects discovered in our QA environment dropped dramatically because we were running the tests in predecessor environments; the tests became informal entry criteria. Test projects were costing about the same and taking about the same amount of time, but quality was increasing significantly. In fact, the team's quality ranking within the company, based on production availability of our systems, improved from worst to first in about a two-year period.

In addition to the quality improvements, we gained a great deal of confidence in our ability to refactor our systems and move them through environments because coverage had increased substantially and test execution had become relatively effortless. Furthermore, the clarity, usability, and credibility of the tests led to more collaborative test failure investigations. It was not uncommon to see developers, testers, and business analysts huddled around a screen or camped in a conference room discussing the significance of patterns of red cells on a test result table, discovering and resolving issues in minutes where formerly it had taken hours or days of asynchronous communication. While there are many other ways that we have continued to improve our testing, nothing has been as "game changing" as our move to automated ATDD with Fit.

Greg McNelly
Progressive Insurance

Tighter Cross-Functional Team Integration – Crisp Visible Story Completion Criteria – Automation Yields Reduced Testing Time

I am an engineering manager for a major publishing company. The adoption of Story Acceptance Testing with the FitNesse framework has resulted in tighter cross-functional integration between development and QA team members. Acceptance tests are written on a per story basis at the start of the sprint. The tests and the results are rendered visually in an easy to understand table format—they are even comprehensible by nontechnical business stakeholders. Because the application under development is business logic intensive and has a minimal UI, the demo at the sprint review meeting consists primarily of running and viewing the test results.

On previous projects, the functional testing efforts were entirely manual and very time consuming. To ensure a stable release, it was necessary to implement a feature freeze 2+ months in advance of the release date. With the manual approach to testing, the sprint would frequently end with untested stories. Adoption of the FitNesse framework provides nearly instantaneous feedback regarding the completion status of each story.

Based on the rapid ROI of the FitNesse adoption for this project, all subsequent new projects will adopt a test automation strategy. Currently, QA is writing the tests. Going forward, I anticipate that a broader audience (business analysts and Product Owners) will contribute to test development.

Gary Marcos
http://www.linkedin.com/in/agile1

What Is Your Story?

Share your success on how ATDD improved your organization with others. Send your story to ken.pugh@netobjectives.com or visit http://atdd.biz.

Summary

- The Who, What, When, Where, Why, and How have been explained.
- The experiences and benefits have been documented.
- What are you waiting for? Why not try it?

Index

A

B

C

D

E

F

G-H

I

J-K

Q-R

S

U

V

W-X-Y-Z

Your purchase of ***Lean-Agile Acceptance Test-Driven Development*** includes access to a free online edition for 45 days through the Safari Books Online subscription service. Nearly every Addison-Wesley Professional book is available online through Safari Books Online, along with more than 5,000 other technical books and videos from publishers such as Cisco Press, Exam Cram, IBM Press, O'Reilly, Prentice Hall, Que, and Sams.

SAFARI BOOKS ONLINE allows you to search for a specific answer, cut and paste code, download chapters, and stay current with emerging technologies.

Activate your FREE Online Edition at www.informit.com/safarifree

STEP 1: Enter the coupon code: SAZSREH.

STEP 2: New Safari users, complete the brief registration form.
Safari subscribers, just log in.

If you have difficulty registering on Safari or accessing the online edition, please e-mail customer-service@safaribooksonline.com

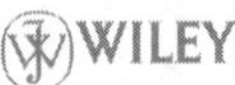